Microsoft® Office Word® 2010 M

Ober • Johnson • Zimmerly

11e

GREGG
College Keyboarding
& Document Processing

Connect
Learn
Succeed™

Connect
Learn
Succeed™

Microsoft® Office Word® 2010 Manual to accompany
Gregg College Keyboarding & Document Processing, Eleventh Edition
Scot Ober, Jack E. Johnson, and Arlene Zimmerly

Published by McGraw-Hill, a business unit of The McGraw-Hill Companies, Inc., 1221 Avenue of the Americas, New York, NY 10020. Copyright © 2011 by The McGraw-Hill Companies, Inc. All rights reserved. Previous editions © 1957, 1964, 1970, 1979, 1984, 1989, 1994, 1997, 2002, 2006, and 2008.

3 4 5 6 7 8 9 0 DOC/DOC 1 0 9 8 7 6 5 4 3 2 1

ISBN 978-0-07-731937-3
MHID 0-07-731937-0

Vice President/Editor in Chief: *Elizabeth Haefele*
Vice President/Director of Marketing: *John E. Biernat*
Executive editor: *Scott Davidson*
Director of Development, Business Careers: *Sarah Wood*
Editorial coordinator: *Alan Palmer*
Marketing manager: *Tiffany Wendt*
Lead digital product manager: *Damian Moshak*
Senior digital product manager: *Lynn M. Bluhm*
Digital product specialist: *Randall Bates*
Director, Editing/Design/Production: *Jess Ann Kosic*
Project manager: *Marlena Pechan*
Senior production supervisor: *Janean A. Utley*
Senior designer: *Marianna Kinigakis*
Senior photo research coordinator: *Lori Kramer*
Digital production coordinator: *Brent Dela Cruz*
Digital developmental editor: *Kevin White*
Outside development house: *Debra Matteson*
Cover credit: © *Robert Adrian Hillman/Shutterstock*
Cover design: *Jessica M. Lazar*
Interior design: *Jessica M. Lazar and Laurie J. Entringer, BrainWorx Studio, Inc.*
Typeface: *11/13.5 Adobe Garamond Pro*
Compositor: *Lachina Publishing Services*
Printer: RR Donnelley, Crawfordsville

www.mhhe.com

Contents

REFERENCE MANUAL — R-1

GETTING STARTED — 1
Word Manual Features — 1
GDP—Word Settings — 2
Appendixes A, B, and C — 3
GDP—Help — 3

LESSON 21 Orientation to Word Processing—A — 4
GDP—Start Word — 4
Choose a Command — 6
  From the Ribbon — 6
  From the Mini Toolbar or Shortcut Menu — 8
  From the Keyboard — 8
  From the Quick Access Toolbar — 9
File—Open — 10
GDP—Quit Word — 11

LESSON 22 Orientation to Word Processing—B — 12
Navigate in a File — 12
File—Save — 14
File—Close — 16
File—New — 16
Switch Windows — 17

LESSON 23 Orientation to Word Processing—C — 19
Select Text — 19
Bold — 21
Undo/Redo a Command — 22
Help — 24

LESSON 24 Orientation to Word Processing—D — 27
Print Preview — 27
Spelling and Grammar Check — 28
  AutoCorrect — 30
Show/Hide Formatting — 32
Zoom — 34
Print — 35

LESSON 25 E-Mail Messages   37
   GDP—Scoring   37
   GDP—Proofreading Viewer   37
   E-Mail a Document   37
   GDP—Reference Manual   40

LESSON 28 Envelopes and Labels   42
   Envelopes   42
   View Gridlines   44
   Labels   44

LESSON 29 Memos and E-Mail With Attachments   47
   E-Mail—Attachments   47

LESSON 30 Correspondence Review   48
   Italic and Underline   48

LESSON 31 One-Page Business Reports   49
   Alignment   49
   Font—Size   50

LESSON 32 Multipage Business Reports   52
   Page Number   52
   Page Break   54
   Widow/Orphan Control   56

LESSON 33 Rough-Draft Business Reports With Lists   59
   Bullets and Numbering   59

LESSON 34 Multipage Academic Reports With Lists   62
   Line Spacing   62

LESSON 35 More Rough-Draft Reports   64
   Cut and Copy   64
   Paste   66

LESSON 36 Boxed Tables   69
   Table—Insert   69
   Table—AutoFit to Contents   72

LESSON 37 Open Tables With Titles   73
   Table—Merge Cells   73
   Table—Borders   74

LESSON 38 Open Tables With Column Headings   77
  Table—Align Bottom   77
  Table—Center Horizontally   78
  Table—Center Page   79

LESSON 39 Ruled Tables With Number Columns   81
  Table—Align Text Right   81
  Table—Borders, Ruled   82

**LESSON 44 Letters With Indented Displays and
Copy Notations and E-Mail With Copies**   84
  Indentation   84
    Increase and Decrease Indent   85
  E-Mail—Copies   85

LESSON 45 Letters in Modified-Block Style   87
  Tab Set—Ruler Tabs   87

**LESSON 46 Left-Bound Business Reports With Indented
Displays and Footnotes**   90
  Margins   90
  Footnotes   91

LESSON 47 Reports in APA Style   94
  Headers   94

LESSON 49 Report Citations   97
  Indentation—Hanging   97
  AutoCorrect—Hyperlink   99

LESSON 50 Preliminary Report Pages   102
  Tab Set—Dot Leaders   102

LESSON 51 Resumes   105
  Font   105
  Table—Change Column Width   107

LESSON 67 Special Correspondence Features   109
  Sort   109

LESSON 68 More Special Correspondence Features   111
  Table—Shading   111
  E-Mail—Blind Copies   112

LESSON 69 Multipage Memos With Tables 114
Find and Replace 114

LESSON 73 Procedures Manual 117
Footers 117

LESSON 74 Reports Formatted in Columns 119
Columns 119
Hyphenation 122

LESSON 76 Tables With Source Notes or Footnotes 125
Table—Text Direction 125
Table—Insert, Delete, and Move Rows or Columns 126

LESSON 78 Tables in Landscape Orientation 131
Page Orientation 131

LESSON 79 Multipage Tables 132
Table—Repeating Table Heading Rows 132

LESSON 80 Tables With Predesigned Formats 133
Table—Styles 133

LESSON 81 International Formatting—Canada 136
Paper Size 136

LESSON 82 International Formatting—Mexico 138
Symbol—Insert 138

LESSON 86 Formal Report Project—A 140
Styles 140

LESSON 88 Formal Report Project—C 143
Clip Art—Insert 143
Text Wrapping 144
Object Anchor 146

LESSON 89 Formal Report Project—D 148
File—Insert 148
Bookmarks and Hyperlinks 149

LESSON 90 Formal Report Project—E 152
Cover Page—Insert 152

LESSON 92 Medical Office Documents—B   154
  Table—Tab   154

LESSON 98 Legal Office Documents—C   158
  Line Numbering   158

LESSON 101 Using Correspondence Templates   160
  Templates—Correspondence   160

LESSON 102 Using Report Templates   165
  Templates—Report   165

LESSON 103 Designing Letterheads   169
  Text Boxes   169
  Font—Small Caps   173

LESSON 104 Designing Notepads   175
  Print Options   175

LESSON 106 Designing Cover Pages   178
  WordArt   178

LESSON 107 Designing Announcements and Flyers   181
  Table—Move   181
  Page Color   182

LESSON 111 Designing an Online Resume   183
  Table—Borders and Shading, Custom   183
    Theme   185

LESSON 112 Form Letters—A   188
  Mail Merge—Letters   188
    Letters—Main Document   188
    Letters—Data Source File   189
    Letters—Placeholders   190
    Letters—Merge   192

LESSON 115 Form Letters With Envelopes and Labels—D   196
  Mail Merge—Envelopes and Labels   196
    Envelopes—Main Document   196
    Envelopes—Data Source File and Placeholders   197
    Labels—Main Document   198
    Labels—Data Source File and Placeholders   199
    Envelopes and Labels—Merge   200

APPENDIX A Using Microsoft Word in the Workplace 204
  Start Word From Windows 204
  Quit Word From Windows 204
  GDP—Word Settings 204
    Style Set—Word 2003 205
    Default Font Size—Table 205
    Status Bar 205
    AutoCorrect Options 205
    AutoFormat As You Type Options 206
    Spelling 207
  Style Set—Word 2010 207
    Style Gallery—Word 2010 208
  Templates 208

APPENDIX B Using GDP Features in Document Processing 209
  GDP—Feature Index 209
  GDP—Reference Initials 209

APPENDIX C Saving a Word File in PDF Format 210

Reference Manual

COMPUTER SYSTEM
keyboard, R-2B
parts of, R-2A

CORRESPONDENCE
application letter, R-12B
attachment notation, R-4D, R-7C
blind copy notation, R-5B
block style, R-3A
body, R-3A
company name, R-5B
complimentary closing, R-3A
copy notation, R-3C, R-5B
date line, R-3A
delivery notation, R-3C, R-4A, R-5B
e-mail, R-5C–D
enclosure notation, R-3B, R-5B
envelope formatting, R-6A
executive stationery, R-4A
half-page stationery, R-4B
indented displays, R-3A
inside address, R-3A
international address, R-3D, R-5A
letter folding, R-6B
letterhead, R-3A
lists, R-3B–C, R-5B, R-12C–D
memo, R-4D, R-7C, R-9C
modified-block style, R-3B, R-3D
multiline lists, R-3B, R-5B, R-12C–D
multipage, R-5A–B, R-8A–D, R-13C
on-arrival notation, R-5A
open punctuation, R-4C
page number, R-5A–B, R-8A–D,
    R-10A–D, R-13C
personal-business, R-3D, R-12B
postscript notation, R-5B
quotation, long, R-3A
reference initials, R-3A, R-4D, R-5B
return address, R-3D, R-12B
salutation, R-3A
simplified style, R-3C
single-line lists, R-3C, R-12C–D
standard punctuation, R-3A
subject line, R-3C, R-4D, R-5A,
    R-7C
tables in, R-4D, R-5A, R-13C–D
window envelope, folding for, R-6B
window envelope, formatted for,
    R-4C
writer's identification, R-3A

EMPLOYMENT DOCUMENTS
application letter, R-12B
resume, R-12A

FORMS
R-14A

LANGUAGE ARTS
abbreviations, R-22
adjectives and adverbs, R-20
agreement, R-19
apostrophes, R-17
capitalization, R-21
colons, R-18
commas, R-15 to R-16
grammar, R-19 to R-20
hyphens, R-17
italics (or underline), R-18
mechanics, R-21 to R-22
number expression, R-21 to R-22
periods, R-18
pronouns, R-20
punctuation, R-15 to R-18
quotation marks, R-18
semicolons, R-16
sentences, R-19
underline (or italics), R-18
word usage, R-20

PROOFREADERS' MARKS
R-14C

REPORTS
academic style, R-8C–D
agenda, meeting, R-11A
APA style, R-10A–B
author/page citations, R-10C
author/year citations, R-10A
bibliography, R-9B
business, R-8A–B, R-9A
byline, R-8A, R-10A
citations, R-9D, R-10A–D
date, R-8A
endnotes, R-8C–D, R-9C
footnotes, R-8A–B, R-9A
hanging indent, R-10D
header, R-10A–B, R-10D
headings, R-9D, R-10C
headings, main, R-10A
headings, paragraph, R-8A, R-8C,
    R-9A
headings, side, R-8A–C, R-9A
indented display, R-8B, R-8D
itinerary, R-11C
left-bound, R-9A
legal document, R-11D
line numbers, R-11D
lists, R-8A, R-8C, R-9A, R-9C,
    R-11A, R-12A, R-12C–D
margins, R-9D
memo report, R-9C
minutes of a meeting, R-11B
MLA style, R-10C–D
multiline lists, R-8A, R-8C, R-11A,
    R-12A, R-12C–D

multipage academic, R-8C–D
multipage business, R-8A–B
outline, R-7A
page number, R-8B, R-8D, R-10A–B
paragraph heading, R-8A, R-9C
quotation, long, R-8B, R-8D
references page, APA style, R-10B
resume, R-12A
side heading, R-8A, R-9C
single-line lists, R-9A, R-9C, R-11A,
    R-12A, R-12C–D
spacing, R-9D
special features, R-9D
subheadings, R-10A
subject line, 2-line, R-9C
subtitle, R-8A
table of contents page, R-7D
tables in, R-8B
title, R-7A–B, R-8A–C, R-10A,
    R-10C
title, 2-line, R-8C, R-9A, R-10A,
    R-10C
title page, R-7B
transmittal memo, R-7C
works-cited page, MLA style, R-10D

TABLES
2-line column heading, R-13B
body, R-13A
bottom-aligned, R-13A–B
boxed, R-5A, R-8B, R-13A
braced column headings, R-13A
capitalization, columns, R-13D
column headings, R-4D, R-5A, R-8B,
    R-13A–D
dollar signs, R-8B, R-13A–B, R-13D
heading block, R-5, R-8B, R-13A–D
in correspondence, R-4D, R-5A,
    R-13C
in reports, R-8B
note, R-8B, R-13A
number, R-8B, R-13C
numbers in, R-4D, R-8B, R-13A–C
open, R-13B
percent signs, R-13B, R-13D
ruled, R-4D, R-13C
source, R-8B
special features, R-13D
subtitle, R-8B, R-13A–B, R-13D
table number, R-8B, R-13C
tables, R-4D, R-5A, R-8B, R-13A–C
title, R-5A, R-8B, R-13A–D
total line, R-13A, R-13C–D
vertical placement, R-13D

U.S. POSTAL SERVICE STATE ABBREVIATIONS
R-14B

Reference Manual

A. MAJOR PARTS OF A COMPUTER SYSTEM

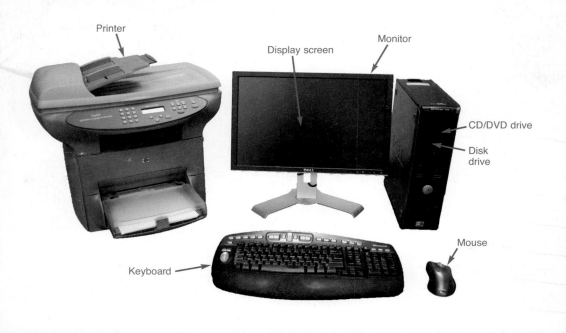

Printer

Display screen

Monitor

CD/DVD drive

Disk drive

Mouse

Keyboard

B. THE COMPUTER KEYBOARD

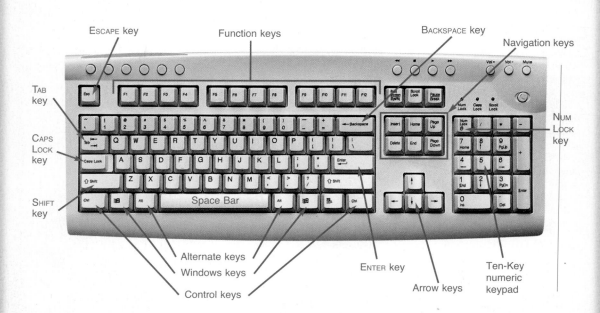

ESCAPE key

Function keys

BACKSPACE key

Navigation keys

TAB key

CAPS LOCK key

SHIFT key

NUM LOCK key

Alternate keys

Windows keys

Control keys

ENTER key

Arrow keys

Ten-Key numeric keypad

Reference Manual

A. BUSINESS LETTER IN BLOCK STYLE

(with standard punctuation and indented display)

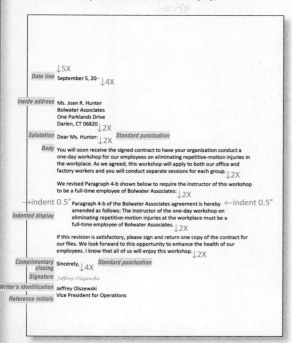

Date line ↓5X
September 5, 20— ↓4X

Inside address Ms. Joan R. Hunter
Bolwater Associates
One Parklands Drive
Darien, CT 06820 ↓2X

Salutation Dear Ms. Hunter: *Standard punctuation* ↓2X

Body You will soon receive the signed contract to have your organization conduct a one-day workshop for our employees on eliminating repetitive-motion injuries in the workplace. As we agreed, this workshop will apply to both our office and factory workers and you will conduct separate sessions for each group. ↓2X

We revised Paragraph 4-b shown below to require the instructor of this workshop to be a full-time employee of Bolwater Associates: ↓2X

→indent 0.5" Paragraph 4-b of the Bolwater Associates agreement is hereby ←indent 0.5"
Indented display amended as follows: The instructor of the one-day workshop on eliminating repetitive-motion injuries at the workplace must be a full-time employee of Bolwater Associates. ↓2X

If this revision is satisfactory, please sign and return one copy of the contract for our files. We look forward to this opportunity to enhance the health of our employees. I know that all of us will enjoy this workshop. ↓2X

Complimentary closing Sincerely, *Standard punctuation* ↓4X

Signature *Jeffrey Olszewski*

Writer's identification Jeffrey Olszewski
Vice President for Operations

Reference initials

B. BUSINESS LETTER IN MODIFIED-BLOCK STYLE

(with multiline list and enclosure notation)

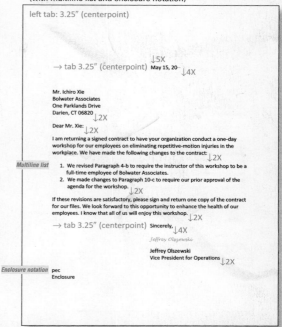

left tab: 3.25" (centerpoint)

→ tab 3.25" (centerpoint) ↓5X
May 15, 20— ↓4X

Mr. Ichiro Xie
Bolwater Associates
One Parklands Drive
Darien, CT 06820 ↓2X

Dear Mr. Xie: ↓2X

I am returning a signed contract to have your organization conduct a one-day workshop for our employees on eliminating repetitive-motion injuries in the workplace. We have made the following changes to the contract: ↓2X

Multiline list
1. We revised Paragraph 4-b to require the instructor of this workshop to be a full-time employee of Bolwater Associates.
2. We made changes to Paragraph 10-c to require our prior approval of the agenda for the workshop. ↓2X

If these revisions are satisfactory, please sign and return one copy of the contract for our files. We look forward to this opportunity to enhance the health of our employees. I know that all of us will enjoy this workshop. ↓2X

→ tab 3.25" (centerpoint) Sincerely, ↓4X

Jeffrey Olszewski

Jeffrey Olszewski
Vice President for Operations ↓2X

Enclosure notation pec
Enclosure

C. BUSINESS LETTER IN SIMPLIFIED STYLE

(with subject line, single-line list; enclosure, delivery, and copy notations)

↓5X
October 5, 20— ↓4X

Mr. Dale P. Griffin
Bolwater Associates
One Parklands Drive
Darien, CT 06820 ↓3X

Subject line WORKSHOP CONTRACT ↓3X

I am returning the signed contract, Mr. Griffin, to have your organization conduct a one-day workshop for our employees on eliminating repetitive-motion injuries in the workplace. We have amended the following sections of the contract: ↓2X

Single-line list
- Paragraph 4-b
- Table 3
- Attachment 2 ↓2X

If these revisions are satisfactory, please sign and return one copy of the contract for our files. We look forward to this opportunity to enhance the health of our employees. I know that all of us will enjoy this workshop. ↓4X

Rogena Kyles

ROGENA KYLES, DIRECTOR ↓2X

iww
Enclosure notation Enclosure
Delivery notation By e-mail
Copy notation c: Legal Department

D. PERSONAL-BUSINESS LETTER IN MODIFIED-BLOCK STYLE

(with international address and return address)

left tab: 3.25" (centerpoint)

→ tab 3.25" (centerpoint) ↓5X
July 15, 20— ↓4X

Mr. Luis Fernandez
Vice President
Arvon Industries, Inc.
21 St. Claire Avenue East
International address Toronto, ON M4T IL9
CANADA ↓2X

Dear Mr. Fernandez: ↓2X

As a former employee and present stockholder of Arvon Industries, I wish to protest the planned sale of the Consumer Products Division. ↓2X

According to published reports, consumer products accounted for 19 percent of last year's corporate profits, and they are expected to account for even more this year. In addition, Dun & Bradstreet predicts that consumer products nationwide will outpace the general economy for the next five years.

I am concerned about the effect that this planned sale might have on overall corporate profits, on our cash dividends for investors, and on the economy of Melbourne, where the two consumer-products plants are located. Please ask your board of directors to reconsider this matter. ↓2X

→ tab 3.25" (centerpoint) Sincerely, ↓4X

Jeanine Ford

Jeanine Ford
Return address 901 East Benson, Apt. 3
Fort Lauderdale, FL 33301
U.S.A.

A. BUSINESS LETTER ON EXECUTIVE STATIONERY

(7.25" × 10.5"; 1" side margins; with delivery notation)

↓5X
July 18, 20— ↓4X

Mr. Rodney Eastwood
BBL Resources
523 Northern Ridge
Fayetteville, PA 17222 ↓2X

Dear Rodney: ↓2X

I see no reason why we should continue to consider the locality around Geraldton for our new plant. Even though the desirability of this site from an economic view is undeniable, there is not sufficient housing readily available for our workers. ↓2X

In trying to control urban growth, the city has been turning down the building permits for much new housing or placing so many restrictions on foreign investment as to make it too expensive.

Please continue to seek out other areas of exploration where we might form a joint partnership. ↓2X

Sincerely, ↓4X

Jennifer Gwatkin

Jennifer Gwatkin, Director ↓2X

mme
By fax

Delivery notation

B. BUSINESS LETTER ON HALF-PAGE STATIONERY

(5.5" × 8.5"; 0.75" side margins)

↓4 X
July 18, 20— ↓4X

Mr. Aristeo Olivas
BBL Resources
52A Northern Ridge
Fayetteville, PA 17222 ↓2X

Dear Aristeo: ↓2X

We should discontinue considering Geraldton for our new plant. Housing is not readily available.

Please seek out other areas of exploration where we might someday form a joint partnership. ↓2X

Sincerely, ↓4X

Chimere Jones

Chimere Jones, Director ↓2X

adk

C. BUSINESS LETTER FORMATTED FOR A WINDOW ENVELOPE

(with open punctuation)

↓5X
July 18, 20— ↓3X

Ms. Reinalda Guerrero
BBL Resources
52A Northern Ridge
Fayetteville, PA 17222 ↓3X

Dear Ms. Guerrero   *Open punctuation* ↓2X

I see no reason why we should even continue to consider the locality around Geraldton for our new plant. Even though the desirability of this site from an economic view is undeniable, there is insufficient housing readily available for our workers. ↓2X

In trying to control urban growth, the city has been turning down the building permits for new housing or placing so many restrictions on foreign investment as to make it too expensive.

Please continue to seek out other areas of exploration where we might form a joint partnership. ↓2X

Sincerely   *Open punctuation* ↓4X

Augustus Mays

Augustus Mays
Vice President for Operations ↓2X

woc

D. MEMO

(with ruled table, left- and right-aligned columns, and attachment notation)

↓5X →tab
MEMO TO: Nancy Price, Executive Vice President ↓2X

FROM: Arlyn J. Bunch, Operations *ajb*

DATE: July 18, 20—

SUBJECT: New Plant Site ↓2X

As you can see from the attached letter, I've informed BBL Resources that I see no reason why we should continue to consider the locality around Geraldton for our new plant. Even though the desirability of this site from an economic standpoint is undeniable, there is insufficient housing available. In fact, as of June 25, the number of appropriate single-family houses listed for sale within a 25-mile radius of Geraldton was as follows: ↓2X

Ruled table

Agent	Units
Belle Real Estate	123
Castleton Homes	11
Red Carpet	9
Geraldton Homes	5

↓1X

In addition, in trying to control urban growth, Geraldton has been either turning down building permits for new housing or placing excessive restrictions on them. Because of this deficiency of housing for our employees, we have no choice but to look elsewhere. ↓2X

woc
Attachment notation   Attachment

A. MULTIPAGE BUSINESS LETTER

(page 1; with on-arrival notation, international address, subject line, and boxed table)

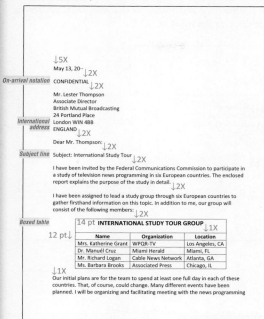

B. MULTIPAGE BUSINESS LETTER

(page 2; with page number; multiline list; company name; and enclosure, delivery, copy, postscript, and blind copy notations)

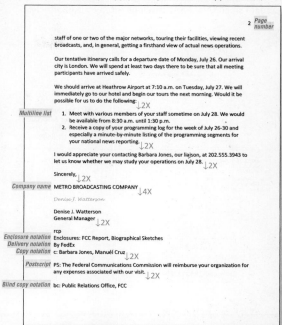

C. E-MAIL MESSAGE IN MICROSOFT OUTLOOK

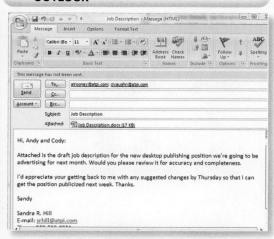

D. E-MAIL MESSAGE IN MSN HOTMAIL

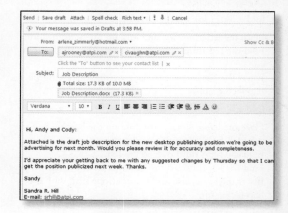

A. FORMATTING ENVELOPES

A standard large (No. 10) envelope is 9.5 by 4.125 inches. A standard small (No. 6¾) envelope is 6.5 by 3.625 inches.

A window envelope requires no formatting, since the letter is formatted and folded so that the inside address is visible through the window.

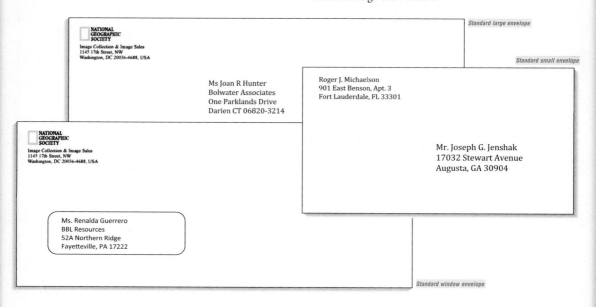

Standard large envelope

NATIONAL
GEOGRAPHIC
SOCIETY
Image Collection & Image Sales
1145 17th Street, NW
Washington, DC 20036-4688, USA

Ms Joan R Hunter
Bolwater Associates
One Parklands Drive
Darien CT 06820-3214

Standard small envelope

Roger J. Michaelson
901 East Benson, Apt. 3
Fort Lauderdale, FL 33301

Mr. Joseph G. Jenshak
17032 Stewart Avenue
Augusta, GA 30904

NATIONAL
GEOGRAPHIC
SOCIETY
Image Collection & Image Sales
1145 17th Street, NW
Washington, DC 20036-4688, USA

Ms. Renalda Guerrero
BBL Resources
52A Northern Ridge
Fayetteville, PA 17222

Standard window envelope

B. FOLDING LETTERS

To fold a letter for a large envelope:

1. Place the letter *face up,* and fold up the bottom third.
2. Fold the top third down to 0.5 inch from the bottom edge.
3. Insert the last crease into the envelope first, with the flap facing up.

To fold a letter for a small envelope:

1. Place the letter *face up,* and fold up the bottom half to 0.5 inch from the top.
2. Fold the right third over to the left.
3. Fold the left third over to 0.5 inch from the right edge.
4. Insert the last crease into the envelope first, with the flap facing up.

To fold a letter for a window envelope:

1. Place the letter *face down* with the letterhead at the top, and fold the bottom third of the letter up.
2. Fold the top third down so that the address shows.
3. Insert the letter into the envelope so that the address shows through the window.

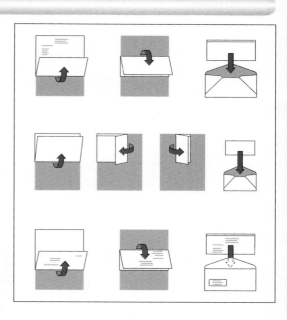

A. OUTLINE

(with 2-line title)

right tab: 0.3"
left tabs: 0.4", 0.7"

↓5X
2-line title   14 pt   **AN ANALYSIS OF THE SCOPE AND EFFECTIVENESS
OF ONLINE ADVERTISING** ↓2X

12 pt ↓ **The Status of Point-and-Click Selling** ↓2X

Jonathan R. Evans ↓2X

January 19, 20-- ↓2X

I. INTRODUCTION ↓2X
II. SCOPE AND TRENDS IN INTERNET ADVERTISING
   A. Internet Advertising
   B. Major Online Advertisers
   C. Positioning and Pricing
   D. Types of Advertising ↓2X
III. ADVERTISING EFFECTIVENESS
   A. The Banner Debate
   B. Increasing Advertising Effectiveness
   C. Measuring ROI

IV. CONCLUSION

→ tab 0.3"
→ tab 0.4"
→ tab 0.7"

B. TITLE PAGE

(with 2-line title)

center page ↓

2-line title   14 pt   **AN ANALYSIS OF THE SCOPE AND EFFECTIVENESS
OF ONLINE ADVERTISING** ↓2X

12 pt ↓ **The Status of Point-and-Click Selling** ↓12X

Submitted to ↓2X

Luis Torres
General Manager
ViaWorld, International ↓12X

Prepared by ↓2X

Jonathan R. Evans
Assistant Marketing Manager
ViaWorld, International ↓2X

January 19, 20--

C. TRANSMITTAL MEMO

(with 2-line subject line and attachment notation)

↓5X →tab
MEMO TO: Luis Torres, General Manager ↓2X

FROM: Jonathan R. Evans, Assistant Marketing Manager *jre*

DATE: January 19, 20--

2-line subject line   **SUBJECT:**   An Analysis of the Scope and Effectiveness of Current Online
→tab Advertising in Today's Marketplace ↓2X

Here is the final report analyzing the scope and effectiveness of Internet
advertising that you requested on January 5. ↓2X

The report predicts that the total value of the business-to-business e-commerce
market will continue to increase by geometric proportions. New technologies
aimed at increasing Internet ad interactivity and the adoption of standards for
advertising response measurement and tracking will contribute to this increase.
Unfortunately, as discussed in this report, the use of "rich media" and interactivity
in Web advertising will create its own set of problems.

I enjoyed working on this assignment, Luis, and learned quite a bit from my
analysis of the situation. Please let me know if you have any questions about the
report. ↓2X

plw
Attachment notation   Attachment

D. TABLE OF CONTENTS

left tab: 0.5"
right dot-leader tab: 6.5"

↓5X
14 pt **CONTENTS** ↓2X

12 pt ↓ INTRODUCTION .... →tab 6.5" 1 ↓2X

SCOPE AND TRENDS IN ONLINE ADVERTISING .... 3 ↓2X

→tab 0.5" Internet Advertising Spending .... →tab 6.5" 4
   Major Online Advertisers 5
   Positioning and Pricing 7
   Types of Advertising .... 8 ↓2X

ADVERTISING EFFECTIVENESS 9

   The Banner Debate 9
   Increasing Advertising Effectiveness 11
   Measuring ROI 12

CONCLUSION 13

APPENDIX

   Sample Internet Advertising 15
   Proposed WEFA Standards 18

BIBLIOGRAPHY 19

Reference Manual

A. MULTIPAGE BUSINESS REPORT

(page 1; with side and paragraph headings, multiline list, footnote references, and footnotes)

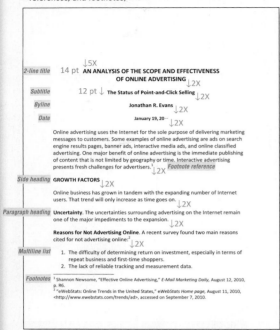

B. MULTIPAGE BUSINESS REPORT

(last page; with page number, indented display, side heading, boxed table with table number and note, and footnote)

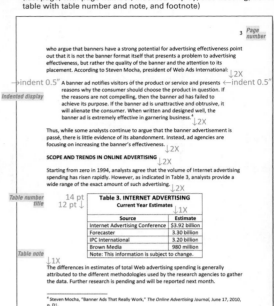

C. MULTIPAGE ACADEMIC REPORT

(page 1; with 2-line title, endnote references, and multiline list)

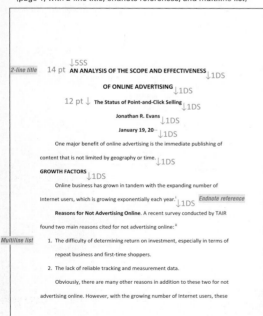

D. MULTIPAGE ACADEMIC REPORT

(last page; with page number, indented display, and endnotes)

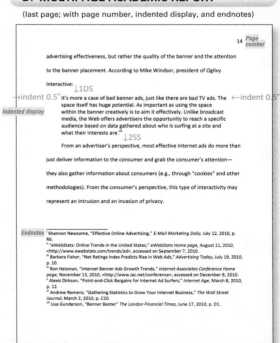

A. LEFT-BOUND BUSINESS REPORT

(page 1; with 2-line title, single-line list, and footnotes)

left margin: 1.5"
right margin: *default 1"*

↓5X
2-line title 14 pt **AN ANALYSIS OF THE SCOPE AND EFFECTIVENESS**
OF ONLINE ADVERTISING ↓2X

12 pt ↓ **The Status of Point-and-Click Selling** ↓2X

Jonathan R. Evans ↓2X

January 19, 20-- ↓2X

Online advertising uses the Internet for the sole purpose of delivering marketing messages to customers. Some examples of online advertising are as follows: ads on search engine results pages, banner ads, interactive media ads, and e-mail marketing. One major benefit of online advertising is the immediate publishing of content that is not limited by geography or time. Interactive advertising presents new challenges for advertisers.[1] ↓2X

GROWTH FACTORS ↓2X

Online business has grown in tandem with the expanding number of Internet users. That trend will only increase as time goes on. ↓2X

Uncertainty. The uncertainties surrounding advertising on the Internet remain one of the major impediments to the expansion. All of the Internet advertising industry is today in a state of flux. ↓2X

Reasons for Not Advertising Online. A recent survey found two main reasons cited for not advertising online:[2] ↓2X

Single-line list
   1. The difficulty of determining return on investment.
   2. The lack of reliable tracking and measurement data.

Footnotes
[1] Shannon Newsome, "Effective Online Advertising," *E-Mail Marketing Daily,* July 12, 2010, p. R6.
[2] "eWebStats: Online Trends in the United States," *eWebStats Home page,* August 11, 2010, <http://www.ewebstats.com/trends/ad>, accessed on September 7, 2010.

B. BIBLIOGRAPHY

(for business or academic style using either endnotes or footnotes)

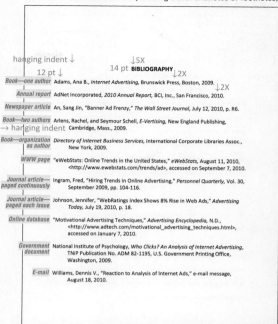

hanging indent ↓ ↓5X
12 pt ↓ 14 pt **BIBLIOGRAPHY** ↓2X

Book—one author Adams, Ana B., *Internet Advertising,* Brunswick Press, Boston, 2009. ↓2X

Annual report AdNet Incorporated, *2010 Annual Report,* BCI, Inc., San Francisco, 2010. ↓2X

Newspaper article An, Sang Jin, "Banner Ad Frenzy," *The Wall Street Journal,* July 12, 2010, p. R6.

Book—two authors Arlens, Rachel, and Seymour Schell, *E-Vertising,* New England Publishing,
→ hanging indent Cambridge, Mass., 2009.

Book—organization as author Directory of Internet Business Services, International Corporate Libraries Assoc., New York, 2009.

WWW page "eWebStats: Online Trends in the United States," *eWebStats,* August 11, 2010, <http://www.ewebstats.com/trends/ad>, accessed on September 7, 2010.

Journal article—paged continuously Ingram, Fred, "Hiring Trends in Online Advertising," *Personnel Quarterly,* Vol. 30, September 2009, pp. 104-116.

Journal article—paged each issue Johnson, Jennifer, "WebRatings Index Shows 8% Rise in Web Ads," *Advertising Today,* July 19, 2010, p. 18.

Online database "Motivational Advertising Techniques," *Advertising Encyclopedia,* N.D., <http://www.adtech.com/motivational_advertising_techniques.html>, accessed on January 7, 2010.

Government document National Institute of Psychology, *Who Clicks? An Analysis of Internet Advertising,* TNIP Publication No. ADM 82-1195, U.S. Government Printing Office, Washington, 2009.

E-mail Williams, Dennis V., "Reaction to Analysis of Internet Ads," e-mail message, August 18, 2010.

C. MEMO REPORT

(page 1, with 2-line subject line, endnote references, and single-line list)

↓5X →tab
MEMO TO: Luis Torres, General Manager ↓2X

FROM: Jonathan R. Evans, Assistant Marketing Manager *jre*

DATE: January 19, 20--

2-line subject line **SUBJECT:** An Analysis of the Scope and Effectiveness of Current Online
→tab Advertising in Today's Marketplace ↓2X

Online advertising uses the Internet and World Wide Web for the sole purpose of delivering marketing messages to customers. Some examples of online advertising are ads on search engine results pages, banner ads, interactive media ads, social network site advertising, online classified advertising, advertising networks, and e-mail marketing, including e-mail spam. ↓2X

One major benefit of online advertising is the immediate publishing of information and content that is not limited by geography or time. To that end, the emerging area of interactive advertising presents fresh challenges for advertisers.[1] *Endnote reference* Such challenges are opportunities for growth.

GROWTH FACTORS ↓2X

Online business has grown in tandem with the expanding number of Internet users. That trend will only increase as time goes on. ↓2X

Uncertainty. The uncertainties surrounding advertising on the Internet remain one of the major impediments to the expansion. All of the Internet advertising industry is today in a state of flux.

Reasons for Not Advertising Online. A recent survey found two main reasons cited for not advertising online:[2] ↓2X

Single-line list
   1. The difficulty of determining return on investment.
   2. The lack of reliable tracking and measurement data.

D. FORMATTING REPORTS

Margins, Spacing, and Indents. Begin the first page of each section (for example, the table of contents, first page of the body, and bibliography pages) 2 inches from the top of the page. Begin other pages 1 inch from the top. Use 1-inch default side and bottom margins for all pages. For a left-bound report, add 0.5 inch to the left margin. Single-space business reports. Double-space academic reports and indent paragraphs.

Titles and Headings. Center the title in 14-pt. font. Single-space multiline titles in a single-spaced report, and double-space multiline titles in a double-spaced report. Insert 1 blank line before and after all parts of a heading block (may include the title, subtitle, author, and/or date), and format all lines in bold. Format side headings in bold, at the left margin, with 1 blank line before and after them. Format paragraph headings at the left margin for single-spaced reports and indented for double-spaced reports in bold, followed by a period in bold and one space.

Citations. Format citations using Word's footnote (or endnote) feature.

Margins, Spacing, Headings, and Citations for APA- or MLA-Style Reports. See page R-10.

Reference Manual

A. REPORT IN APA STYLE

(page 3; with header, 2-line title, byline, main heading, subheading, and citations)

top, bottom, and side margins: *default* (1")
double-space throughout

Online Advertising 3 *Header*

2-line title   An Analysis of the Scope and Effectiveness

of Online Advertising

Byline   Jonathan R. Evans

→ tab   Online advertising uses the Internet for the sole purpose of delivering

marketing messages to customers. Some examples of online advertising are ads

on search engine results pages, banner ads, interactive media ads, online

classifieds, advertising networks, and e-mail marketing (Gunderson, 2011, p. D1).   *Citation*

One major benefit of online advertising is the immediate publishing of

content that is not limited by geography or time. To that end, interactive

advertising presents fresh challenges for advertisers (Newsome, 2010).

Main heading   Growth Factors

Online business has grown in tandem with the expanding number of

Internet users. That trend will only increase as time goes on (Arlens & Schell).

Subheading *Uncertainty* ◄—— Italic

The uncertainties surrounding Internet advertising are impeding its

expansion. A recent survey found two main reasons cited for not advertising

online. The first is the difficulty of determining return on investment, especially in

terms of repeat business and first-time shoppers. The second is the lack of reliable

tracking and measurement data ("eWebStats," 2010).

B. REFERENCES IN APA STYLE

(page 14; with header)

top, bottom, and side margins: *default* (1")
double-space throughout

Online Advertising 14 *Header*

hanging indent ↓   References

Book—one author   Adams, A. B. (2009). *Internet advertising and the upcoming electronic upheaval.*

→ hanging indent   Boston: Brunswick Press.

Annual report   AdNet Incoporated. (2010). *2010 annual report.* San Francisco: BCI, Inc.

Newspaper article   An, S. J. (2010, July 12). Banner ad frenzy. *The Wall Street Journal,* p. R6.

Book—two authors   Arlens, R., & Seymour, S. (2010). *E-vertising.* Cambridge, MA: New England

Publishing.

Book—organization   Directory of business and financial services. (2009). New York: International
as author

Corporate Libraries Association.

WWW page   eWebStats: Advertising revenues and trends. (n.d.). New York: eMarketer.

Retrieved August 11, 2010, from

http://www.emarketer.com/ewebstats/2507manu.ad

Journal article—   Ingram, F. (2009). Trends in online advertising. *Personnel Quarterly, 20,* 804-816.
paged continuously

Journal article—   Johnson, J. (2010, July 19). WebRatings Index shows 4% rise in Web ads.
paged each issue

Advertising Today, 39, 18.

Online database   Motivational advertising techniques. (2010, January). *Advertising Encyclopedia.*

Retrieved January 7, 2010, from http://www.adtech.com/ads.html

Government document   National Institute of Psychology (2009). *Who clicks? An analysis of Internet*

advertising (TNIP Publication No. ADM 82-1195). Washington, DC.

C. REPORT IN MLA STYLE

(page 1; with header, heading, 2-line title, and citations)

top, bottom, and side margins: *default* (1")
double-space throughout

Evans 1 *Header*

Heading   Jonathan R. Evans

Professor Inman

Management 302

19 January 20--

2-line title   An Analysis of the Scope and Effectiveness

of Online Advertising

→ tab   Online advertising uses the Internet for the sole purpose of delivering

marketing messages to customers. Some examples of online advertising are ads

on search engine results pages, banner ads, interactive media ads, social network

site advertising, online classifieds, and e-mail marketing (Gunderson D1).   *Citation*

One major benefit of online advertising is the immediate publishing of

information and content that is not limited by geography or time. To that end,

interactive advertising presents fresh challenges for advertisers (Newsome 59).

Online business has grown in tandem with the expanding number of

Internet users. That trend will only increase as time goes on (Arlens & Schell 376-

379). The uncertainties surrounding Internet advertising remain one of the major

impediments to the expansion. A recent survey found two main reasons cited for

not advertising online. The first is the difficulty of determining return on

investment. The second is the lack of reliable tracking and measurement data.

D. WORKS CITED IN MLA STYLE

(page 14; with header and hanging indent)

top, bottom, and side margins: *default* (1")
double-space throughout

Evans 14 *Header*

hanging indent ↓   Works Cited

Book—one author   Adams, Ana. B. *Internet Advertising and the Upcoming Electronic Upheaval.*

→ hanging indent   Boston: Brunswick Press, 2009.

Annual report   AdNet Incoporated. *2010 Annual Report.* San Francisco: BCI, Inc., 2010.

Newspaper article   An, Sang Jin. "Banner Ad Frenzy." *The Wall Street Journal,* 12 July 2010: R6.

Book—two authors   Arlens, Rachel, and Seymour Schell. *E-vertising.* Cambridge, MA: New England

Publishing, 2009.

Book—organization   Corporate Libraries Association. *Directory of Business and Financial Services.* New
as author

York: Corporate Libraries Association, 2009.

WWW page   "eWebStats: Advertising Revenues and Trends." 11 Aug. 2009. 7 Jan. 2010

<http://www.emarketer.com/ewebstats/ad>.

Journal article—   Ingram, Frank. "Trends in Online Advertising." *Personnel Quarterly* 20 (2010):
paged continuously

804-816.

Journal article—   Johnson, June. "WRI shows 4% rise in Web ads." *WebAds Today* 19 July 2010: 18.
paged each issue

Online database   Motivational Advertising Techniques. 2010. Advertising Encyclopedia. 7 Jan. 2010

<http://www.adtech.com/ads.html>.

Government document   National Institute of Psychology. *Who clicks?* TNIP Publication No. ADM 82-1195.

Washington, DC. GPO: 2010.

E-mail   Williams, Dan V. "Reaction to Internet Ads." E-mail to the author. 18 Aug. 2010.

A. MEETING AGENDA

↓5X
14 pt **MILES HARDWARE EXECUTIVE COMMITTEE** ↓2X
12 pt ↓ **Meeting Agenda** ↓2X
June 7, 20-- ↓2X

Numbered list: default format

1. Call to order
2. Approval of minutes of May 5 meeting
3. Progress report on building addition and parking lot restrictions (Norman Hodges and Anthony Pascarelli)
4. May 15 draft of Five-Year Plan
5. Review of National Hardware Association annual convention
6. Employee grievance filed by Ellen Burrows (John Landstrom)
7. New expense-report forms (Anne Richards)
8. Announcements
9. Adjournment

B. MINUTES OF A MEETING

↓5X
14 pt **RESOURCE COMMITTEE** ↓2X
12 pt ↓ **Minutes of the Meeting** ↓2X
March 13, 20-- ↓1X

ATTENDANCE	The Resource Committee met on March 13, 20--, at the Airport Sheraton in Portland, Oregon, with all members present. Michael Davis, chairperson, called the meeting to order at 2:30 p.m. ↓1X
APPROVAL OF MINUTES	The minutes of the January 27 meeting were read and approved as presented.
OLD BUSINESS	The members of the committee reviewed the sales brochure on electronic copyboards and agreed to purchase one for the conference room. Cynthia Giovanni will secure quotations from at least two suppliers.
NEW BUSINESS	The committee reviewed a request from the Purchasing Department for three new computers. After extensive discussion regarding the appropriate use of the computers and software to be purchased, the committee approved the request.
ADJOURNMENT	The meeting was adjourned at 4:45 p.m. The next meeting is scheduled for April 13 in Suite B. ↓2X Respectfully submitted, ↓4X *D. S. Madsen* D. S. Madsen, Secretary

(Note: Table shown with "View Gridlines" active.)

C. ITINERARY

↓5X
14 pt **PORTLAND SALES MEETING** ↓2X
12 pt ↓ **Itinerary for Dorothy Turner** ↓2X
March 12-15, 20-- ↓1X

THURSDAY, MARCH 12 ↓1X	
5:10 p.m.-7:06 p.m.	Flight from Detroit to Portland; Northwest 83 (800-555-1212); e-ticket; Seat 8D; nonstop. ↓2X Jack Weatherford (Home: 503-555-8029; Office: 503-555-7631) will meet your flight on Thursday, provide transportation during your visit, and return you to the airport on Saturday morning. Airport Sheraton (503-555-4032) King-sized bed, nonsmoking room; late arrival guaranteed; Reservation No. 302M6-02. ↓1X
FRIDAY, MARCH 13	
9 a.m.-5:30 p.m.	Portland Sales Meeting 1931 Executive Way, Suite 10 Portland, OR 97211 (503-555-7631)
SATURDAY, MARCH 14	
7:30 a.m.-2:47 p.m.	Flight from Portland to Detroit; Northwest 360; e-ticket; Seat 9a; nonstop.

(Note: Table shown with "View Gridlines" active.)

D. LEGAL DOCUMENT

(with line numbers)

left tabs: 1", 3.25"
right tab: 6.5"

line numbers (court documents only)

```
 1   STATE OF NEVADA                          → tab 6.5" IN DISTRICT COURT ↓2X
 2
 3   COUNTY OF CLARK                           NORTHEAST JUDICIAL DISTRICT ↓2X
 4
 5   JOHN C. SMITH       → tab 3.25" →    NO. ___1 space, 20 underscores___
 6   209 East Clark Avenue                ) tab 6.5"
 7   Las Vegas, NV 89155-1603             )
 8                                        )
 9   → tab 1" Plaintiff, → tab 3.25" )
10                                        )
11        vs.                             )    → tab 6.5" SUMMONS
12                                        )
13   FAITH GEORGIA                        )
14                                        )
15        Defendant.                      )
16                                            ↓2X
17   THE STATE OF NEVADA TO THE ABOVE-NAMED DEFENDANT: ↓2X
18
19   → tab 1" You are hereby summoned and required to appear and defend
20   against the Complaint in this action, which is hereby served upon you by serving
21   upon the undersigned an Answer or other proper response within twenty (20)
22   days after the service of the Summons and Complaint upon you, exclusive of the
23   day of service. ↓2X
24
25        If you fail to do so, judgment by default will be taken against you for
26   the relief demanded in the Complaint.
27
28        SIGNED this ___ day of July, 20--. ↓2X
29   1 space;                        underscores to the right margin
30   5 underscores; → tab 3.25" Jim Roe → tab 6.5" Attorney at Law
31   1 space                     229 South Civic Way
32                               Laughlin, NV 89029-2648
33                               Telephone: 702-555-1205
34                               Attorney for Plaintiff
35
```

A. RESUME

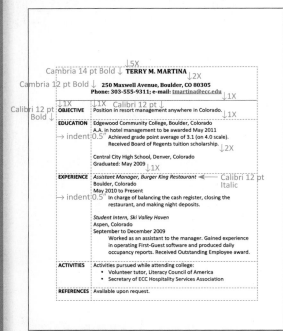

(Note: Table shown with "View Gridlines" active.)

B. APPLICATION LETTER IN BLOCK STYLE

(with return address)

↓5X
March 1, 20--
↓4X

Mr. Lou Mansfield, Director
Human Resources Department
Rocky Resorts International
P.O. Box 1412
Denver, CO 80214
↓2X
Dear Mr. Mansfield:
↓2X
Please consider me an applicant for the position of concierge for Suite Retreat, as advertised in last Sunday's *Denver Times*.
↓2X
I will receive my A.A. degree in hotel management from Edgewood Community College in May and will be available for full-time employment immediately. In addition to my extensive coursework in hospitality services and business, I've had experience in working for a ski lodge similar to Suite Retreats in Aspen. As a lifelong resident of Colorado and an avid skier, I would be able to provide your guests with any information they request.

After you've reviewed my enclosed resume, I would appreciate having an opportunity to discuss with you why I believe I have the right qualifications and personality to serve as your concierge. I can be reached at 303-555-9311.
↓2X
Sincerely,
↓4X
Terry M. Martina

Return address   Terry M. Martina
250 Maxwell Avenue, Apt. 8
Boulder, CO 80305
↓2X
Enclosure

C. FORMATTING LISTS

Numbers or bullets are used in documents to call attention to items in a list and to increase readability. If the sequence of the list items is important, use numbers rather than bullets.

- Insert 1 blank line before and after the list.
- Use Word's default format for all lists in either single- or double-spaced documents, including lists in documents such as a meeting agenda. Any carryover lines will be indented automatically.
- Use the same line spacing (single or double) between lines in the list as is used in the rest of the document.

The three bulleted and numbered lists shown at the right are all formatted correctly.

D. EXAMPLES OF DIFFERENT TYPES OF LISTS

According to the Internet Advertising Bureau, the following are the most common types of advertising on the Internet:

- Banner ads that feature some type of appropriate animation to attract the viewer's attention and interest.
- Sponsorship, in which an advertiser sponsors a content-based Web site.
- Interstitials, ads that flash up while a page downloads.

There is now considerable controversy about the effectiveness of banner advertising. As previously noted, a central goal of banner advertisements is to

*****

According to the Internet Advertising Bureau, the following are the most common types of advertising on the Internet, shown in order of popularity:

1. Banner ads
2. Sponsorship
3. Interstitials

There is now considerable controversy about the effectiveness of banner advertising. As previously noted, a central goal of banner advertisements is to

*****

According to the Internet Advertising Bureau, the following are the most common types of advertising on the Internet:

- Banner ads that feature some type of appropriate animation to attract the viewer's attention and interest.

- Sponsorship, in which an advertiser sponsors a Web site.

- Interstitials, ads that flash up while a page downloads.

There is now considerable controversy about the effectiveness of banner advertising. As previously noted, a central goal of banner advertisements is to

A. BOXED TABLE

(with subtitle; bottom-aligned and braced column headings; left- and right-aligned columns; total line and table note)

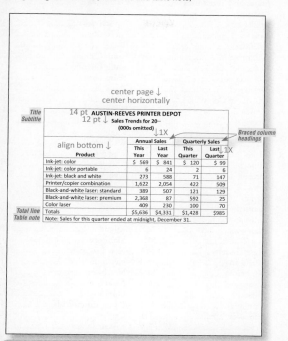

B. OPEN TABLE

(with 2-line title; 2-line centered, bottom-aligned column headings; left- and right-aligned columns; column entries with dollar and percent signs)

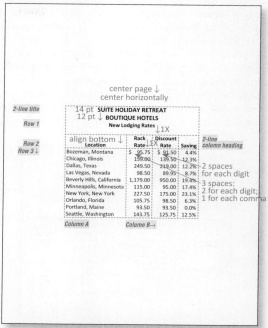

(Note: Table shown with "View Gridlines" active.)

C. RULED TABLE

(with table number, title, centered column headings, and total line)

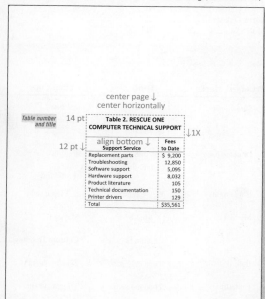

(Note: Table shown with "View Gridlines" active.)

D. FORMATTING TABLES

The three basic styles of tables are boxed, open, and ruled. Tables have vertical columns (Column A), horizontal rows (Row 1), and intersecting cells (Cell A1). Center a table vertically that appears alone on the page. Insert 1 blank line before and after a table that appears within a document. Automatically adjust column widths and horizontally center all tables.

Heading Block. Merge any cells in Row 1, and type the heading block. Center and bold throughout. Type the title in all-caps, 14-pt. font, and the subtitle in upper- and lowercase, 12-pt. font. If a table has a number, type *Table* in upper- and lowercase. Follow the table number with a period and 1 space. Insert 1 blank line below the heading block.

Column Headings. Center column headings. Type in upper- and lowercase and bold. Bottom-align all column headings if a row includes a 2-line column heading. Merge desired cells for braced headings.

Column Entries. Left-align text columns, and right-align number columns. Capitalize only the first word and proper nouns in column entries.

Column Entry Dollar and Percent Signs. Insert the dollar sign only before the amount in the first entry and before a total amount entry. Align the dollar sign with the longest amount in the column, inserting spaces after the dollar sign as needed (allowing for 2 spaces for each digit and 1 space for each comma). Repeat the percent sign for each number in each column entry (unless the column heading identifies the data as percentages).

Table Note and Total Line. For a note line, merge the cells of the last row and use "Note" followed by a colon. For a total line, add a top and bottom border, use "Total" or "Totals" as appropriate, and add a percent or dollar sign if needed.

A. FORMATTING BUSINESS FORMS

Many business forms can be created and filled in by using templates that are provided within commercial word processing software. Template forms can be used "as is" or they can be edited. Templates can also be used to create customized forms for any business.

When a template is opened, the form is displayed on screen. The user can then fill in the necessary information, including personalized company information. Data are entered into cells or fields, and you can move quickly from field to field with a single keystroke—usually by pressing Tab or Enter.

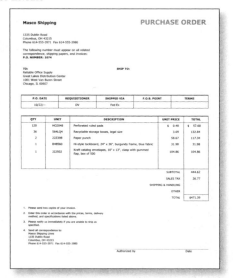

B. U.S. POSTAL SERVICE ABBREVIATIONS

(for States, Territories, and Canadian Provinces)

States and Territories

Alabama	AL
Alaska	AK
Arizona	AZ
Arkansas	AR
California	CA
Colorado	CO
Connecticut	CT
Delaware	DE
District of Columbia	DC
Florida	FL
Georgia	GA
Guam	GU
Hawaii	HI
Idaho	ID
Illinois	IL
Indiana	IN
Iowa	IA
Kansas	KS
Kentucky	KY
Louisiana	LA
Maine	ME
Maryland	MD
Massachusetts	MA
Michigan	MI
Minnesota	MN
Mississippi	MS
Missouri	MO
Montana	MT
Nebraska	NE
Nevada	NV
New Hampshire	NH
New Jersey	NJ
New Mexico	NM
New York	NY
North Carolina	NC
North Dakota	ND
Ohio	OH
Oklahoma	OK
Oregon	OR
Pennsylvania	PA
Puerto Rico	PR
Rhode Island	RI
South Carolina	SC
South Dakota	SD
Tennessee	TN
Texas	TX
Utah	UT
Vermont	VT
Virgin Islands	VI
Virginia	VA
Washington	WA
West Virginia	WV
Wisconsin	WI
Wyoming	WY

Canadian Provinces

Alberta	AB
British Columbia	BC
Labrador	LB
Manitoba	MB
New Brunswick	NB
Newfoundland	NF
Northwest Territories	NT
Nova Scotia	NS
Ontario	ON
Prince Edward Island	PE
Quebec	PQ
Saskatchewan	SK
Yukon Territory	YT

C. PROOFREADERS' MARKS

Proofreaders' Marks		Draft	Final Copy
⌒	Omit space	data base	database
∨ or ∧	Insert	if hes not going	if he's not going,
≡	Capitalize	Maple street	Maple Street
⌿	Delete	a final draft	a draft
#	Insert space	allready to	all ready to
when	Change word	and if you	and when you
/	Use lowercase letter	our President	our president
¶	Paragraph	… to use it.¶We can	… to use it. We can
•••	Don't delete	a true story	a true story
○	Spell out	the only ①	the only one
∽	Transpose	they all see	they see all

Proofreaders' Marks		Draft	Final Copy
SS	Single-space	first line / second line	first line / second line
ds	Double-space	first line / second line	first line / second line
⌐	Move right	Please send	Please send
⌐	Move left	May I	May I
∿	Bold	Column Heading	**Column Heading**
ital	Italic	Time magazine	*Time* magazine
u/l	Underline	Time magazine	Time magazine readers
♂	Move as shown	readers will see	will see

Language Arts For Business

(50 "must-know" rules)

PUNCTUATION

Commas

RULE 1
, direct address
(L. 21)

Use commas before and after a name used in direct address.
> Thank you, John, for responding to my e-mail so quickly.
> Ladies and gentlemen, the program has been canceled.

RULE 2
, independent clause
(L. 27)

Use a comma between independent clauses joined by a coordinate conjunction (unless both clauses are short).
> Ellen left her job with IBM, and she and her sister went to Paris.
> But: Ellen left her job with IBM and went to Paris with her sister.
> But: John drove and I navigated.

Note: An independent clause is one that can stand alone as a complete sentence. The most common coordinate conjunctions are *and, but, or,* and *nor*.

The under-line calls attention to a point in the sentence where a comma might mistakenly be inserted.

RULE 3
, introductory expression
(L. 27)

Use a comma after an introductory expression (unless it is a short prepositional phrase).
> Before we can make a decision, we must have all the facts.
> But: In 2004 our nation elected a new president.

Note: An introductory expression is a group of words that come before the subject and verb of the independent clause. Common prepositions are *to, in, on, of, at, by, for,* and *with*.

RULE 4
, direct quotation
(L. 41)

Use a comma before and after a direct quotation.
> James said, "I shall return," and then left.

RULE 5
, date
(L. 51)

Use a comma before and after the year in a complete date.
> We will arrive on June 2, 2006, for the conference.
> But: We will arrive on June 2 for the conference.

RULE 6
, place
(L. 51)

Use a comma before and after a state or country that follows a city (but not before a ZIP Code).
> Joan moved to Vancouver, British Columbia, in May.
> Send the package to Douglasville, GA 30135, by Express Mail.
> But: Send the package to Georgia by Express Mail.

Reference Manual

<table>
<tr><td>

RULE 7
, series
(L. 61)

</td><td>

Use a comma between each item in a series of three or more.

We need to order paper, toner, and font cartridges for the printer.
They saved their work, exited their program, and turned off their computers when they finished.

Note: Do not use a comma after the last item in a series.

</td></tr>
<tr><td>

RULE 8
, transitional expression
(L. 61)

</td><td>

Use a comma before and after a transitional expression or independent comment.

It is critical, therefore, that we finish the project on time.
Our present projections, you must admit, are inadequate.
But: You must admit our present projections are inadequate.

Note: Examples of transitional expressions and independent comments are *in addition to*, *therefore*, *however*, *on the other hand*, *as a matter of fact*, and *unfortunately*.

</td></tr>
<tr><td>

RULE 9
, nonessential expression
(L. 71)

</td><td>

Use a comma before and after a nonessential expression.

Andre, who was there, can verify the statement.
But: Anyone who was there can verify the statement.
Van's first book, *Crisis of Management*, was not discussed.
Van's book *Crisis of Management* was not discussed.

Note: A nonessential expression is a group of words that may be omitted without changing the basic meaning of the sentence. Always examine the noun or pronoun that comes before the expression to determine whether the noun needs the expression to complete its meaning. If it does, the expression is *essential* and does *not* take a comma.

</td></tr>
<tr><td>

RULE 10
, adjacent adjectives
(L. 71)

</td><td>

Use a comma between two adjacent adjectives that modify the same noun.

We need an intelligent, enthusiastic individual for this job.
But: Please order a new bulletin board for our main conference room.

Note: Do not use a comma after the second adjective. Also, do not use a comma if the first adjective modifies the combined idea of the second adjective and the noun (for example, *bulletin board* and *conference room* in the second example above).

</td></tr>
</table>

Semicolons

<table>
<tr><td>

RULE 11
; no conjunction
(L. 97)

</td><td>

Use a semicolon to separate two closely related independent clauses that are not joined by a conjunction (such as *and, but, or*, or *nor*).

Management favored the vote; stockholders did not.
But: Management favored the vote, but stockholders did not.

</td></tr>
<tr><td>

RULE 12
; series
(L. 97)

</td><td>

Use a semicolon to separate three or more items in a series if any of the items already contain commas.

Staff meetings were held on Thursday, May 7; Monday, June 7; and Friday, June 12.

Note: Be sure to insert the semicolon *between* (not within) the items in a series.

</td></tr>
</table>

Hyphens

RULE 13
- number
(L. 57)

Hyphenate compound numbers between twenty-one and ninety-nine and fractions that are expressed as words.

> Twenty-nine recommendations were approved by at least three-fourths of the members.

RULE 14
- compound adjective
(L. 67)

Hyphenate compound adjectives that come before a noun (unless the first word is an adverb ending in -ly).

> We reviewed an up-to-date report on Wednesday.
> But: The report was up to date.
> But: We reviewed the highly rated report.

Note: A compound adjective is two or more words that function as a unit to describe a noun.

Apostrophes

RULE 15
' singular noun
(L. 37)

Use 's to form the possessive of singular nouns.

> The hurricane's force caused major damage to North Carolina's coastline.

RULE 16
' plural noun
(L. 37)

Use only an apostrophe to form the possessive of plural nouns that end in s.

> The investors' goals were outlined in the stockholders' report.
> But: The investors outlined their goals in the report to the stockholders.
> But: The women's and children's clothing was on sale.

RULE 17
' pronoun
(L. 37)

Use 's to form the possessive of indefinite pronouns (such as someone's or anybody's); do not use an apostrophe with personal pronouns (such as hers, his, its, ours, theirs, and yours).

> She could select anybody's paper for a sample.
> It's time to put the file back into its cabinet.

Colons

RULE 18
: explanatory material
(L. 91)

Use a colon to introduce explanatory material that follows an independent clause.

> The computer satisfies three criteria: speed, cost, and power.
> But: The computer satisfies the three criteria of speed, cost, and power.
> Remember this: only one coupon is allowed per customer.

Note: An independent clause can stand alone as a complete sentence. Do not capitalize the word following the colon.

Periods

RULE 19
. polite request
(L. 91)

Use a period to end a sentence that is a polite request.

> Will you please call me if I can be of further assistance.

Note: Consider a sentence a polite request if you expect the reader to respond by doing as you ask rather than by giving a yes-or-no answer.

Quotation Marks

RULE 20
" direct quotation
(L. 41)

Use quotation marks around a direct quotation.

> Harrison responded by saying, "Their decision does not affect us."
> But: Harrison responded by saying that their decision does not affect us.

RULE 21
" title
(L. 41)

Use quotation marks around the title of a newspaper or magazine article, chapter in a book, report, and similar terms.

> The most helpful article I found was "Multimedia for All."

Italics (or Underline)

RULE 22
title or title
(L. 41)

Italicize (or underline) the titles of books, magazines, newspapers, and other complete published works.

> Grisham's *The Brethren* was reviewed in a recent *USA Today* article.

Reference Manual

GRAMMAR

Sentences

<table>
<tr><td>

RULE 23
fragment
(L. 21)

</td></tr>
</table>

Avoid sentence fragments.

> Not: She had always wanted to be a financial manager. But had not had the needed education.

> But: She had always wanted to be a financial manager but had not had the needed education.

Note: A fragment is a part of a sentence that is incorrectly punctuated as a complete sentence. In the first example above, "but had not had the needed education" is not a complete sentence because it does not contain a subject.

<table>
<tr><td>

RULE 24
run-on
(L. 21)

</td></tr>
</table>

Avoid run-on sentences.

> Not: Mohamed is a competent worker he has even passed the MOS exam.
> Not: Mohamed is a competent worker, he has even passed the MOS exam.
> But: Mohamed is a competent worker; he has even passed the MOS exam.
> Or: Mohamed is a competent worker. He has even passed the MOS exam.

Note: A run-on sentence is two independent clauses that run together without any punctuation between them or with only a comma between them.

Agreement

<table>
<tr><td>

RULE 25
agreement singular
agreement plural
(L. 67)

</td></tr>
</table>

Use singular verbs and pronouns with singular subjects; use plural verbs and pronouns with plural subjects.

> I <u>was</u> happy with <u>my</u> performance.
> <u>Janet and Phoenix were</u> happy with <u>their</u> performance.
> Among the items discussed <u>were</u> our <u>raises and benefits</u>.

<table>
<tr><td>

RULE 26
agreement pronoun
(L. 81)

</td></tr>
</table>

Some pronouns (*anybody, each, either, everybody, everyone, much, neither, no one, nobody,* and *one*) are always singular and take a singular verb. Other pronouns (*all, any, more, most, none,* and *some*) may be singular or plural, depending on the noun to which they refer.

> <u>Each</u> of the employees has finished <u>his or her</u> task.
> <u>Much</u> <u>remains</u> to be done.
> <u>Most</u> of the pie <u>was</u> eaten, but <u>most</u> of the cookies <u>were</u> left.

<table>
<tr><td>

RULE 27
agreement intervening words
(L. 81)

</td></tr>
</table>

Disregard any intervening words that come between the subject and verb when establishing agreement.

> That <u>box</u>, containing the books and pencils, <u>has</u> not been found.
> <u>Alex</u>, accompanied by Tricia and Roxy, <u>is</u> attending the conference and taking <u>his</u> computer.

<table>
<tr><td>

RULE 28
agreement nearer noun
(L. 101)

</td></tr>
</table>

If two subjects are joined by *or, either/or, neither/nor,* or *not only/but also,* make the verb agree with the subject nearer to the verb.

> Neither the coach nor the <u>players</u> <u>are</u> at home.
> Not only the coach but also the <u>referee</u> <u>is</u> at home.
> But: <u>Both</u> the coach and the referee <u>are</u> at home.

Pronouns

RULE 29
nominative pronoun
(L. 107)

Use nominative pronouns (such as *I, he, she, we, they,* and *who*) as subjects of a sentence or clause.

> The programmer and <u>he</u> are reviewing the code.
> Barb is a person <u>who</u> can do the job.

RULE 30
objective pronoun
(L. 107)

Use objective pronouns (such as *me, him, her, us, them,* and *whom*) as objects of a verb, preposition, or infinitive.

> The code was reviewed by the programmer and <u>him</u>.
> Barb is the type of person <u>whom</u> we can trust.

Adjectives and Adverbs

RULE 31
adjective/adverb
(L. 101)

Use comparative adjectives and adverbs (*-er, more,* and *less*) when referring to two nouns or pronouns; use superlative adjectives and adverbs (*-est, most,* and *least*) when referring to more than two.

> The <u>shorter</u> of the <u>two</u> training sessions is the <u>more</u> helpful one.
> The <u>longest</u> of the <u>three</u> training sessions is the <u>least</u> helpful one.

Word Usage

RULE 32
accept/except
(L. 117)

***Accept* means "to agree to"; *except* means "to leave out."**

> All employees <u>except</u> the maintenance staff should <u>accept</u> the agreement.

RULE 33
affect/effect
(L. 117)

***Affect* is most often used as a verb meaning "to influence"; *effect* is most often used as a noun meaning "result."**

> The ruling will <u>affect</u> our domestic operations but will have no <u>effect</u> on our Asian operations.

RULE 34
farther/further
(L. 117)

***Farther* refers to distance; *further* refers to extent or degree.**

> The <u>farther</u> we drove, the <u>further</u> agitated he became.

RULE 35
personal/personnel
(L. 117)

***Personal* means "private"; *personnel* means "employees."**

> All <u>personnel</u> agreed not to use e-mail for <u>personal</u> business.

RULE 36
principal/principle
(L. 117)

***Principal* means "primary"; *principle* means "rule."**

> The <u>principle</u> of fairness is our <u>principal</u> means of dealing with customers.

MECHANICS

Capitalization

RULE 37
≡ sentence
(L. 31)

Capitalize the first word of a sentence.
> Please prepare a summary of your activities.

RULE 38
≡ proper noun
(L. 31)

Capitalize proper nouns and adjectives derived from proper nouns.
> Judy Hendrix drove to Albuquerque in her new Pontiac convertible.

Note: A proper noun is the official name of a particular person, place, or thing.

RULE 39
≡ time
(L. 31)

Capitalize the names of the days of the week, months, holidays, and religious days (but do not capitalize the names of the seasons).
> On Thursday, November 25, we will celebrate Thanksgiving, the most popular holiday in the fall.

RULE 40
≡ noun #
(L. 77)

Capitalize nouns followed by a number or letter (except for the nouns *line, note, page, paragraph,* and *size*).
> Please read Chapter 5, which begins on page 94.

RULE 41
≡ compass point
(L. 77)

Capitalize compass points (such as *north, south,* or *northeast*) only when they designate definite regions.
> From Montana we drove south to reach the Southwest.

RULE 42
≡ organization
(L. 111)

Capitalize common organizational terms (such as *advertising department* and *finance committee*) only when they are the actual names of the units in the writer's own organization and when they are preceded by the word *the*.
> The report from the Advertising Department is due today.
> But: Our advertising department will submit its report today.

RULE 43
≡ course
(L. 111)

Capitalize the names of specific course titles but not the names of subjects or areas of study.
> I have enrolled in Accounting 201 and will also take a marketing course.

Number Expression

RULE 44
general
(L. 47)

In general, spell out numbers zero through ten, and use figures for numbers above ten.
> We rented two movies for tonight.
> The decision was reached after 27 precincts sent in their results.

Reference Manual

RULE 45
# figure 	
(L. 47)
	Use figures for
	• **Dates. (Use _st, d,_ or _th_ only if the day comes before the month.)**
	  The tax report is due on April 15 (not _April 15th_).
	  We will drive to the camp on the 23d (or _23rd_ or _23rd_) of May.
	• **All numbers if two or more _related_ numbers both above and below ten are used in the same sentence.**
	  Mr. Carter sent in 7 receipts, and Ms. Cantrell sent in 22.
	  But: The 13 accountants owned three computers each.
	• **Measurements (time, money, distance, weight, and percent).**
	  The $500 statue we delivered at 7 a.m. weighed 6 pounds.
	• **Mixed numbers.**
	  Our sales are up 9½ (or _9.5_) percent over last year.

RULE 46
# word 	
(L. 57)
	Spell out
	• **A number used as the first word of a sentence.**
	  Seventy-five people attended the conference in San Diego.
	• **The shorter of two adjacent numbers.**
	  We have ordered 3 two-pound cakes and one 5-pound cake for the reception.
	• **The words _million_ and _billion_ in round numbers (do not use decimals with round numbers).**
	  Not: A $5.00 ticket can win $28,000,000 in this month's lottery.
	  But: A $5 ticket can win $28 million in this month's lottery.
	• **Fractions.**
	  Almost one-half of the audience responded to the question.

Abbreviations

RULE 47 abbreviate none (L. 67)	**In general business writing, do not abbreviate common words (such as _dept._ or _pkg._), compass points, units of measure, or the names of months, days of the week, cities, or states (except in addresses).** Almost one-half of the audience indicated they were at least 5 <u>feet</u> 8 inches tall. **Note:** Do not insert a comma between the parts of a single measurement.
RULE 48 abbreviate measure (L. 87)	**In technical writing, on forms, and in tables, abbreviate units of measure when they occur frequently. Do not use periods.** 14 oz 5 ft 10 in 50 mph 2 yrs 10 mo

RULE 49
abbreviate lowercase
(L. 87)
	In most lowercase abbreviations made up of single initials, use a period after each initial but no internal spaces.
	  a.m. p.m. i.e. e.g. e.o.m.
	  Exceptions: mph mpg wpm

RULE 50
abbreviate =
(L. 87)
	In most all-capital abbreviations made up of single initials, do not use periods or internal spaces.
	  OSHA PBS NBEA WWW VCR MBA
	  Exceptions: U.S.A. A.A. B.S. Ph.D. P.O. B.C. A.D.

Getting Started

You can use Microsoft® Word for Windows (Word) to create anything from a simple e-mail message to a lengthy report with features, such as a preformatted cover page, footnotes, and stylized tables. The *Gregg College Keyboarding & Document Processing Manual for Microsoft Word 2010* (Word Manual) explains step by step how to create attractive, professional business documents using Word. It is a handy, permanent reference you can use on the job to review frequently used features and shortcuts.

The Word Manual is used in conjunction with your textbook and "GDP" (Gregg Document Processing—the shortened name of the associated course software) to develop the keyboarding and document processing skills needed for success in today's workplace. You will launch Word from GDP, complete the hands-on practice exercises in the Word Manual, and then type related document processing jobs in the textbook. This learning sequence is an effective, efficient way to become an accomplished Word user.

Word Manual Features

Each word processing feature is explained, illustrated, and then followed by a hands-on practice exercise in which you will use a new Word feature to format a document similar to the ones you will type in the textbook for that lesson. A handy list of keyboard shortcuts, a list of Word commands and their lesson of introduction, and an index are included on the inside and back covers of the Word Manual.

The following conventions are used throughout:

- Commands, tabs, groups, buttons, and other names or keyboard combinations used in step-by-step directions are shown in bold. For example, "Click the **File** tab, and click **Save**."
- When you see a key combination used in a direction, press and hold down the first key while you press the second key; then release both keys. For example, "On the keyboard, press **CTRL + S** to save a file."
- Words you are to type are shown in a different font. For example, "Type Agenda as the report title."

The following icons are used throughout:

🔴	**Attention**	Identifies important, broad-based information.
🔵	**Help**	Identifies troubleshooting steps to guide you when Word behaves unexpectedly or to help you remedy common mistakes.
🔵	**Tip**	Identifies helpful Word tips or provides guidance for using Word outside of GDP (such as at work or at home) where settings can vary.
🔴	**Hands On**	Identifies the beginning of a practice exercise.
🔵	**GO TO** **Textbook**	Identifies the end of a practice exercise and directs you to open your textbook to the corresponding lesson to study formatting and type the document processing jobs.
🔵	**REFER TO** **Word Manual**	Directs you to open a different lesson in the Word Manual for related information.
🔵	**REFER TO** **Reference Manual**	Directs you to open the Reference Manual found in the front pages of your Word Manual and textbook to review model documents and other helpful information.

🔵 An electronic reference manual can be accessed via GDP. See Lesson 25 for details.

The following terms (for a right-handed mouse) are used throughout:

- **Point.** Move the mouse until the mouse pointer on the screen is pointing to and resting over the desired item.
- **Click.** Point to an item; then press and quickly release the left mouse button without moving the mouse.
- **Double-click.** Point to an item; then press and quickly release the left mouse button twice without moving the mouse.
- **Drag.** Point to an item, hold down the left mouse button while moving the mouse, and release at the end of the selection.
- **Right-click.** Point to an item; then press and quickly release the right mouse button.
- **Select.** Highlight text.

GDP—Word Settings

🔵 **REFER TO**
Word Manual

Appendix A: GDP—Word
Settings
L. 24: Spelling and
Grammar Check

In order to create a standardized, trouble-free computing environment, GDP automatically opens Word documents with the Word 2003 Style Set already in place. This style uses preset margins, line spacing, and font choices, which are discussed in detail in Appendix A.

🛈 It is very important that before you begin typing any job in Word, you first manually set (or verify) certain Word options so that Word features will behave as expected! See Appendix A, GDP—Word Settings, for details.

In the workplace, most users customize Word. Therefore, understanding fundamental Word settings and learning to adjust and customize these settings is very helpful. Customized settings will generally not change unless you reset them.

🛈 Screen shots in this manual may vary slightly (title bars, tabs, and so forth) from the Word screens you see when you open a Word document from GDP. Word marks various spelling and grammar errors with red, blue, and green wavy lines. Also, Word is distributed in a variety of versions, and some Word features (such as Help and Clip Art) include Web-based content that changes. These slight differences are not cause for concern.

Appendixes A, B, and C

Refer to Appendix A, Using Microsoft Word in the Workplace, for tips on using Word outside of GDP (such as at work), for information on Word options you must manually set (or verify) while working in GDP, for troubleshooting steps for Word settings, or for guidance using the Word 2010 Style Set as an alternative to the Word 2003 Style Set. You should use only the Word 2003 Style Set within GDP.

Refer to Appendix B, Using GDP Features in Document Processing, for an index to the GDP features that are relevant to document processing jobs and their order of introduction in the Word Manual.

Refer to Appendix C, Saving a Word File in PDF Format, for steps to save a Word document in PDF format.

GDP—Help

GDP features that you will use when you begin to type practice exercises and document processing jobs are introduced in this manual on a "need-to-know" basis. When a relevant GDP feature is introduced, you will use GDP's Help for details and specific steps. Explore GDP Help to familiarize yourself with this valuable reference tool.

Orientation to Word Processing—A

REFER TO Word Manual

Appendix A: Start Word From Windows

Before you type any GDP job in Word, first manually set (or verify) certain Word options! See Appendix A, GDP—Word Settings, for details.

GDP—Start Word

See GDP Help for specific steps to start Word to begin either a practice exercise or a document processing job. Document processing jobs begin in Lesson 25 with Correspondence 25-1.

To verify your Word version and system information:

1. From the **File** tab, click **Help**.
2. In the right pane, under **About Microsoft Word**, note the version that is displayed.
3. For other relevant details (such as your operating system and version), click the **Additional Version and Copyright Information** link; in the **About Microsoft Office Word** window, click **System Info**; click **OK** when finished.

PRACTICE

1. Note that GDP launched Word and opened a blank, unnamed document.

   In future practice exercises, GDP will typically launch Word and automatically open a document with an assigned name and content in place.

   Depending upon your Windows settings, file extensions may or may not appear in Word's title bar. Notify your instructor before changing any Windows settings. At home, consult Windows Help for steps to display file extensions.

2. Study the illustration that follows this list; then use the mouse pointer to point to each item in the list on your Word window. To point to an item, move the mouse until the on-screen mouse pointer rests on the desired item. The pointer takes on different shapes, depending on the current task and on where it is positioned on the screen.

   • **File** tab. Displays the Backstage view with file management features, such as Save, Open, Close, New, Print, and Save & Send. The Recent Documents pane on the right lists recently opened documents. The Help, Options, and Exit buttons are at the bottom of the menu.

PRACTICE (continued)

- **Quick Access toolbar.** Displays frequently used commands, such as Save and Undo. You can add Word commands to customize it.
- **Title bar.** Displays the name of the current document and the name of the application program. In the next illustration, the file is generically named as *Document1*.
- **Ribbon.** Displays tabs, such as Home and Page Layout, for quick access to popular Word commands that are organized into groups.
- **Tab.** Includes groups of frequently used commands related specifically to that tab. For example, under the Home tab, the groups are Clipboard, Font, Paragraph, Styles, and Editing.
- **Group.** Displays groups of commands related to that tab. For example, the Clipboard group includes Paste, Cut, and Copy.
- **Dialog Box Launcher.** Displays a dialog box or task pane with more options related to that group.
- **Ruler.** Horizontal ruler used to set tabs, margins, and indents.
- **View Ruler button.** Displays the horizontal and vertical rulers. This toggle button turns the ruler display on and off.
- **Insertion point.** Shows where text will be inserted next.
- **Mouse pointer.** Shows the position of the mouse. The context-sensitive pointer changes dynamically with the task at hand.
- **Vertical scroll box.** Displays different parts of a document as you drag it up or down.
- **Vertical scroll bar.** Displays one screen of the document at a time as you click on it.
- **Status bar.** Displays information about a document, such as the current page and number of words in the document.
- **Vertical Page Position.** Displays the vertical page position of the insertion point as measured from the top of the page. (If you do not see this item in your Word screen, see Appendix A, GDP—Word Settings, Status Bar, for steps to display it.)
- **Spelling and Grammar Check button.** Displays proofreading and grammatical errors found in the text of a document.
- **View shortcut buttons.** Display different document views, such as Print Layout and Full Screen Reading.

  Use **Print Layout** view (Word's default view) unless otherwise directed. To change to **Print Layout** view, click the **Print Layout** view button.

- **Zoom buttons.** Apply different zoom settings.
- **Zoom slider.** Displays a faraway or close-up view when you drag the slider arrow or click the minus or plus signs.

Note: Keep this document open and continue reading.

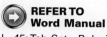
REFER TO
Word Manual
L. 45: Tab Set—Ruler Tabs

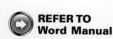
REFER TO
Word Manual
Appendix A: GDP—Word
Settings, Status Bar

REFER TO
Word Manual
L. 24: Spelling and
Grammar Check

Print Layout view button

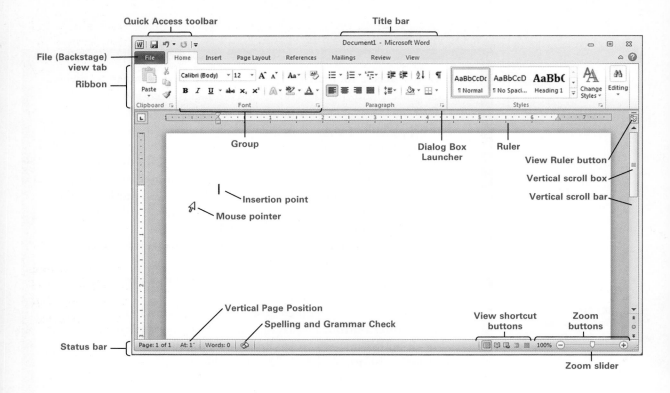

Choose a Command

A command directs Word to perform some action. For example, you can click on a button to direct Word to print a document or insert a table. You can choose commands from the Ribbon, from Mini toolbars, from shortcut menus, or from the keyboard using shortcut keys.

FROM THE RIBBON

The Ribbon includes the File, Home, Insert, Page Layout, References, Mailings, Review, and View default tabs. Each tab organizes commands into groups of related features. When you click a tab, the Ribbon displays only the command groups related to that tab.

If your mouse has a scroll button, click the **Home** tab and roll your mouse scroll button to move from one group to the next. Click any button in a group to execute a given command or display a submenu. Click any list arrow to display a submenu. Click any Dialog Box Launcher diagonal arrow to open a related dialog box or task pane.

To display a ScreenTip: Point to a button (or any item) in each group, and pause briefly. Read the helpful information that displays for that feature. The next illustration shows the ScreenTip that displays for the Bold button.

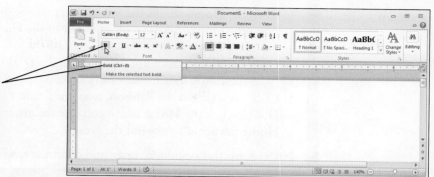

When you point to the command button in each group and pause briefly, you will see a helpful ScreenTip including any keyboard shortcuts, such as CTRL + B for Bold.

Word's Live Preview allows you to see how formatting options, such as font colors and Quick Styles, will look if applied. For example, if you select text and pause over a button (such as a font color button), a Live Preview of the new formatting appears. When you point to the next style, the Live Preview is updated. After previewing, click the desired choice to apply it.

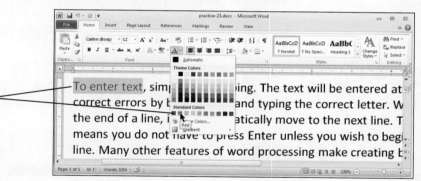

By selecting text (the text shown in red was selected first) and then pointing to various formatting choices, you can instantly see a "live preview" of how those choices would appear.

To increase the screen space for the document to more easily view the **Live Preview**, double-click any tab to collapse the Ribbon groups. To expand the groups, double-click any tab again.

Or: Press **CTRL + F1**.

Minimize the Ribbon button

Or: Click the **Minimize the Ribbon** button in the upper-right-hand corner of the Word window.

Some tabs are "dynamic" and appear only "on demand" as you work on a given task. For example, if you insert a picture and click it, an on-demand Picture Tools tab appears on the Ribbon with a context-sensitive Format tab and related groups. When you click away from the picture, the contextual tab disappears.

PRACTICE (continued)

1. Click the **Home** tab on the **Ribbon** to make it the active tab.
2. From the **Quick Access** toolbar, point to the **Undo** button, and note the **ScreenTip**.
3. From the **Home** tab, **Font** group, click the **Dialog Box Launcher**.
4. Note the commands in the **Font** dialog box, and click **Cancel**.
5. Click each tab on the **Ribbon**; note the group names for each tab.
6. Double-click the **Home** tab to collapse the groups; double-click the **Home** tab again to expand the groups.

Note: Keep this document open and continue reading.

FROM THE MINI TOOLBAR OR SHORTCUT MENU

Frequently used commands appear in Mini toolbars for quick access. For example, if you select some text and point to the top part of the selected text, a faded Mini toolbar appears. When you move your mouse over the faded Mini toolbar, it brightens so you can click the desired command. You can right-click the selected text to make the Mini toolbar appear along with a context-sensitive shortcut menu.

Point to the "top" part of the selected text or right-click the selected text to display the Mini Font toolbar.

PRACTICE (continued)

1. Type your first name, and double-click it to select it.
2. Point to the top of the selected text; note the faded **Mini Font** toolbar.
3. Point to the faded **Mini Font** toolbar until it brightens; then click away from the toolbar.
4. Select your first name again, right-click, and note the solid **Mini Font** toolbar and the related choices in the shortcut menu.

Note: Keep this document open and continue reading.

FROM THE KEYBOARD

Key combination shortcuts that start with the CTRL key, such as CTRL + C to copy, and others, such as F1 for Help, are used as an alternative to a mouse to execute a command. If a button has a keyboard shortcut, the key combination will be displayed in a ScreenTip when you point to a button. A handy list of keyboard shortcuts appears on the inside cover of this manual.

Keyboard shortcuts (also known as Key Tips) are available for every button on the Ribbon as an alternative to a mouse click. Press **ALT** to make the **Key Tip** badges appear and to move you out of text entry mode into command mode. Then press the desired **Key Tip** badge letter to make all the **Key Tips** for the commands appear. If you press the wrong **Key Tip** badge letter, press **ESC** to back up one level.

When the **Key Tips** are displayed, use the directional arrow keys to move around the **Ribbon** left or right through the tabs or from the **Home** or **Insert** tab, up to the **Quick Access** toolbar. The **Key Tips** will disappear—tap **ALT** twice to make them reappear. When the desired command is in view, press **ENTER** to activate it. Press the **TAB** key and **SHIFT + TAB** to cycle through commands.

 PRACTICE (continued)

1. On the **Ribbon**, click the **Home** tab.
2. From the **Font** group, point to the **Italic** button, and note the **ScreenTip** and the key combination shortcut, **CTRL + I**.
3. If necessary, double-click your name to select it again.
4. Tap **ALT** to make the **Key Tip** badges appear; then tap **H** on the keyboard to make the **Key Tip** badges appear in the groups under the **Home** tab. (Wait a few seconds for the **Key Tips** to appear.)
5. Press **1** on the keyboard to bold your name.
6. Tap **ALT** to make the **Key Tip** badges appear; then press the up arrow on the keyboard to move up to the **Quick Access** toolbar from the **Home** and **Insert** tabs.
7. Press the down, left, and right arrows to move around the tabs.
8. Tap **ALT** to make the **Key Tip** badges appear; then press the **TAB** key and **SHIFT + TAB** to cycle through commands.

Note: Keep this document open and continue reading.

FROM THE QUICK ACCESS TOOLBAR

The Quick Access toolbar is located above the File and Home tabs. This customizable toolbar displays frequently used commands, such as Save, Undo, and Repeat.

To add a favorite command to the toolbar: Click the list arrow to the right of the **Quick Access** toolbar; then click the desired choice. Click **More Commands** to add additional commands.

To remove a command from the toolbar: Click the list arrow to the right of the **Quick Access** toolbar; then uncheck the desired choice.

PRACTICE (continued)

1. Click the **Home** tab on the **Ribbon** to make it the active tab.
2. From the **Quick Access** toolbar, click the **Undo** button repeatedly until you return to a blank screen.
3. Click the list arrow to the right of the **Quick Access** toolbar, and check **Quick Print**; note the new **Quick Print** icon on the toolbar, which sends your entire document to the default printer immediately when clicked.
4. Click the list arrow to the right of the **Quick Access** toolbar, and uncheck **Quick Print**; note the **Quick Print** icon is removed.

Note: Keep this document open and continue reading.

File—Open

Open button

To open a file:

1. Click the **File** tab, and click the **Open** button.

   Or: Press **CTRL + O**.

   When you click the **File** tab, **Recent**, a list of recently opened documents appears under the **Recent Documents** pane. To open a recent document, click the desired document name. To keep a file permanently in the **Recent Documents** list, click the dimmed **Pin** button to the right of the document name. To release a document, click the **Pin** again.

2. Note that the **Open** dialog box appears.

   The appearance of your dialog box varies depending on your computer, your Windows version, and your Windows settings. File extensions may or may not appear. Consult Windows Help for steps to display file extensions.

3. Browse to the desired location and file; then double-click the desired file to open it.

   Consult Windows Help for steps to browse to a file. If the desired file does not display, you likely have a file filter in effect. Consult Windows Help for steps to display **All Files** (*.*) when you are browsing. If the list of files is too long to display all at once, scroll through the list until the desired file is visible.

PRACTICE (continued)

 In future practice exercises, GDP will typically launch Word and automatically open a document with an assigned name and content in place ready for your input. In this exercise, you will practice opening a file manually.

1. Open the file named *practice-21*.
2. Note that the title bar displays the file name *practice-21*.

Note: Keep this document open and continue reading below.

GDP—Quit Word

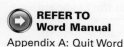 **REFER TO**
Word Manual

Appendix A: Quit Word
From Windows

See GDP Help for specific steps to quit Word to end a practice exercise or a document processing job and return to GDP.

PRACTICE (continued)

From this point forward, "Return to GDP" means that you follow the standard steps to quit Word and return to GDP as explained in GDP Help.

1. Return to GDP.
2. If you are prompted to save changes, click **No**.

 GO TO
Textbook

See GDP Help for specific steps to repeat or edit this practice exercise.

Orientation to Word Processing—B

Navigate in a File

The insertion point (a blinking vertical bar) shows where text will appear in the document as you type. After scrolling, click at the desired point in the document to move the insertion point. Do not confuse the mouse pointer with the blinking insertion point (cursor). The mouse pointer is typically either an arrow or I-beam symbol that shows the location of the mouse pointer on the screen.

To navigate through the document:

Page number ScreenTip

To Navigate	With the Mouse	With the Keyboard
Anywhere	Click where desired to position the cursor.	Use the arrow keys to move the cursor.
Through the document	Click the scroll bar (the area above or below the scroll box) to display the previous or next screen.	Press **PAGE UP** or **PAGE DOWN** to move up or down a screen at a time.
To a specific page	Drag the **vertical scroll box** until the desired page appears in the **Page number ScreenTip**.	Press **CTRL + F**; click the **Search Document** box list arrow, **Go To**; in the **Enter page number box**, type the desired page; click **Go To**, **Close**.
To the beginning or end of a document	Drag the **vertical scroll box** to the top or bottom of the **vertical scroll bar**.	Press **CTRL + HOME** or **CTRL + END** to move to the start or the end of a document.
To the beginning or end of a line	Click at the beginning or end of the line.	Press **HOME** to move to the beginning of a line or **END** to move to the end.
Through the pages (Refer to the illustration that follows.)	Press **ALT + CTRL + HOME** to display browse options. Click the **Browse by Page** button; then click the double arrows to browse up or down.	With the **Browse by Page** button active, press **CTRL + PAGE DOWN** or **CTRL + PAGE UP** to browse up or down a page at a time.

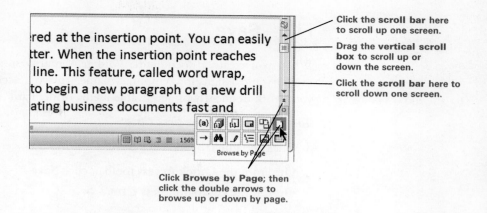

red at the insertion point. You can easily
tter. When the insertion point reaches
line. This feature, called word wrap,
to begin a new paragraph or a new drill
ating business documents fast and

Click the **scroll bar** here
to scroll up one screen.

Drag the **vertical scroll
box** to scroll up or
down the screen.

Click the **scroll bar** here to
scroll down one screen.

Browse by Page

Click **Browse by Page**; then
click the double arrows to
browse up or down by page.

PRACTICE

1. Manually open the file named *practice-22*.

   In future practice exercises, GDP will typically launch Word and automatically open a document with an assigned name and content in place.

2. Locate the mouse pointer (an I-beam symbol) and the insertion point (in front of the first word) on the Word screen for *practice-22*.
3. Move the mouse pointer over the **Ribbon**; note that it changes from an I-beam to an arrow.
4. Move the insertion point to the end of the document.
5. Move the insertion point just to the left of the "T" in "This" in line 3.
6. Press **BACKSPACE**; then press the **SPACE BAR** to replace the deleted space.
7. Press **DELETE**; then type T to replace the deleted letter.
8. Move to the beginning of the same line (line 3).
9. Move to the beginning of the document.

Note: Keep this document open and continue reading.

File—Save

When you create a document, Word temporarily stores it in the computer's memory and assigns it a temporary name. To avoid accidental loss of data, save your work frequently on removable media or the hard drive.

To save a file for the first time:

1. Click the **File** tab, and click **Save**.

   Or: From the **Quick Access** toolbar, click **Save**.

   Or: On the keyboard, press **CTRL + S**.

2. After the **Save As** window appears, browse to the desired folder.

   🌑 The appearance of the **Save As** dialog box will differ depending on your computer, your Windows version, and your Windows settings. File extensions may or may not appear. Consult Windows Help for help with displaying file extensions and browsing to folders and files.

3. If necessary, click the list arrow in the **Save as type** box, and click **Word Document (*.docx)** to save the file as a Word 2010 document. Word automatically adds the extension *.docx* to your file name, so you don't need to type it.

4. Type the desired file name in the **File name** box, and click **Save**.

   💡 Word automatically inserts an initial file name in the File name box, which usually consists of the first few words in the document. While the temporary file name is still highlighted, type your preferred file name. The temporary name will be deleted automatically and replaced with the name you type. A file name can include upper- and/or lowercase letters, numbers, spaces, and a few common symbols, such as the hyphen or underline.

Save button

To save an existing document: Click the **File** tab; click **Save**.

Or: On from the Quick Access toolbar, click **Save**.

Or: On the keyboard, press **CTRL + S**.

⚠️ When GDP opens a Word document to begin a document processing job, typically a document with an assigned name opens automatically. When you use Save, you will not need to type a file name since the file was already assigned a specific name. However, in this practice exercise, you will use the Save and Save As commands to manually save a file.

To save an existing file under a different name or to keep the original version of a file and then make changes to the newly saved file, click the **File** tab, and click **Save As**. In the **Save As** window, in the **File name** box, the existing document name will be highlighted. Browse to a new location if desired, type the new file name, and click **Save**.

See Appendix C, Saving a Word File in PDF Format, for steps to save a Word document in PDF format.

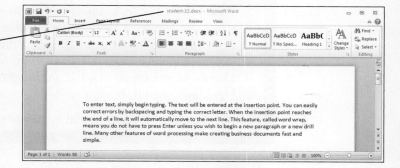

PRACTICE (continued)

1. Move to the end of the document, and press **ENTER** 2 times.
2. Type your first and last name.
3. Click the **File** tab, and click the **Save As** button.
4. Save this file with the new file name *student-22*, and click **Save**. Your screen should now look similar to this.

> To enter text, simply begin typing. The text will be entered at the insertion point. You can easily correct errors by backspacing and typing the correct letter. When the insertion point reaches the end of a line, it will automatically move to the next line. This feature, called word wrap, means you do not have to press Enter unless you wish to begin a new paragraph or a new drill line. Many other features of word processing make creating business documents fast and simple.

Note: Keep this document open and continue reading.

Note that the file name changes to *student-22.docx* after saving. Depending upon your Windows settings, the file extension "docx" may not appear in the title bar.

File—Close

To close a file: Click the **File** tab, and click **Close**.

Or: On the keyboard, press **CTRL + W**.

Close button

Or: Click the **Close** button in the upper-right-hand corner of the window, which turns red when you rest the mouse over it.

If the file is a new, unsaved document or an existing document to which you made changes, you will be prompted to save the document. Follow the prompts to save or discard the file as desired.

PRACTICE (continued)

1. Move the insertion point to the top of the document, and type today's date; use the **BACKSPACE** key to correct any errors.
2. Press **ENTER** 2 times to insert 1 blank line after the date.
3. Close the document by carefully following one of the steps just explained—do *not* close Word! (*Hint*: Press **CTRL + W** to ensure that you close the document but leave Word open.)
4. Do not save changes. The file, *student-22*, will close, and you will see a blank unnamed document.

Note: Keep the blank document open and continue reading.

File—New

When you start Word outside of GDP, a new blank document (named *Document1* or *Document2*, etc.) appears on the screen, ready for you to begin typing. When you finish and close that document using the **Close** button, Word will also close unless there is an additional Word document open.

To close the Word file but keep Word open: On the keyboard, press **CTRL + F4**.

Or: Click the **File** tab, and click **Close**.

Then, either open an existing document or create a new document to continue working.

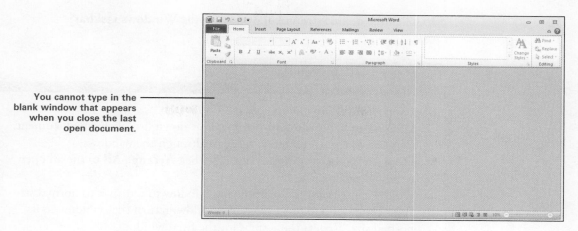

You cannot type in the blank window that appears when you close the last open document.

To create a new document: Press **CTRL + N**.

New button (active)

Or: Click the **File** Tab, and click **New**; under **Available Templates**, double-click the **Blank document** button.

 PRACTICE (continued)

1. Press **CTRL + N** to create a new blank document, and type your name.
2. Note the generic file name in the title bar.
3. Open the file named *practice-22*.

Note: Keep these documents open and continue reading.

Switch Windows

You do not need to close one document before opening another. Several documents can be open at the same time, and you can switch back and forth among them.

To switch windows:

1. Click the **View** tab.
2. From the **Window** group, click **Switch Windows**, and click the desired window from the drop-down list.

Or: Press **CTRL + F6** on the keyboard repeatedly to toggle through available windows.

Or: Click **Arrange All** to tile all open windows. To return each window to normal size, switch windows and click the **Maximize** button in the upper-right-hand corner of each window or double-click the title bar.

Or: Click the desired document button on the **Windows taskbar**.

 PRACTICE (continued)

1. From the **Window** group, click the **View** tab.
2. Click **Switch Windows**; from the drop-down list, click any document.
3. Press **CTRL + F6** repeatedly to toggle through the windows.
4. From the **Window** group, **View** tab, click **Arrange All** to tile all open windows side by side.
5. Double-click the title bar in the top window to return it to normal size.
6. Press **CTRL + F6** to open the next window; return that window to its normal size. Repeat these steps for the final window.
7. Close all open files without saving, and return to GDP.

 GO TO
Textbook

Orientation to
Word Processing—C

Select Text

To modify existing text: First select the text you want to change as described next. After you select text, make any changes you wish, such as italicizing, moving, or deleting the text. Selected text appears highlighted as shown:

> To enter text, simply begin typing. The text v
> correct errors by backspacing and typing the
> the end of a line, it will automatically move t —— Selected text is
> means you do not have to press Enter unless   highlighted.
> line. Many other features of word processing
> simple.

To select (highlight) text using the mouse:

To Select	Do This
Any amount of text	Point and drag over the text you want to select.
Any amount of continuous text	Position the insertion point at the beginning of the desired text. Hold down **SHIFT**, and press the right and down arrow keys to extend the selection; or click at the end of the selection.
A word (and the space after it)	Double-click the word.
A line	Click in the **Selection bar** to the left of the line.
A sentence (and the space after it)	Hold down **CTRL** and click anywhere in the sentence.
A paragraph	Double-click in the **Selection bar** next to the paragraph (or triple-click anywhere in the paragraph).
The entire document	Triple-click anywhere in the **Selection bar** (or press **CTRL + A**).

To deselect text (that is, cancel the operation): Click anywhere on the screen or press any arrow key.

PRACTICE

Beginning with Lesson 23, most practice exercises will automatically open a file with an assigned name and with content included ready for input.

AutoCorrect Options button

From this point forward, GDP will typically launch Word and automatically open a document with an assigned name and content in place ready for input as you follow the steps in the practice exercise.

1. Move the insertion point to the beginning of the document.
2. Press **TAB** to indent the first line of the paragraph. (If an **AutoCorrect Options** lightning bolt button appears, click it; and click **Stop Setting Indent on Tabs and Backspace**.) Note that the words "can easily" move to the beginning of the second line.

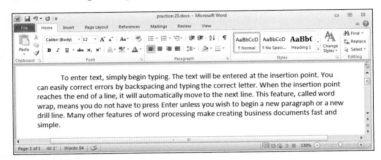

3. Select the word "automatically" in the third line by double-clicking anywhere in the word; then delete the word by pressing **BACKSPACE**.
4. Move the insertion point immediately to the left of "T" in "This" in line 3. Delete the space to the left by pressing **BACKSPACE**; then start a new paragraph at this point by pressing **ENTER** 2 times. Press **TAB** to indent the line.

REFER TO
Word Manual
Appendix A: GDP—Word Settings, AutoFormat As You Type Options

If the second paragraph is indented automatically when you press **ENTER**, see Appendix A for help.

5. Select the second paragraph by double-clicking the **Selection bar** area next to the paragraph or by triple-clicking anywhere in the paragraph.

Selection bar area ——

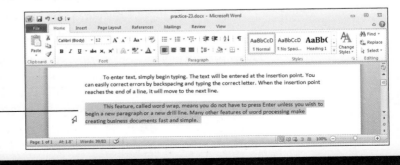

6. Select the entire document by pressing **CTRL + A**. Now deselect the document by clicking anywhere on the screen or by pressing any directional arrow key. (Pressing an arrow key deselects the text and moves the insertion point to the beginning or end of the document.)

7. Select the words "word processing" in the last sentence. In their place, type `Microsoft Word for Windows`. Your screen should now look similar to the following illustration:

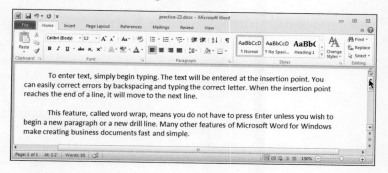

Note: Keep this document open and continue reading.

Bold

One way of making text (such as a title) stand out is to format it in bold. You can either bold the text as you type or bold existing text. The Bold button "toggles." Clicking the button once activates Bold; clicking the button again turns it off.

To bold text as you type:

B
Bold button

This is bold text.

This is not bold.

1. From the **Home** tab, **Font** group, click the **Bold** button.

   Or: On the keyboard, press **CTRL + B**.

2. Type the text you want to appear in bold.

3. Click the **Bold** button or press **CTRL + B** again to turn off bold, and note that the text appears in bold on the screen.

To bold existing text:

1. Select the text you want to appear in bold.

    To bold (or unbold) a single word, click inside the word and bold (or unbold) it. It is not necessary to select the word first.

2. Click the **Bold** button.

   Or: Press **CTRL + B**.

To remove bold formatting:

1. Select the text or click inside a single word.
2. Click the **Bold** button.

   Or: Press **Ctrl + B** again.

PRACTICE (continued)

1. Move to the end of the first paragraph. Space 1 time after the period, turn on bold, type `Amazing!`, and then turn off bold.
2. Select "word wrap" in line 4, and bold both words.
3. Remove the bold formatting from "Amazing!" in line 3.
4. In the last sentence, select and then bold "Word for Windows."
5. In the last sentence, click inside "Microsoft" but do not select it; then bold it. Your text should now look similar to this:

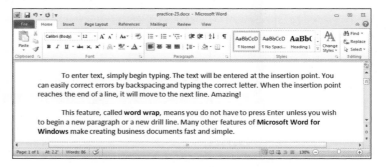

Note: Keep this document open and continue reading.

Undo/Redo a Command

To cancel a command before it has been executed or to deselect text: Press **Esc**, click elsewhere on the screen, or tap any directional arrow key. Once a command has been executed and you realize you made a mistake, you can usually reverse the last several actions.

Undo button

To undo the most recent action: From the **Quick Access** toolbar, click the **Undo** button.

Or: Press **Ctrl + Z**.

To undo an action other than the most recent one: Press the **Undo** button or **CTRL + Z** repeatedly, or click the arrow to the right of the **Undo** button to display a list of recent actions. The most recent action is at the top. Select and click the action you want to undo. Clicking an action anywhere below the first one undoes all actions up to and including the selected action.

Redo button

To redo a command: From the **Quick Access** toolbar, click the **Redo** button.

Or: Press **CTRL + Y**.

Repeat button

The **Redo** button is inactive until you first use **Undo**. Then it toggles between **Redo** and **Repeat** as you work.

PRACTICE (continued)

1. Move the insertion point to the end of the document.
2. Press **ENTER** 2 times to begin a new paragraph.
3. Press **TAB**. Type this sentence:

   ```
   Word processing makes sense (and cents) in the
   contemporary office.
   ```

4. Use **Undo** to undo (delete) the sentence you just typed.
5. Use **Redo** to reinsert the sentence. Your text should look similar to this:

   > To enter text, simply begin typing. The text will be entered at the insertion point. You can easily correct errors by backspacing and typing the correct letter. When the insertion point reaches the end of a line, it will move to the next line. Amazing!
   >
   > This feature, called **word wrap**, means you do not have to press Enter unless you wish to begin a new paragraph or a new drill line. Many other features of **Microsoft Word for Windows** make creating business documents fast and simple.
   >
   > Word processing makes sense (and cents) in the contemporary office.

Note: Keep this document open and continue reading.

Help

Word's extensive online Help is available in many places throughout Word, and help is available in a variety of formats including demos, discussion groups, and training courses.

 Because Word is distributed in a variety of versions with slight differences in each and because it includes Web-based content that changes, your Word Help feature may differ from the steps described below. These differences are not cause for concern. If your features differ, explore any Help features of interest on your own.

To open the Word Help home page:

Microsoft Word Help button

1. Click the **Microsoft Office Word Help** button in the upper-right-hand corner of the Word window.

   Or: On the keyboard, press **F1**.

   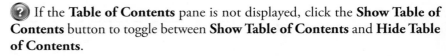 You might have to press the **Help** button a second time to open the **Word Help** home page.

2. Type any keywords in the search box, and click the **Search** button.
3. In the **Table of Contents** pane, click **Getting help** for some excellent Word resources.

   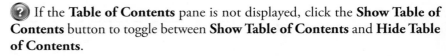 If the **Table of Contents** pane is not displayed, click the **Show Table of Contents** button to toggle between **Show Table of Contents** and **Hide Table of Contents**.

Show Table of Contents button

4. Click the **Home** button any time to return to the **Word Help** home page, and explore the various links.

To get help while in a dialog box: Click the **Help** button. (It looks like a question mark and appears in the upper-right-hand corner of the Word window next to the Close button.)

Or: On the keyboard, press **F1**.

PRACTICE (continued)

If your Help features differ, explore any Help features of interest on your own.

1. Click the **Microsoft Word Help** button.
2. Type bold in the **Search** box, and click the **Search** button.

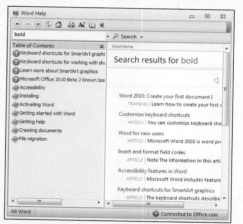

3. In the **Search results for bold** list, click any related link for information.
4. In the **Table of Contents** pane, click any desired link, and explore the results.
5. If you have an Internet connection, click any link that looks like it requires an online connection, and explore it.
6. Click the **Home** button to return to the **Word Help** home page.
7. Scroll to the bottom of the screen, and explore the options.

PRACTICE (continued)

8. From the **Home** tab, **Font** group, click the **Dialog Box Launcher**; click the **Help** button to open the **Word Help** window.
9. Close the **Word Help** window.
10. Save the changes to *practice-23* and return to GDP.

   See GDP Help for specific steps to edit or restart a practice file.

Orientation to Word Processing—D

24

Print Preview

To preview a document before printing:

1. Click the **File** tab, **Print**, to open the **File** view (also known as the **Backstage** view).

   Or: On the keyboard, press **CTRL + P** or **CTRL + F2**.

2. Note that your formatted document appears as a full page on the right side of the screen, and note the options under **Print**, **Printer**, and **Settings**.

3. Note the **Zoom** slider in the lower-right-hand corner of the screen, which you can use to adjust the zoom level of the print preview for that document.

   See Zoom on page 34 for details on using the Zoom features.

4. Press **Esc** or click the **Home** tab to exit the **File** view and return to the document to make any desired document edits.

Zoom slider

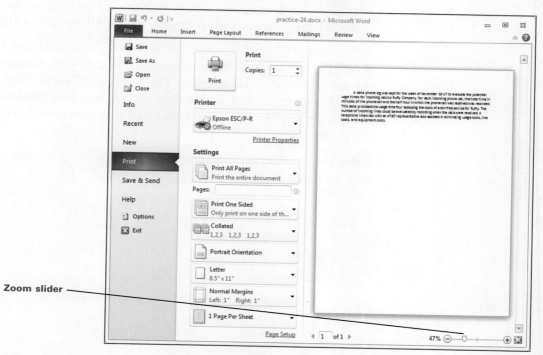

PRACTICE

1. Click the **File** tab, **Print**. Your screen should look similar to the preceding illustration.
2. Drag the **Zoom slider** left and right to adjust the zoom level.
3. Press **Esc** to return to the normal document window.

Note: Keep this document open and continue reading.

Spelling and Grammar Check

Word's spelling and grammar tool checks your document for spelling, grammar, and typographical errors. When the automatic spelling and grammar checking feature is active, spelling and grammar are checked as you type. Word marks possible spelling errors with a red, wavy line; possible grammatical and typographical spacing errors with a green, wavy line; and possible incorrect spelling of a word relative to the context (meaning) of the word in that sentence with a blue, wavy line.

To correct a spelling error immediately: Right-click the word marked with the red (or blue), wavy line to display suggested spellings or corrections; then click the desired choice, such as **Ignore**, **Ignore All**, or **Add to Dictionary**.

To correct a grammar error immediately: Right-click the word marked with a green, wavy line; click the desired choice; or click **Grammar**, and click the desired choice, such as **Ignore Once**, or click **Cancel** if the choices don't apply. For more detailed information, click **About This Sentence**. Verify that the spacing between words and before and after punctuation is correct. Adjust any spaces as needed.

(?) If your spelling and grammar tools are not working as expected, verify that they are active.

To activate your spelling and grammar tools: Click the **File** tab, **Options**. Click the **Proofing** group. Under **When correcting spelling and grammar in Word**, verify that these boxes are checked; then click **OK**:

- **Check spelling as you type**
- **Use contextual spelling**
- **Mark grammar errors as you type**
- **Check grammar with spelling**

Many Word users prefer to check spelling only and find the grammar check and the corresponding green underlines distracting. If you do not wish to check grammar, uncheck the grammar options.

To manually check spelling and grammar:

1. From the **Review** tab, **Proofing** group, click the **Spelling and Grammar** button.

   Or: On the keyboard, press **F7**.

   Or: On the status bar, click the **Spelling and Grammar Check** button when errors are present. Point to the button with the red X, and note the **ScreenTip:** "Proofing errors were found. Click to correct." Click the button to move to each error. If no errors are found, the button displays a blue check mark, and this **ScreenTip** displays: "No proofing errors."

2. Note that Word scrolls through the document. If the program finds a problem, it displays the **Spelling and Grammar** dialog box.

3. Each time Word stops for a spelling error, do one of the following:
   - If the word in the **Not in Dictionary** box is spelled correctly, click **Ignore Once** (or **Ignore All** if you want the speller to ignore all occurrences of this word in your document). Use caution because once you click **Ignore**, Word will no longer mark that text as an error, even if you spell-check the document again.
   - To add the word in question to the custom dictionary so that it will not be marked again, click **Add to Dictionary**. Use caution to avoid adding an incorrectly spelled word to the dictionary.
   - If a word in the **Suggestions** list is the correct spelling, select that word, and then click **Change**.
   - If the correct word is not displayed in the **Suggestions** list, click on the highlighted word in the **Not in Dictionary** box, type the correction, and then click **Change**.

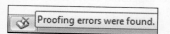

Spelling and Grammar Check button (errors)

Spelling and Grammar Check button (no errors)

Omitted words, misused words, or typographical errors that form a new word (such as "sing" for "sign") are often missed by Word's spell check! Always proofread documents carefully before submitting them.

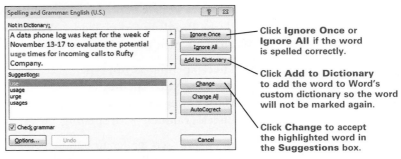

Click **Ignore Once** or **Ignore All** if the word is spelled correctly.

Click **Add to Dictionary** to add the word to Word's custom dictionary so the word will not be marked again.

Click **Change** to accept the highlighted word in the **Suggestions** box.

💡 *To remove an incorrectly spelled word from Word's dictionary:* Click the **File** tab, **Options**. From the **Proofing** group, under **When correcting spelling in Microsoft Office Programs**, click **Custom Dictionaries**. From the **Custom Dictionaries** window, click **Edit Word List**. In the **CUSTOM.DIC** window, click the desired word, edit it as desired, and click **OK** 3 times.

Word's grammar check is often unreliable. Use caution before accepting any suggested changes!

4. Each time Word stops for a grammar error, do one of the following:
   - Compare the description of the error with the suggested correction in the **Suggestions** box.
   - If the change is appropriate, click **Change**.
   - If the change is not appropriate, click **Ignore Once** or **Ignore All**.
5. When the dialog box appears with the message "The spelling and grammar check is complete," click **OK**.

AUTOCORRECT

🔘 **REFER TO Word Manual**

Appendix A: GDP—Word Settings, AutoCorrect Options

Word will automatically correct some common typographical errors immediately after you type them—often without your noticing. For example, if you type "teh" and press the SPACE BAR, Word will automatically change "teh" to "the" on the fly as you type.

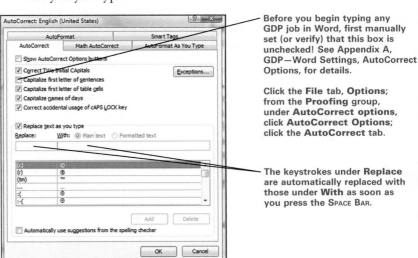

Before you begin typing any GDP job in Word, first manually set (or verify) that this box is unchecked! See Appendix A, GDP—Word Settings, AutoCorrect Options, for details.

Click the **File** tab, **Options**; from the **Proofing** group, under **AutoCorrect options**, click **AutoCorrect Options**; click the **AutoCorrect** tab.

The keystrokes under **Replace** are automatically replaced with those under **With** as soon as you press the SPACE BAR.

PRACTICE (continued)

1. Verify that your spelling and grammar check tools are active. (Refer to page 29 for steps.)
2. Type this sentence after the last line in the paragraph:

   `Usage costs is a significant factor to be studied carefully.`

3. Next, press **CTRL + HOME** to move to the top of the document; note the words marked with a red, wavy underline and a green, wavy underline. Adjust your zoom level for a closer look.

> A data phone log was kept for the week of November 13-17 to evaluate the potential usge times for incoming calls to Rufty Company. For each incoming phone call, the total time in minutes of the phone call and the half hour in which the phone call was received was recorded. This data provided the usage time four assessing the costs of a toll-free service for Rufty. The numberof incoming lines could be evaluated by recording when the calls were received. A telephone interview with an AT&T representative also assisted in eliminating usage costs, line costs, and equipment costs. Usage costs is a significant factor to be studied carefully.

4. From the **Review** tab, **Proofing** group, click the **Spelling and Grammar** button.

   Or: On the keyboard, press **F7**.

   a. Word displays "usge" in the **Not in Dictionary** box and suggests "usage" as a possible change. Click **Change** to accept this suggestion.
   b. Word displays "Rufty" in the **Not in Dictionary** box and suggests "Rutty" instead. However, the "Rufty" is correct, and it occurs throughout the document. Click **Ignore All** so that Word will not mark this word again.
   c. Word displays "numberof" in the **Not in Dictionary** box and provides a suggested spelling. Click the correct suggestion. Then click **Change**.
   d. Word displays "Usage costs is" in the **Subject-Verb Agreement** box and displays a suggestion in the **Suggestions** box. Click **Change**.

   ❓ If Word displays a message saying the spelling check is complete without checking grammar, verify that your grammar check tool is active. Refer to page 29 for details.

   e. When Word displays the dialog box with the message "The spelling and grammar check is complete," click **OK**.
   f. Carefully proofread the document after running the spell checker. Note that this error has not been corrected. In line 4, "four" should be "for." Because "four" is in Word's internal dictionary, it was not marked. Change "four" to "for."

PRACTICE (continued)

5. Your lines should now look similar to the following illustration. Save the document.

> A data phone log was kept for the week of November 13-17 to evaluate the potential usage times for incoming calls to Rufty Company. For each incoming phone call, the total time in minutes of the phone call and the half hour in which the phone call was received was recorded. This data provided the usage time for assessing the costs of a toll-free service for Rufty. The number of incoming lines could be evaluated by recording when the calls were received. A telephone interview with an AT&T representative also assisted in eliminating usage costs, line costs, and equipment costs. Usage costs are a significant factor to be studied carefully.

Note: Keep this document open and continue reading.

Show/Hide Formatting

When you press a nonprinting key, such as TAB or ENTER, Word inserts a formatting mark into the document. For example, pressing TAB inserts a tab character (→) and indents the line. Pressing ENTER inserts a paragraph mark (¶) and starts a new paragraph. Word defines a paragraph as any text or graphic that is followed by a ¶ mark. Formatting marks do not appear on the printed document.

 The directions "insert 1 hard return" or "press ENTER 1 time" are synonymous.

¶
Show/Hide ¶ button

To display formatting marks on the screen: From the **Home** tab, **Paragraph** group, click the **Show/Hide ¶** button.

Or: On the keyboard, press **CTRL + SHIFT + 8**.

On the keyboard, press **SHIFT + F1** to display formatting marks and open the **Reveal Formatting** pane with detailed formatting information.

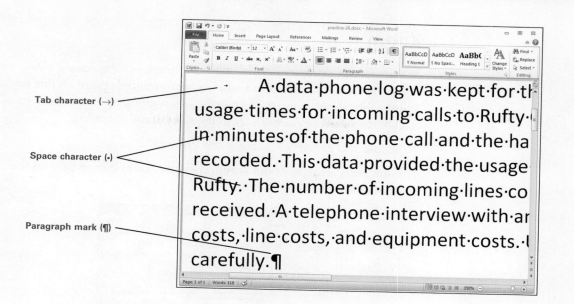

Tab character (→)

Space character (·)

Paragraph mark (¶)

A·data·phone·log·was·kept·for·th
usage·times·for·incoming·calls·to·Rufty·
in·minutes·of·the·phone·call·and·the·ha
recorded.·This·data·provided·the·usage
Rufty.··The·number·of·incoming·lines·co
received.·A·telephone·interview·with·ar
costs,·line·costs,·and·equipment·costs.·l
carefully.¶

PRACTICE (continued)

1. From the **Home** tab, **Paragraph** group, click the **Show/Hide ¶** button.

   Or: Press **CTRL + SHIFT + 8** to display the formatting marks.

2. Point to the different formatting marks shown on the screen, such as the tab character, space character, and paragraph mark.

3. From the **Home** tab, **Paragraph** group, click the **Show/Hide ¶** button.

   Or: Press **CTRL + SHIFT + 8** to hide the formatting marks.

4. Select "November 13-17," and apply bold formatting.
5. With the text still selected, press **SHIFT + F1**.
6. Read the information in the **Reveal Formatting** task pane.
7. Close the **Reveal Formatting** task pane.

Note: Keep this document open and continue reading.

Zoom

As you format documents, you will need to zoom in to take a closer look at details or zoom out to display a whole page or multiple pages on one screen. To adjust zoom settings, use the View tab, Zoom group options, or use the Zoom level button and the Zoom slider to the right of the status bar.

To adjust the zoom level using the View tab:

1. From the **View** tab, **Zoom** group, click the **Zoom** button to open the **Zoom** dialog box.

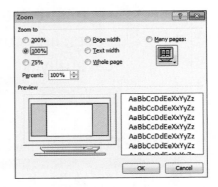

2. Note the choices under **Zoom to**.
3. As you click a **Zoom to** option, note the **Preview**.
4. Click the desired view; then click **OK**.
5. Note the buttons in the **Zoom** group for **One Page**, **Two Pages**, and **Page Width**.

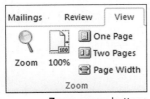

Zoom group buttons

To adjust the zoom level using the Zoom level button and the Zoom slider to the right of the status bar:

1. Click the **Zoom level** button (the percentage on the slider on the slider bar) to display the **Zoom** dialog box. The same choices described earlier can be found there.
2. Click the **Zoom Out** and **Zoom In** buttons as desired.
3. Drag the **Zoom slider** as desired.

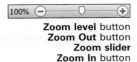

Zoom level button
Zoom Out button
Zoom slider
Zoom In button

💡 To hide the marginal white space at the top and bottom of a page, point to the top or bottom edge of any page until the mouse pointer displays double boxed arrows pointing down and up and double-click. Repeat these steps to show white space.

PRACTICE (continued)

1. Open *practice-24-zoom*.
2. Click the **Zoom Out** button repeatedly until 2 whole pages display.
3. Click the **Zoom In** button repeatedly until the **Zoom level** button shows **100%**.
4. Drag the **Zoom slider** until the **Zoom level** button shows about **300%**.
5. Turn on **Show/Hide ¶**, and note the detailed formatting marks.
6. Click the **Zoom level** button to display the **Zoom** dialog box.
7. Under **Zoom to**, click **Text Width**; click **OK**.
8. From the **View** tab, **Zoom** group, click the **One Page** button, the **Two Pages** button, the **Page Width** button, and finally, the **100%** button.
9. Close *practice-24-zoom*.

Note: Keep the remaining document open and continue reading.

Print

To print the document displayed on the screen:

1. Save your document.
2. Click the **File** tab, and click **Print**.

   Or: On the keyboard, press **CTRL + P**.

   Use **Quick Print** to immediately print a copy of the entire document on your default printer. See Lesson 21 for steps to add Quick Print to the Quick Access toolbar.

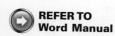

REFER TO
Word Manual

L. 21: Choose a Command, From the Quick Access Toolbar

3. Click the desired print options under **Print**, **Printer**, and **Settings**.

Click the list arrow next to **Print All Pages**; then click the desired choice from the drop-down list.

To print the page currently displayed in **Print Preview**, browse to the desired page, and click **Print Current Page**.

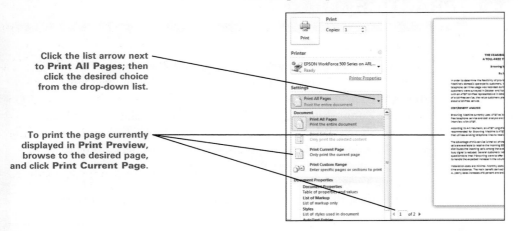

To print only a selected part of a document, select the desired text. Click the **File** tab, **Print**. Click the list arrow next to **Print All Pages**; then click **Print Selection**.

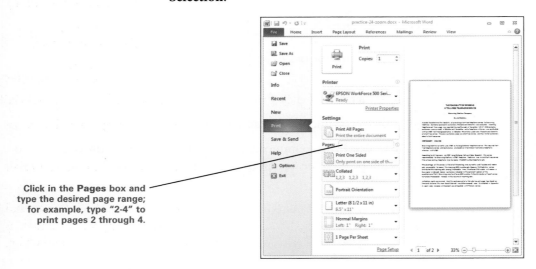

Click in the **Pages** box and type the desired page range; for example, type "2-4" to print pages 2 through 4.

PRACTICE (continued)

1. Print 2 copies of *practice-24*.
2. Save changes to *practice-24*, and return to GDP.

Check with your instructor before printing anything!

GO TO
Textbook

E-Mail Messages

Before you type any GDP job in Word, first manually set (or verify) certain Word options! See Appendix A, GDP—Word Settings, for details.

REFER TO Word Manual

L. 21: GDP—Start Word; GDP—Quit Word

Correspondence 25-1 (an e-mail message) is the first document processing job in the textbook. You will use several GDP features regularly from this point on as you work through your document processing jobs—**Scoring**, **Proofreading Viewer**, and the **GDP Reference Manual**.

See GDP Help for specific steps to begin and end a document processing job and to return to GDP.

GDP—Scoring

In GDP when you finish a document processing job and quit Word, GDP will provide instructions for submitting your document for scoring and for reviewing your results.

See GDP Help for details and specific steps for GDP's Scoring feature.

GDP—Proofreading Viewer

GDP's Proofreading Viewer helps you edit a previous attempt at a document processing job.

See GDP Help for details and specific steps for GDP's Proofreading Viewer features.

See Lesson 69, Find and Replace, for steps to use Find and Replace to find and replace incorrect spaces that might be missed when you proofread, such as an extra space between words or sentences or an extra trailing space following any punctuation in the last line of a paragraph.

E-Mail a Document

REFER TO Reference Manual

R-5C: E-Mail Message in Microsoft Outlook

R-5D: E-Mail Message in MSN Hotmail

An open Word document can be sent as the actual e-mail message, or the document can be sent as an e-mail attachment. However, to send any e-mail via Word, Microsoft Outlook must be the default e-mail software client. If you do not use Outlook, complete steps 1–7 only. To send an open Word document as the actual e-mail message, first add the Send to Mail Recipient command to the Quick Access toolbar.

E-mail choices vary, depending on your e-mail software. Most message screens include the To, Cc, and Subject boxes with options to display a Bcc box. The attachment feature is often displayed as a paper clip icon.

To send an open Word document as the actual e-mail message:

1. Open the desired Word file.
2. Click the list arrow next to the **Quick Access** toolbar, and click **More Commands** from the bottom part of the drop-down menu.
3. In the right pane, in the **Choose commands from** list box, click the list arrow; click **All Commands**.
4. Scroll down the list, and click **Send to Mail Recipient**.
5. Click **Add>>**; click **OK**.

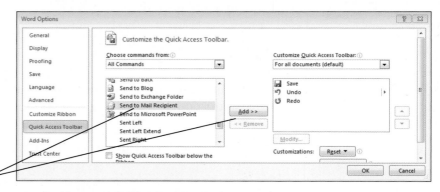

Click Send to Mail Recipient; then click Add>> to add the command to the Quick Access toolbar.

To remove the **Send to Mail Recipient** button from the **Quick Access** toolbar, right-click the button and click **Remove from Quick Access** toolbar.

6. From the **Quick Access** toolbar, click **Send to Mail Recipient**.
7. Note that an e-mail header appears at the top of the document and that the **Subject** box contains the document file name.

If an e-mail header does not appear, your e-mail software is not compatible with this feature and you cannot continue. To hide the e-mail header, click the **Send to Mail Recipient** button again.

8. Fill in the e-mail header boxes as desired, replacing the document's name that appears by default in the **Subject** box with the desired subject line; click **Send a Copy** to send the e-mail; close the document.

To send an open Word document as an e-mail attachment:

1. Open the desired Word file, click the **File** tab, **Save & Send**; under **Save & Send**, verify that **Send Using E-mail** is active; then under the **Send Using E-mail** pane, click **Send as Attchment**.
2. Follow step 8 in the previous section.

See Appendix C, Saving a Word File in PDF Format, for steps to send an open Word document as an e-mail attachment in the more generic PDF format.

PRACTICE

Do not send an e-mail message without consulting your instructor!

Before you begin this exercise, first manually set (or verify) certain Word options so that Word behaviors described in steps 5 and 6 will occur as expected! See Appendix A, GDP—Word Settings, AutoFormat As You Type Options, for details.

From now on, before you complete any practice exercise, first read the related Formatting section in your textbook in preparation for the practice exercise document.

1. Press **ENTER** to insert blank lines in *practice-25* as many times as needed to arrange the e-mail message in correct format as shown in Lesson 25-F, E-Mail Messages, in the textbook.
2. Click directly before "Uploading" in the first paragraph; type this paragraph; then press **ENTER** 2 times after the paragraph:

```
As soon as you complete Lesson 10, please schedule
a technique check with me. I'll send you an
appointment schedule tomorrow. Choose a convenient
appointment time and reply to my e-mail message
when you have made a selection.
```

In Word, lines wrap automatically to a second line as you approach the right margin. Do not press **ENTER** when you see a line break in the copy to be typed, which inserts a hard return and forces an incorrect line break. Press **ENTER** only between paragraphs, not within a paragraph.

3. Click the **Show/Hide ¶** button to view ¶ formatting marks, which indicate a hard return. Your document should look like the one that follows. If your line endings are different, remove any unwanted hard returns.

Hi,·Students:¶
¶
As·soon·as·you·complete·Lesson·10,·please·schedule·a·technique·check·with·me.·I'll·send·you·an·
appointment·schedule·tomorrow.·Choose·a·convenient·appointment·time·and·reply·to·my·e-
mail·message·when·you·have·made·a·selection.¶
¶
Uploading·your·lessons·on·time·and·on·a·regular·basis·is·absolutely·critical·to·your·success·in·an·
online·course.·The·grace·period·for·turning·in·your·work·ends·next·week,·so·work·hard·this·
week·to·get·on·schedule.·Send·me·an·e-mail·message·if·you·have·any·questions.¶
¶
Professor·Charlene·Morimoto¶
E-mail:·cmorimoto@fastmail.net¶

---

4. Click directly after "me" just before the period at the end of the first sentence, and type this:
```
--the sooner, the better
```

REFER TO
Word Manual
Appendix A: GDP—Word Settings, AutoFormat as You Type Options

PRACTICE (continued)

**REFER TO
Word Manual**

L. 49: AutoCorrect—
Hyperlink

5. Note that after you type both hyphens (--) followed by "the" and then press the **SPACE BAR**, a solid, formatted dash (—) appears.
6. Click directly after the last character in the e-mail address, and press **ENTER**; note that the e-mail address is converted to a hyperlink.
7. Type this on the line below the e-mail address:
   Phone: 323-555-4000
8. With your instructor's permission, follow the steps on page 38 to send an open Word document as the actual e-mail message.
9. Fill in any desired address in the **To** box.
10. Delete the file name in the **Subject** box, type Weekly Announcement, Keyboarding Online, and click **Send a Copy**. Your message should look similar to this:

Click the Send to Mail Recipient button once to display the e-mail header and again to hide it.

Formatted em dash

Automatic hyperlink

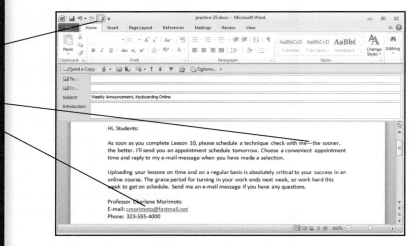

Note: Keep this document open and continue reading.

GDP—Reference Manual

In addition to the printed Reference Manual found in the front of your Word Manual and textbook, an electronic Reference Manual is available when you are working inside GDP and Word. You should routinely refer to both the electronic GDP Reference Manual and the printed Reference Manual as you complete the practice exercises and document processing jobs.

See GDP Help for details and specific steps for GDP's online Reference Manual.

GO TO
Textbook

PRACTICE (continued)

1. Open GDP's online Reference Manual.
2. Explore the contents and index features until you find information on the formatting of e-mail messages. Try using "e-mail" or "writer's identification" as keywords when you search.
3. Compare this information to the printed Reference Manual pages R-5C, E-Mail Message in Microsoft Outlook/Internet Explorer, and R-5D, E-Mail Message in MSN Hotmail, found in the front of your Word Manual and textbook.
4. Save changes to *practice-25*, and return to GDP.

Envelopes and Labels

Envelopes

If you type a letter first and then add an envelope, Word automatically inserts the inside address into the envelope Delivery address box.

To create an envelope:

1. From the **Mailings** tab, **Create** group, click the **Envelopes** button.
2. Click the **Envelopes** tab if necessary.

Word searches your current document for an inside address and inserts it into the **Delivery address** box.

A No. 10 envelope is the default setting. Click **Options** below the **Preview** window to select another envelope size.

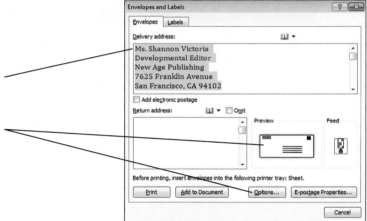

3. If a letter includes an inside address, the **Delivery address** box should display the inside address automatically. Edit the address if necessary. If an inside address is not present, type the delivery address now.
4. Type a return address; if your envelope has a printed return address, delete information in the **Return address** box, or check **Omit**.
5. Insert an envelope into your printer; click **Print**.

   To save the envelope with the document or to change to a different printer, click **Add to Document**.

1. Press **ENTER** 5 times above the date, delete the date, and type the current date; from the **Mailings** tab, **Create** group, click the **Envelopes** button. Your screen should look similar to this (the **Return address** box may be different):

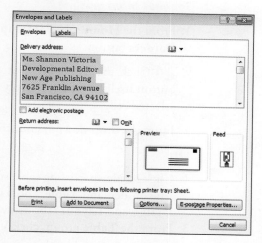

2. Check the **Omit** box to omit the return address, click **Add to Document**, and view the envelope at the top of the page.

    ❓ As an alternative, insert a No. 10 envelope into the printer, click **Print** in the **Envelopes and Labels** dialog box, and print the envelope, which would look like this:

3. From the **File** tab, click **Close** to close the file, but do not return to GDP. When prompted to save changes to the file, click **Yes**. Word will remain open but no document will be displayed.

Note: Keep Word open and continue reading.

View Gridlines

Word's label feature automatically creates a table structure using the exact dimensions of the selected label product. Since the table structure does not have printed borders, a blank page will appear unless you use View Gridlines to display light blue gridlines around the cell boundaries.

To view table gridlines:

1. From the **Home** tab, **Paragraph** group, click the list arrow next to the **Borders** button.

   ❓ Click the list arrow next to the **Borders** button and not the **Borders** button itself, or you will apply the currently displayed border to the table or selected cell.

2. From the drop-down menu, click **View Gridlines**.

Or:

1. Click inside an existing table structure.
2. The on-demand **Table Tools** tab appears on the ribbon with on-demand **Design** and **Layout** tabs below it. Click the **Layout** tab.
3. From the **Table** group, click **View Gridlines**.

Or: From the **Design** tab, **Table Styles** group, click the list arrow next to the **Borders** button; click **View Gridlines**.

   💡 Do not confuse **View Gridlines** as explained in this lesson with **Gridlines** under the **View** tab, **Show** group, which is used to align drawing objects and other things.

Labels

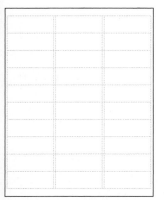

Avery US Letter 5160 label page—**View Gridlines** active.

It is usually more convenient to print a page of labels and affix them to an envelope than it is to adjust your printer to print envelopes. Labels can be affixed to blank envelopes in place of a typed return address or a delivery address. You can create a single label or a page full of labels.

A variety of labels are available from a good office supply vendor. Note the vendor, label number, and/or the label dimensions because you will be asked to specify the label type when you create labels.

To create and print a single label:

1. Open a new file; from the **Mailings** tab, **Create** group, click the **Labels** button.
2. Click the **Labels** tab.

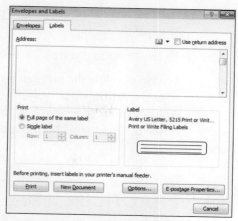

3. Type the mailing address in the **Address** box.

   🛈 If you open the **Envelopes and Labels** dialog box from an existing document that includes an address such as a business letter, Word will search for an address and insert it automatically.

4. Clear the check box for **Use return address**, if necessary.
5. Under **Print**, click **Single label**.
6. Click the **Options** button to open the **Label Options** dialog box.

Click the desired vendor from the **Label vendors** box.

Click the desired product from the **Product number** box. Note the label details under **Label information**.

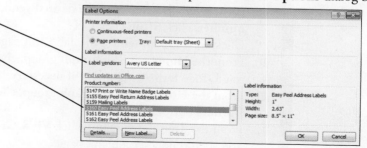

7. Click the list arrow in the **Label Vendors** box to display the list of vendors; click **Avery US Letter** (or the desired vendor).
8. Under **Product number**, click **5160 Easy Peel Address Labels** (or the desired product number); click **OK**, **Print**.

To create and print a full page of the same label:

1. Open a new file; from the **Mailings** tab, **Create** group, click the **Labels** button; click the **Labels** tab.
2. Type the mailing address in the **Address** box.
3. If necessary, clear the check box for **Use return address**.
4. Under **Print**, click **Full page of the same label**.
5. Click the **Options** button.
6. Click the list arrow in the **Label Vendors** box to display the list of vendors; click **Avery US Letter** (or any desired label vendor); under **Product number**, click **5160 Easy Peel Address Labels** (or any desired product number); click **OK**.

7. Click **New Document**, and print the document.
8. Close the document; when prompted to save changes, click the desired choice.

To create and print a page of labels with different information on each label:

1. Skip step 4 in the previous set of steps, and delete any text that might appear in the **Address** box.
2. After completing step 7 in the previous set of steps and before printing, type the different label information in each separate box of the blank label form as desired.

 PRACTICE (continued)

1. Open a new, blank Word file. (*Hint:* Press **CTRL + N**.)
2. From the **Mailings** tab, **Create** group, click the **Labels** button.
3. In the **Envelopes and Labels** dialog box, click the **Labels** tab.
4. Select and delete any text that might appear in the **Address** box.
5. Clear the check box for **Use return address** if needed.
6. Under **Print**, click **Full page of the same label**.
7. Click the **Options** button.
8. Click **Avery US Letter** as the desired vendor; under **Product number**, click **5160**; click **OK**.
9. Click **New Document** to display a full page of empty labels.
10. From the **Home** tab, **Paragraph** group, click the **Show/Hide ¶** button to hide formatting marks if necessary.
11. From the **Home** tab, **Paragraph** group, click the list arrow next to the **Borders** button.
12. From the drop-down menu, click **View Gridlines** to hide gridlines. You should now see a blank page.
13. Click **View Gridlines** again to display the nonprinting gridlines.
14. Type the first block of information in the first label; press **TAB** twice, or click in the next label (middle label in first row), and type the second block of information in the next label:

```
Ms. Renee Milfuggia
Stevenson Corporation
1479 Monroe Street
Gastonia, NC 28054

Mr. George Shawley
1014 South Marietta Street
Grove City, PA 16127
```

15. Close the document without saving changes.
16. Return to GDP.

 GO TO
Textbook

Memos and E-Mail
With Attachments

E-Mail—Attachments

The steps to attach a file to an e-mail message vary depending upon your e-mail program. A special symbol (such as a paper clip) denotes an attachment. Refer to your e-mail software's Help feature for steps to include an attachment.

To send an e-mail message with an attachment from Word:

1. With your instructor's permission, follow the steps in Lesson 25, E-Mail a Document, and the steps below to e-mail a document.
2. Fill in any desired address in the **To** box.
3. Click the **File** (paper clip icon) button on the e-mail toolbar.
4. From the **Insert File** dialog box, browse to the desired file, click **Insert**, and verify that the desired file is listed in the **Attach** box.

 To remove an attachment, right-click the file name in the **Attach** box, and click **Clear**.

Do not send an e-mail message without consulting your instructor!

GO TO
Textbook

PRACTICE

1. Follow the steps in Lesson 25, E-Mail a Document, to e-mail a document.
2. In the **To** box, fill in any desired address.
3. In the **Subject** box type this:
   MedNet Contact Information
4. Click the **File** (paper clip icon) button on the e-mail toolbar.
5. From the **Insert File** dialog box, browse to *practice-29-attachment* and click **Insert**.
6. Verify that the desired file is listed in the **Attach** box.
7. Clear the attached file, and attach it again.
8. Save *practice-29*, and return to GDP.

Correspondence Review

Italic and Underline

To italicize or underline text as you type:

Italic button

1. From the **Home** tab, **Font** group, click the **Italic** or **Underline** button.

   Or: Press **CTRL + I** (italic) or **CTRL + U** (underline).

U

Underline button

2. Type the text you want italicized or underlined; then click the **Italic** or **Underline** button again to turn off italic or underline.

plain text

italic text

<u>underlined</u> text

To italicize or underline existing text:

1. Select the text to be italicized or underlined; or for a single word, simply click inside the word.
2. Click the **Italic** or **Underline** button.

   Or: Press **CTRL + I** or **CTRL + U**.

 Italic and Underline are toggle buttons. Click the button once to activate the feature and again to deactivate it. To undo this formatting, select the text and then click the desired button.

PRACTICE

1. Type the first line—underline "not" and italicize the book title, *To Kill a Mockingbird*; press **ENTER** 1 time, and type the second sentence exactly as shown:

   ```
   I will not have time to read To Kill a Mockingbird
   before Friday.
   I will have time to read This Old House.
   ```

2. In line 2, underline "will" and italicize the book title "This Old House."
3. In line 1, remove the underline from "not." Your copy should look like this:

   I will **not** have time to read *To Kill a Mockingbird* before Friday.
   I <u>will</u> have time to read *This Old House.*

4. Save changes to *practice-30*, and return to GDP.

GO TO Textbook

One-Page Business Reports

Alignment

Alignment buttons (**Align Text Left** button active)

Four types of alignment are available for text:

- **Left.** Aligns text flush with the left margin (default setting), leaving an uneven right edge.
- **Right.** Aligns text flush with the right margin, leaving an uneven left edge.
- **Centered.** Centers the text between the left and right margins.
- **Justified.** Aligns text flush with both the left and the right margins.

To change text alignment:

1. Click in the desired line or paragraph, or select the desired text.
2. From the **Home** tab, **Paragraph** group, click the desired alignment button.

   Or: From the **Home** tab, **Paragraph** group, click the **Dialog Box Launcher.** From the **Indents and Spacing** tab, under **General**, click the down arrow to the right of the **Alignment box.** Click the desired alignment, and click **OK**.

   Or: On the keyboard, press **CTRL + L** (left alignment); **CTRL + E** (center alignment); **CTRL + R** (right alignment); **CTRL + J** (justified alignment).

PRACTICE

1. Turn on **Show/Hide ¶**, and press **ENTER** 5 times to position the insertion point 2 inches from the top of the page.
2. Type the report title, MICHIGAN AVENUE VETERINARY CLINIC (DRAFT), and press **ENTER** 2 times.
3. Type the report subtitle, Recent Trends, and press **ENTER** 2 times.
4. Type the byline, Marcus Smith, and press **ENTER** 2 times.
5. Type the date, July 1, and press **ENTER** 2 times.
6. Note that all the newly typed lines are flush with the left margin because the document originally opened with left-aligned paragraphs.
7. Select the title, subtitle, byline, and date; bold and center the lines.
8. Change paragraph 1 to justified alignment; note that all lines in that paragraph are aligned flush with both the left and right margins.

9. Change paragraph 2 to right alignment; note that all lines in that paragraph are flush with the right margin. Your document should now look similar to this:

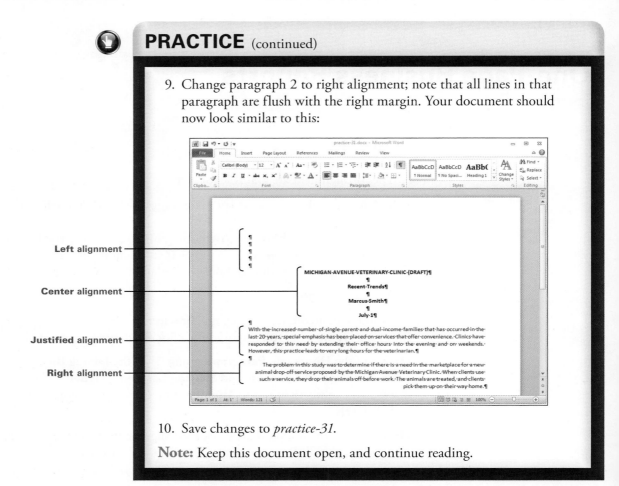

10. Save changes to *practice-31*.

Note: Keep this document open, and continue reading.

Font—Size

Font size is measured in points; 1 point (pt.) is equal to $\frac{1}{72}$ of an inch. The point size refers to the height of a character. Thus, a 12-pt. font is $\frac{1}{6}$ of an inch tall. Here are some examples of different font sizes you can use.

10-pt. Font Size

12-pt. Font Size

18-pt. Font Size

24-pt. Font Size

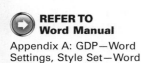

**REFER TO
Word Manual**

Appendix A: GDP—Word Settings, Style Set—Word 2003

GDP's Word 2003 style set changes the default font from Calibri 11 to Calibri 12. You can easily change the font size in any text you type. However, avoid using too many font sizes in the same document.

To change the font size:

1. Position the insertion point where you want to begin using the new font size (or select the text you want to change).
2. From the **Home** tab, **Font** group, click the down arrow to the right of the **Font Size** box; click the desired font size.

Font Size box

Or: Click the **Grow Font** or **Shrink Font** buttons as desired.

Grow Font button

Or: Press **CTRL + SHIFT + >** to increase the font size, or press **CTRL + SHIFT + <** to decrease the font size.

Shrink Font button

Or: On the keyboard, press **CTRL + D** to open the **Font** dialog box. From the **Font** tab, under **Size**, click the desired font size; click **OK**.

PRACTICE (continued)

REFER TO
Word Manual

Appendix A: GDP—Word Settings, Status Bar

1. Set alignment to left in both paragraphs.
2. Click inside the title.
3. Look at the **Vertical Page Position** bar on the status bar; note that the insertion point is positioned vertically as follows: **At: 2″**.

   ❓ If the **Vertical Page Position** bar does not appear on the status bar, see Appendix A, GDP—Word Settings, Status Bar.

4. Select the title, and change the font size to 14 points. (*Hint:* Click in the **Selection bar** area for "one-click" line selection.)
5. Click in the blank line below the first paragraph, press **ENTER** 2 times, and move the insertion point up one line.
6. Type the side heading PROBLEM, and bold the heading. Your document should look similar to this:

Title typed in Calibri Bold 14 pt.

Vertical Page Position bar At: 2″

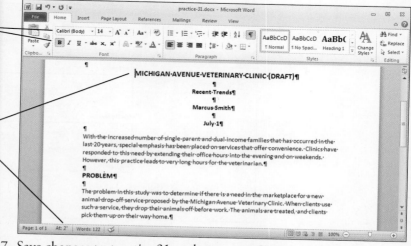

GO TO
Textbook

7. Save changes to *practice-31*, and return to GDP.

Multipage Business Reports

Page Number

REFER TO
Reference Manual
R-8A and R-8B: Multipage
Business Report

REFER TO
Word Manual
L. 47: Headers

Use the Page Number command to insert a right-aligned page number at the top of the second and subsequent pages in a multipage business report or multipage business letter. The Page Number command inserts a page number field code inside the document header.

A header is any information, such as a page number, that appears at the top of every page. The page number field code increases the page number automatically on each page. If you insert a page number by typing it manually, your document will display the same page number on each page. You can suppress the first-page header so that the page number appears only on the second and subsequent pages. The page number on the first page of multipage letters and reports is usually suppressed (removed).

If the **Page Number** feature is not behaving as expected: right-click over the header area, and click **Edit Header**. From the **Design** tab, **Options** group, verify that **Different first page** is unchecked; from the **Design** tab, **Close** group, click **Close Header and Footer**.

To insert a right-aligned page number inside the header:

1. From the **Insert** tab, **Header & Footer** group, click **Page Number**, **Top of Page**, **Plain Number 3**, from the design gallery.

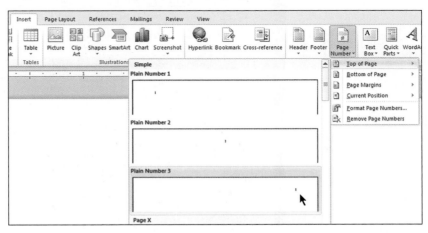

2. Note that you are now inside the **Header** section with the automatic page number highlighted; note that the on-demand **Design** tab appears.

(?) In a left-bound report in which the document margins have been changed, do not press **TAB** to position a page number using the preset tabs—the page number will not be aligned correctly; instead, follow the two previous steps.

To suppress (remove) the page number only on the first page of a multipage document while you are still inside the header:

1. From the **Design** tab, **Options** group, check **Different First Page**.
2. Note the following: you are still in the **First Page Header** section and the page number is suppressed.

To close a header and return to the document body:

1. Double-click anywhere outside the **First Page Header** area inside the document area.

   Or: From the **Design** tab, **Close** group, click the **Close Header and Footer** button.

2. Note the following: any existing header is now dimmed, the document is active, and the **Design** tab has disappeared.

To suppress the page number only on the first page of a multipage document after you have closed the header:

1. Right-click over the header area on any page; click **Edit Header**.
2. From the **Design** tab, **Options** group, check **Different First Page**.
3. Double-click over the body to close the header.

(?) If the page number is still in the **First Page Header**, select the page number (**CTRL + A**), and cut it (**CTRL + X**).

To start page numbering with a different number:

1. From the **Insert** tab, **Header & Footer** group, click **Page Number**, **Top of Page**, **Plain Number 3**, from the gallery of designs.
2. From the **Design** tab, in the **Header & Footer** group, click **Page Number**, **Format Page Numbers**, to display the **Page Number Format** dialog box.
3. From the **Page Number Format** dialog box, under **Page numbering**, click **Start at** and type 3 in the **Start at** box; click **OK**.

To remove a header: From the **Insert** tab, **Header & Footer** group, click **Header**, **Remove Header**. Repeat this on the second page if you have suppressed the header on the first page.

PRACTICE

1. Use the **Page Number** command to insert a header with right-aligned page numbers.
2. Suppress the page number on page 1.
3. In **File** view, preview the document to verify that the page numbers are positioned correctly. (*Hint:* Press **CTRL** + **P**.)

Note that the page number is suppressed (hidden) on the first page and appears on the second page.

Adjust the zoom level until you can see 2 pages at once.

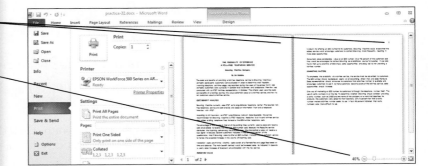

4. Adjust the zoom level until 2 pages display.
5. Click the **Home** tab.
6. Save changes to *practice-32*.

Note: Keep this document open and continue reading.

REFER TO Word Manual

L. 24: Zoom

Page Break

As you type, Word automatically starts a new page when the text on the current page reaches the bottom margin. The page break can change unpredictably to accommodate text as it is added and deleted. These automatic page breaks are not always desirable. Generally speaking, at least 2 continuous lines should remain at the bottom of a page and at least 2 continuous lines should be carried over to the top of the next page.

- A single line at the bottom of a page is known as an "orphan." Never end a page with a single line of a new paragraph or a heading followed by no text.
- A single line of a paragraph (the last line of a paragraph from the previous page) at the top of a page is known as a "widow." You may begin a page with a heading on a line by itself, but never begin a page with 1 line of a paragraph.

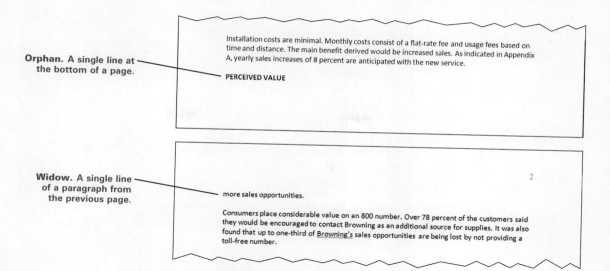

Orphan. A single line at the bottom of a page.

Installation costs are minimal. Monthly costs consist of a flat-rate fee and usage fees based on time and distance. The main benefit derived would be increased sales. As indicated in Appendix A, yearly sales increases of 8 percent are anticipated with the new service.

PERCEIVED VALUE

Widow. A single line of a paragraph from the previous page.

2

more sales opportunities.

Consumers place considerable value on an 800 number. Over 78 percent of the customers said they would be encouraged to contact Browning as an additional source for supplies. It was also found that up to one-third of Browning's sales opportunities are being lost by not providing a toll-free number.

A quick way to fix a widow or orphan is to insert a manual page break, which forces a page to end at a particular spot. No matter what text is added to or deleted from the document, the page will always end at this point unless you later delete the manual page break. A more desirable way to end pages with acceptable breaks and avoid a fixed page break is to use the Widow/Orphan control feature, which you will learn about later.

To insert a manual page break:

1. From the **Home** tab, in the **Paragraph** group, click **Show/Hide ¶** so that you will be able to see the **Page Break** formatting symbol.
2. Click where you want to start a new page.
3. From the **Insert** tab, in the **Pages** group, click **Page Break**.

    Or: On the keyboard, press **CTRL + ENTER**.

To remove a manual page break:

1. From the **Home** tab, in the **Paragraph** group, click **Show/Hide ¶** to see the **Page Break** formatting symbol.
2. Select the **Page Break** formatting symbol; click **DELETE**.

Note: The manual page break in the next illustration was inserted to avoid leaving the side heading as a single line (orphan) at the bottom of the first page.

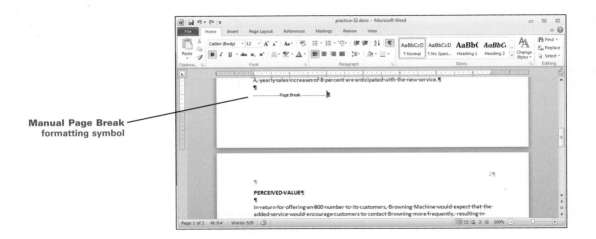

Manual Page Break
formatting symbol

PRACTICE (continued)

1. Turn on **Show/Hide ¶**.
2. Click immediately in front of the side heading "PERCEIVED VALUE."
3. Insert a manual page break.
4. Note the following: the **Page Break** formatting symbol appears on page 1 and the side heading now appears at the top of page 2.
5. Select the **Page Break** formatting symbol and delete it.

Note: Keep this document open and continue reading.

Widow/Orphan Control

The Widow/Orphan control feature, which is on by default, controls widows and orphans without using hard page breaks. However, because a blank line follows a main heading, the Widow/Orphan control feature will keep the heading with that next blank line that follows; but it will not keep the heading, the blank line that follows it, and the first line of the paragraph together. The "Keep with next" option keeps these lines together so that a single heading or a single line of text will not appear as the last line at the bottom of a page.

If you use a Word style to create a heading, Word automatically formats that heading with "Keep with next" paragraph formatting. You will learn about styles in Lesson 86, Styles.

To verify that Widow/Orphan control is on and to fix any one-liners:

1. From the **Home** tab, **Paragraph** group, click the **Dialog Box Launcher.**
2. From the **Paragraph** dialog box, click the **Line and Page Breaks** tab.
3. Under **Pagination**, check **Widow/Orphan control** if needed; click **OK.**

Check Widow/
Orphan control.

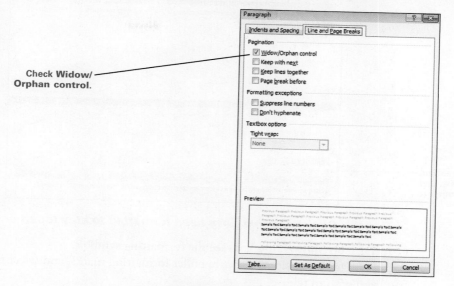

4. Turn on **Show/Hide ¶** to see formatting symbols.
5. Select the lines you wish to keep together. In this example, select the heading at the bottom of page 1 through the first line of the paragraph that follows it.
6. From the **Home** tab, **Paragraph** group, click the **Dialog Box Launcher.**
7. From the **Paragraph** dialog box, click the **Line and Page Breaks** tab.
8. Under **Pagination**, check **Keep with next**; click **OK.**

Do not check **Keep lines together**, or you could get unexpected results.

Check **Keep with next.**

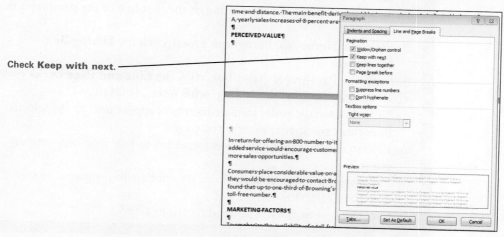

9. Note that the selected lines remain together on the top of page 2.
10. Note that square bullets (formatting marks indicating that this paragraph format option has been applied) appear next to the selected lines. These lines will always remain together on the same page.

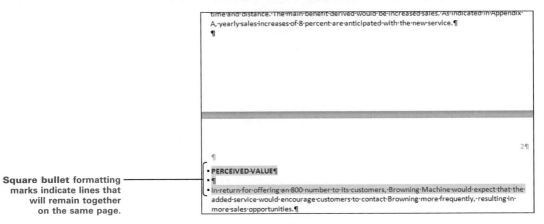

Square bullet formatting marks indicate lines that will remain together on the same page.

To release any lines that have been formatted to stay together:

1. Turn on **Show/Hide ¶** to see the formatting symbols.
2. Look for lines with the square bullet formatting marks, and select the lines you wish to release.
3. From the **Home** tab, **Paragraph** group, click the **Dialog Box Launcher**.
4. From the **Paragraph** dialog box, click the **Line and Page Breaks** tab.
5. Under **Pagination**, uncheck **Keep with next**; click **OK**.

PRACTICE (continued)

1. Select the lines you wish to keep together; in this case, select the heading at the bottom of page 1 through the first line of the paragraph that follows it.
2. From the **Home** tab, **Paragraph** group, click the **Dialog Box Launcher**.
3. From the **Paragraph** dialog box, click the **Line and Page Breaks** tab.
4. Under **Pagination**, check **Keep with next**; click **OK**.
5. Note that square bullet formatting marks appear next to the selected lines that now appear together on page 2.
6. Release the lines that have been formatted to stay together; note the effect.
7. Undo that action so that the lines are once again formatted to stay together. (*Hint:* Press **CTRL + Z**.)
8. Save changes to *practice-32*, and return to GDP.

GO TO
Textbook

Rough-Draft Business Reports With Lists

Bullets and Numbering

Reference Manual
R-12D: Examples of Different Types of Lists

To call attention to a list of items, format them with bullets or numbers. If the sequence of the items is important, use numbers; if not, use bullets. The items in the list are automatically indented from the left margin.

Word's default list indent will be used as standard formatting for lists in the document processing jobs in your textbook and for lists in the practice exercises.

To add bullets or numbers and to end a list:

1. Press **ENTER** as needed to insert 1 blank line above the list.
2. Click the **Bullets** or **Numbering** button, and type your list of items pressing **ENTER** 1 time after each item.
3. Note that a new bullet or number appears each time you press **ENTER**.
4. To end the list, press **ENTER** 2 times. (The second time you press **ENTER**, the numbers or bullets end, and your insertion point moves back to the left margin.)

   Or: Press **ENTER** 1 time, and click either the active, highlighted **Bullets** or **Numbering** button 1 time to release it. Your insertion point should move back to the left margin.

5. Press **ENTER** as needed to insert 1 blank line below the list.

Bullets button

Numbering button

If bullets or numbers are not behaving as expected: Undo all previous actions related to adding bullets or numbers. Type your list of items unformatted, and insert 1 blank line above and below the list by pressing **ENTER** as many times as needed. Select only the text to be formatted as a list. From the **Home** tab, **Paragraph** group, click either the **Bullets** or **Numbering** button.

To remove bullets or numbers from an existing list:

1. Select the desired list, or click anywhere inside the desired line.
2. Click either the **Bullets** or **Numbering** button as appropriate.
3. If necessary, from the **Home** tab, **Paragraph** group, click the **Decrease Indent** button to position the text at the left margin.

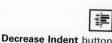
Decrease Indent button

   Or: Right-click and click **Decrease Indent**.

To change the number of the list so that it starts with a particular number:

1. Point to the desired number in the list, and click to select it. (All the numbers in the list should be highlighted, and the desired number should be highlighted in a different color.)
2. Right-click over the desired highlighted list number to display the shortcut menu.
3. Click **Restart at 1** to restart numbering, or click **Continue Numbering** to continue numbering from a previous list in the document or click **Set Numbering Value**, and type the desired value in the **Set value to** box.

   ⑦ If necessary, click the **Numbering** button twice right after this to reset the line number value on the selected lines.

   ⑨ To move a list item, click in the desired line to be moved; then press **ALT + SHIFT + ↑** (the directional up arrow) or **ALT + SHIFT + ↓** (the directional down arrow) as desired.

   ⑨ If you press the **TAB** or **BACKSPACE** key after typing a list and an unwanted indention appears:

1. Click the **File** tab, **Options**.
2. From the **Word Options** window, click **Proofing** in the left pane; then click the **AutoCorrect Options** button on the right.
3. In the **AutoCorrect** window, click the **AutoFormat As You Type** tab; uncheck **Set left- and first-indent with tabs and backspaces**.
4. Click **OK** twice.

PRACTICE

1. Select the four sentences in the middle that end with question marks, and format them as a numbered list using Word's default list indent.
2. Move the insertion point to the end of the document (*Hint:* **CTRL + END**).
3. Click the **Bullets** button.
4. Type the following three list items, pressing **ENTER** 1 time between each sentence.

   ```
   Provide a better understanding of the need for this
   service.
   Define some of the mechanics of the service.
   Provide direction on how to introduce this service.
   ```

5. Press **ENTER** 3 times after the last sentence, noting that the bullets end after you press **ENTER** 2 times and a blank line is inserted the next time you press **ENTER**.

6. Type the following paragraph:

```
Although cat owners also represent a large client
base for the veterinarian, they were excluded from
this study because cats do not have to be licensed.
```

7. Click anywhere inside the last bulleted item, and click the **Bullet** button.
8. Note that the bullet is removed.
9. Click the **Bullet** button again to reverse these steps.
10. Move to the end of the last sentence, press the SPACE BAR 1 time to add a space, type the following sentence, and press ENTER 2 times:

```
Two more questions must be asked:
```

11. Click the **Numbering** button and type each question on a separate line:

```
Should cat owners be surveyed?
Should the same questions be asked?
```

12. Click the first number in this list, and use the shortcut menu to change the number of the list to continue numbering from the previous numbered list. Note that the items are renumbered to 5 and 6.
13. Click over the "5" to select it, right-click, and click **Restart at 1**. Note that the items are renumbered to 1 and 2. Your document should look similar to this:

The following problem was addressed in this study to determine the value of this proposed service to dog owners: What is the feasibility of offering an animal drop-off service to dog owners who are customers of the Michigan Avenue Veterinary Clinic? First, these four questions must be addressed:

1. How much value will the new service provide to dog owners?
2. How many potential clients will transfer from their existing veterinarian to take advantage of this new service?
3. What drop-off hours and pick-up hours are preferred?
4. What level of additional personnel and boarding facilities will be required to offer this service?

The purpose of this study is to determine if the Michigan Avenue Veterinary Clinic should invest the resources needed to introduce and maintain a new animal drop-off service. The proposed study would provide these results:

- Provide a better understanding of the need for this service.
- Define some of the mechanics of the service.
- Provide direction for how to introduce this service.

Although cat owners also represent a large client base for the veterinarian, they were excluded from this study because cats do not have to be licensed. Two more questions must be asked:

1. Should cat owners be surveyed?
2. Should the same questions be asked?

GO TO Textbook

14. Save changes to *practice-33*, and return to GDP.

Multipage Academic Reports With Lists

Line Spacing

REFER TO
Reference Manual
R-8C: Multipage Academic
Report

You can change the line spacing from single to 1.5 lines to add an extra half line of space between typed lines. You can also change to double spacing for an academic report to add an extra blank line between typed lines. The precise amount of space between lines is determined partly by the size of the font in use.

If you change line spacing at the beginning of a document, all paragraphs that you type will reflect the new spacing unless you change the spacing again. If you change the line spacing in an existing paragraph, only the lines of that paragraph are changed.

REFER TO
Word Manual
Appendix A: GDP—Word
Settings, Style Set—Word
2003

The Word 2003 Style Set used in Word documents launched via GDP changes the default line spacing from multiple-line spacing to single-line spacing so that the spacing between lines is not excessively wide. The same style set changes the default spacing after paragraphs from 10 pt. to 0 pt. so that you can continue to press ENTER 2 times to insert a blank line between paragraphs.

To change line spacing for selected text or an entire document: On the keyboard, select the desired text or click **CTRL + A** to select the entire document; then follow any of the steps that follow. If you have just started typing, you don't have to select text—just set the desired line spacing.

- **CTRL + 1** for single spacing
- **CTRL + 5** for 1.5 spacing
- **CTRL + 2** for double spacing

**Line and Paragraph
spacing button**

When you click the list
arrow on the **Line and
Paragraph spacing button**,
you will see a check by
the current line spacing.

Or: From the **Home** tab, **Paragraph** group, click the list arrow on the **Line spacing** button, and click the desired line-spacing option.

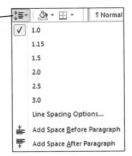

Or:

1. From the **Home** tab, **Paragraph** group, click the **Dialog Box Launcher**.
2. From the **Paragraph** dialog box, click the **Indents and Spacing** tab.
3. Click the down arrow in the **Line spacing** list box, and click the desired line-spacing option; click **OK**.

PRACTICE

1. Select the entire document with **CTRL + A**, and press **CTRL + 2** to change to double-spacing.
2. Turn on **Show/Hide ¶**, and delete the extra blank lines above and below both lists.
3. Click in front of each paragraph, and press **TAB**. The body of your document should look similar to this:

> The following problem was addressed in this study to determine the value of this proposed service to dog owners: What is the feasibility of offering an animal drop-off service to dog owners who are customers of the Michigan Avenue Veterinary Clinic? First, these four questions must be addressed:
>
> 1. How much value will the new service provide to dog owners?
> 2. How many potential clients will transfer from their existing veterinarian to take advantage of this new service?
> 3. What drop-off hours and pick-up hours are preferred?
> 4. What level of additional personnel and boarding facilities will be required to offer this service?
>
> The purpose of this study is to determine if the Michigan Avenue Veterinary Clinic should invest the resources needed to introduce and maintain a new animal drop-off service. The proposed study would provide these results:
>
> - Provide a better understanding of the need for this service.
> - Define some of the mechanics of the service.
> - Provide direction on how to introduce this service.
>
> Although cat owners also represent a large client base for the veterinarian, they were excluded from this study because cats do not have to be licensed.

GO TO
Textbook

4. Save changes to *practice-34*, and return to GDP.

More Rough-Draft Reports

Cut and Copy

Cut, Copy, and **Paste** buttons

You can copy and/or cut and move text from one part of a document to another. To move text means to first cut (delete) the selected text from one location and then paste (insert) it in another location (either in the same document or in a different document). To copy text means to make a copy of the selected text and then insert (paste) it in another location. Copying leaves the original text unchanged. Cut, Copy, and Paste buttons are found on the Home tab, Clipboard group.

The Microsoft Office Clipboard allows you to copy several items, such as text and pictures, from Office documents or other programs and paste them into another Office document. Each time you cut or copy an item, you add it to the collection of items in the Clipboard if the Clipboard is displayed. You can click any item from the list of selected items to paste it into a different place in the current document or move to a new document and paste any item there. You can paste the same item repeatedly.

When you exit all Office programs, the last item that you copied stays on the Clipboard. When you exit all Office programs and restart your computer, all items are cleared from the Office Clipboard.

To display the Office Clipboard in the left pane:

1. From the **Home** tab, in the **Clipboard** group, click the **Dialog Box Launcher**.
2. Click any item under **Click an item to paste** to paste it into your document at the insertion point.
3. Click the **Options** button at the bottom of the pane; then click any desired options for displaying the **Clipboard**.
4. To clear the **Clipboard,** click the **Clear All** button.
5. To close the **Clipboard,** click the **Close** button at the top of the pane.

To cut text:

1. From the **Home** tab, **Clipboard** group, click the **Dialog Box Launcher** to display the **Office Clipboard**.
2. In your document, select the text you want to cut and move.

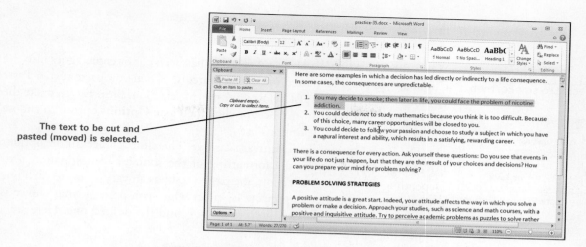

The text to be cut and pasted (moved) is selected.

3. From the **Home** tab, **Clipboard** group, click the **Cut** button.

   Or: On the keyboard, press **CTRL + X**.

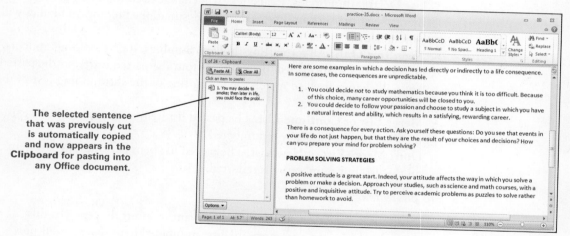

The selected sentence that was previously cut is automatically copied and now appears in the Clipboard for pasting into any Office document.

To copy text:

1. In your document, select the text you want to copy.
2. From the **Home** tab, **Clipboard** group, click the **Copy** button.

   Or: On the keyboard, press **CTRL + C**.

Paste

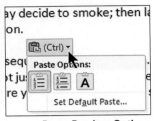

Paste Preview Options
button

When the Clipboard is active, any text that has been cut or copied goes into the Clipboard and can be pasted once or repeatedly. When you paste text, a Paste Options button appears just below your pasted selection. Press **Esc** to make the button disappear for that instance, or click the **Paste Options** button to choose a desired action from the options list.

The Paste Options list is context-sensitive. Therefore, choices in the options list change depending on the formatting of the source and destination text. Depending on the exact selection, the pasted results can vary. Point to each one with the mouse pointer to preview its effect when you paste. If that choice is undesirable, click a different choice until you find the desired one. Here are a few possible choices:

- **Keep Source Formatting.** Pasted text will appear exactly as it did in the source.
- **Use Destination Styles.** Pasted text will change itself to match the formatting style of the surrounding text in the destination. Bolding and italics will be retained.
- **Keep Text Only.** All formatting (bullets, numbers, italics, bolding, indents, graphics, and so forth) will be removed from the pasted text; and the pasted text will change itself to match the formatting of the surrounding text in the destination.
- **Merge List** or **Continue List.** The pasted list item is merged with the existing list and automatically renumbered.
- **Don't Merge List** or **New List.** The pasted list item becomes the last item on the list, but numbering is restarted.

To paste text:

1. Position the insertion point where you want to insert the text. (In this example, the intent is to move the first numbered item that was cut previously to the end of the list. Therefore, the insertion point was placed in the blank line just below the last list item.)
2. From the **Home** tab, **Clipboard** group, click the **Paste** button to make the cut list item reappear in its new location. (In this example, the items are automatically renumbered to reflect the new order.)

   Or: On the keyboard, press **Ctrl + V**.

   Or: On the **Clipboard** pane, under **Click an item to paste**, click the cut item.

Note: Always check the revised text to ensure that you moved exactly what you wanted to move and that numbering, spacing, formatting, and so forth, are correct.

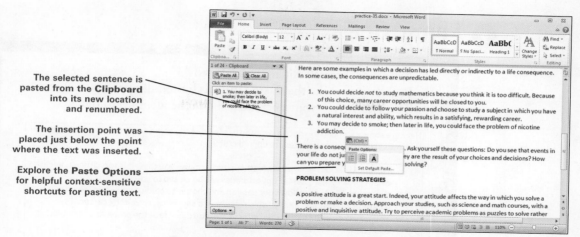

The selected sentence is pasted from the **Clipboard** into its new location and renumbered.

The insertion point was placed just below the point where the text was inserted.

Explore the **Paste Options** for helpful context-sensitive shortcuts for pasting text.

 To move text, you can also point to the selected text and drag and drop it into place in the desired location as an alternative to cutting and pasting. The keyboard shortcuts for cut (**CTRL + X**), copy (**CTRL + C**), and paste (**CTRL + V**) are universal to most Windows programs. Therefore, an item cut or copied in Word could be pasted into an Excel spreadsheet and vice versa.

PRACTICE

1. Display the **Office Clipboard** and clear it.
2. Turn on **Show/Hide ¶**, and select the first numbered item ("You may decide to smoke . . .") including the paragraph symbol at the end. (*Hint:* Click inside the sentence; then press **CTRL** and click.)

   Note: The list number is not highlighted in the selection because it was created using the Numbering feature as opposed to typing it manually. However, the number will be cut along with the text because you included the paragraph symbol in the selection.

3. Cut the selected list item.
4. Note the following: the remaining list items are renumbered and the cut item appears in the **Clipboard** list.
5. Click in the blank line just after the list.
6. Paste the cut list item.
7. Note that the cut and pasted list item is renumbered "3."
8. Click the **Paste Options** button, and click **New List** or **Don't Merge List**.
9. Note that the pasted item is numbered "1."
10. Click the **Paste Options** button, and click **Continue List** or **Merge List**.

PRACTICE (continued)

11. Note that the pasted item is numbered "3."
12. Press **Esc** to make the **Paste Options** button disappear.
13. The list items in your document should be identical to these:

> Here are some examples in which a decision has led directly or indirectly to a life consequence. In some cases, the consequences are unpredictable.
>
> 1. You could decide *not* to study mathematics because you think it is too difficult. Because of this choice, many career opportunities will be closed to you.
> 2. You could decide to follow your passion and choose to study a subject in which you have a natural interest and ability, which results in a satisfying, rewarding career.
> 3. You may decide to smoke; then later in life, you could face the problem of nicotine addiction.
>
> There is a consequence for every action. Ask yourself these questions: Do you see that events in your life do not just happen, but that they are the result of your choices and decisions? How can you prepare your mind for problem solving?

GO TO
Textbook

14. Save changes to *practice-35*, and return to GDP.

Boxed Tables

Table—Insert

REFER TO Reference Manual
R-13A: Boxed Table

Tables have vertical columns (identified by a letter, such as Column A) and horizontal rows (identified by a number, such as Row 1). A table cell (identified by the column letter and row number, such as Cell A1) is created where a column and a row intersect. Thus "President" is located in Cell A1, the intersection of Column A and Row 1 in the example below.

	Column A	Column B
Row 1	President	Juanita Cortes
Row 2	Secretary	Rhonda Butler
Row 3	Treasurer	Rachel Corker
Row 4	Faculty Sponsor	Professor Leon South

A table cell creates fixed boundaries around the text you type just as margins do in a document. Therefore, when you type text within a cell, the text wraps to the next line of the cell when it approaches the right cell border. The cell expands vertically to make room for the next line.

When you first insert a table, Word applies borders to all the cells by default. A boxed table has borders all around. An open table does not have any borders. A ruled table has a border on the top and bottom of Row 2 and the bottom of the last row only. You will learn to remove borders in open and ruled tables in later lessons.

If the font inside any table defaults to 11 pt. rather than 12 pt., see Appendix A, Using Microsoft Word in the Workplace, GDP—Word Settings, Default Font Size—Table, for help.

To insert a table:

1. Position the insertion point where you want the table to start (in this case, at the top of the document).
2. From the **Insert** tab, **Tables** group, click the **Table** button. Then drag to create a table with the desired number of columns and rows.

Table button

Note: A 2-column, 4-row table is shown in the next example. Notice that as you drag, a Live Preview of the table appears in the Word window in the background. When you release the mouse, the table is inserted. An "on-demand" Table Tools tab appears above the Ribbon with a Design tab and Layout tab below it. These on-demand tabs appear when you click inside a table and disappear when you click outside a table.

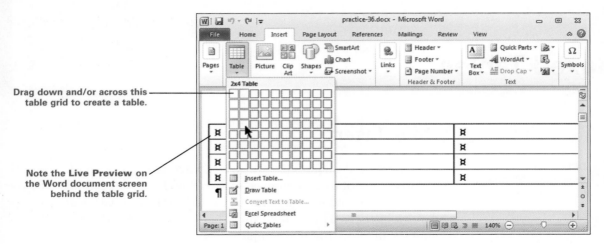

Drag down and/or across this table grid to create a table.

Note the **Live Preview** on the Word document screen behind the table grid.

Or: From the **Insert** tab, **Tables** group, click the **Table** button, **Insert Table**. The **Insert Table** dialog box appears. Type the number of columns you want in the **Number of columns** box; for this example, type 2. Press **TAB**, and type the number of rows in the **Number of rows** box; for this example, type 4. Click **OK** to insert the table into your document.

3. Turn on **Show/Hide ¶**; note that the insertion point is in Cell A1, the table move handle appears above Cell A1, and table end-of-cell markers appear at the beginning of each cell and outside the last cell in any row. (These table formatting codes will be used in later lessons.)

When the insertion point is inside a table, the "on-demand" **Table Tools** and **Design** and **Layout** tabs appear.

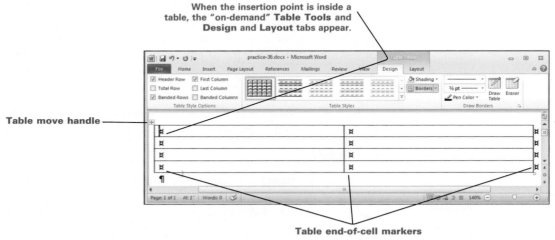

Table move handle

Table end-of-cell markers

4. Type text inside the cells as desired. Cells will expand automatically to accommodate longer text.

If you press **ENTER** by accident, an additional blank line will be added to the cell. Press **BACKSPACE** or click **Undo** to delete the unwanted line.

To move the insertion point from cell to cell: Click the desired cell with the mouse, or press **TAB**.

To move the insertion point to the previous cell: Press **SHIFT + TAB**.

To move the insertion point up or down the rows: Use the arrow keys.

To insert an additional row: Click in the last cell, and press **TAB**.

Or: Turn on **Show/Hide ¶**, click immediately to the right of any row just before the table end-of-cell marker, and press **ENTER**.

To move a row up or down: Click inside the row to be moved; then hold down **ALT + SHIFT +** ↑ or **ALT + SHIFT +** ↓.

PRACTICE

1. Insert a table with 2 columns and 4 rows, click in Cell A1, and type `President`.
2. Press **TAB** to move to Cell B1, and type `Juanita Cortes`.
3. Press **TAB** (not **ENTER**) to move to Cell A2, and continue typing the entries as shown below:

   ```
   Secretary              Rhonda Butler
   Treasurer              Rachel Corker
   Faculty Sponsor        Professor Leon South
   ```

   ? If you are in the last cell of a table (Cell B4 in the example above) and you press **TAB**, an additional row would be inserted. Click the **Undo** button to remove the unwanted row.

4. Turn on **Show/Hide ¶**. Your finished table should look like this:

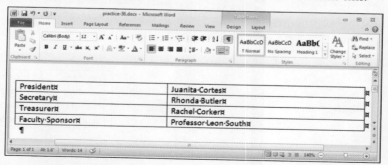

5. Save changes to *practice-36*.

Note: Keep this document open and continue reading.

Table—AutoFit to Contents

To resize the width of columns in a table to fit the contents in that table using AutoFit to Contents:

1. Click anywhere in the table.
2. From **Table Tools, Layout** tab, **Cell Size** group, click the list arrow under **AutoFit**, and click **AutoFit Contents**.

   Or: Right-click any table cell, and click **AutoFit, AutoFit to Contents**.

   Or: Select the table (see Lesson 37), and double-click on the right border of any cell.

    If any of the lines wrap incorrectly when you use the **AutoFit** feature, point to the cell border to the right of the column until you see a double-sided arrow and double-click.

3. Note that the table has been resized to accommodate the longest word or words in each column.

PRACTICE (continued)

1. Right-click anywhere inside the table.
2. Click **AutoFit, AutoFit to Contents**, and turn off **Show/Hide ¶**. Your finished table should look like this:

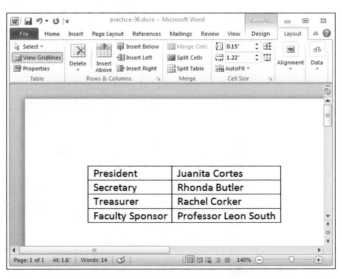

President	Juanita Cortes
Secretary	Rhonda Butler
Treasurer	Rachel Corker
Faculty Sponsor	Professor Leon South

GO TO Textbook

3. Save changes to *practice-36*, and return to GDP.

Open Tables With Titles

Table—Merge Cells

**REFER TO
Reference Manual**
R-13B: Open Table

Table titles (and subtitles, if used) are typed in the first row of a table. Merge all the cells in Row 1 to form one continuous cell; then type the title centered, in bold and all caps, using a 14-pt. font. Type the subtitle on the line below the title centered and in bold in upper- and lowercase, 12-pt. font. Insert 1 blank line below the subtitle or below the title if it appears alone.

To select in a table with Show/Hide ¶ on:

To Select		With Mouse	With Mouse and Keyboard
A cell		Click the **table end-of-cell marker**.	
A row		Click just to the left of the row.	
A column		Click the top border of the column.	
Multiple adjoining cells		Drag across and down as desired.	Click in Cell A1, hold down **SHIFT**, then click in the last cell (B2).
A table		Point to the top corner of the first cell (A1); click the **Table Move Handle**.	Click inside the table; under **Table Tools**, **Layout** tab, **Table** group, click **Select**; Select Table; or press **ALT + SHIFT + 5** on the numeric keypad (with **NUM LOCK** active).
Text in the next or previous cell			Press **TAB** or **SHIFT + TAB**. (Selected text will be deleted with the first keystroke.)

To merge several cells into a single cell:

1. Select the cells you want to merge.

Site Visitation	September 13-16	Alan C. Wingett
On-Site Interviews	September 14-15	Chad Spencer
Preliminary Decisions	September 23	Sherri Jordan
New York Visits	October 4-7	Pedro Martin
Evaluation Conference	October 8	Sherri Jordan
Final Decision	October 10	Gerald J. Pearson

Merge Cells button

2. Under **Table Tools**, **Layout** tab, **Merge** group, click **Merge Cells**, or right-click over the selected row and click **Merge Cells**.
3. Type the desired information in the merged cell, right-click, and click **AutoFit**, **AutoFit to Contents**.

VICE-PRESIDENTIAL SEARCH SCHEDULE Harry Wesson, Coordinator		
Site Visitation	September 13-16	Alan C. Wingett
On-Site Interviews	September 14-15	Chad Spencer
Preliminary Decisions	September 23	Sherri Jordan
New York Visits	October 4-7	Pedro Martin
Evaluation Conference	October 8	Sherri Jordan
Final Decision	October 10	Gerald J. Pearson

PRACTICE

1. Select Row 1, and merge the cells.
2. Type this title in all caps, 14-pt. font size:
   VICE-PRESIDENTIAL SEARCH SCHEDULE
3. Bold and center the text in Row 1.
4. Press **ENTER**, and type this subtitle centered in bold, 12-pt. font size:
   Harry Wesson, Coordinator
5. Press **ENTER** 1 time to insert a blank line after the subtitle.
6. Save changes to *practice-37*.

Note: Keep this document open, and continue reading.

Table—Borders

Borders are the lines that surround each cell within a table. Word applies borders by default when a new table is inserted to create a boxed table. To create an "open" table, remove the borders from a boxed table.

Note: Advanced borders features are covered in these lessons:

- Lesson 39: Remove and apply borders to create a ruled table.
- Lesson 51: Apply a bottom border to the first row of a resume.
- Lesson 86: Apply a border to the bottom of a header.
- Lesson 111: Apply advanced customized borders and shading.

REFER TO
Word Manual
L. 28: View Gridlines

⑦ When borders are removed, use **View Gridlines** to see the light, nonprinting blue gridlines to guide you as you enter text. This table has no borders and gridlines are displayed:

VICE-PRESIDENTIAL SEARCH SCHEDULE Harry Wesson, Coordinator		
Site Visitation	September 13-16	Alan C. Wingett
On-Site Interviews	September 14-15	Chad Spencer
Preliminary Decisions	September 23	Sherri Jordan
New York Visits	October 4-7	Pedro Martin
Evaluation Conference	October 8	Sherri Jordan
Final Decision	October 10	Gerald J. Pearson

To remove borders from a table:

1. From the **Table Tools**, **Layout** tab, **Table** group, click **View Gridlines**, and select the table or the desired cells.
2. From the **Table Tools**, **Design** tab, **Table Styles** group, click the list arrow next to the **Borders** button; then click the desired border to apply it or remove it.

Click the **Borders** button to apply the active border displayed on the **Borders** button.

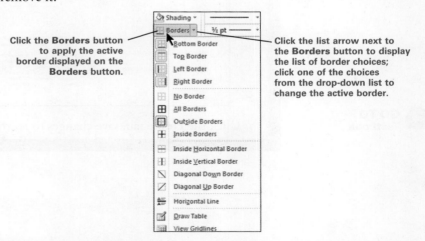

Click the list arrow next to the **Borders** button to display the list of border choices; click one of the choices from the drop-down list to change the active border.

⑦ The most recently used border appears as the active **Borders** button. Be careful to click the list arrow *next to* the **Borders** button and not the **Borders** button itself. If you click the **Borders** button, the currently displayed border on the button will be applied to the table or selected cell.

⬇ Click inside the table to find the **Borders** button under **Table Tools, Design** tab, **Table Styles** group.

3. Repeat the process until the desired borders have been applied or removed.

To remove all borders at once: Select the table; from any **Borders** button, click **No Border**.

To apply borders all at once to all cells: Select the table; from any **Borders** button, click **All Borders**.

PRACTICE (continued)

1. Click inside Cell A1, and automatically adjust the column widths to fit the contents for all columns. (*Hint:* Right-click over the table, and click **AutoFit**, **Auto Fit to Contents**.)
2. Remove borders from this table.
3. Note that blue gridlines are visible.

   ? If gridlines are not visible, from the **Table Tools Layout** tab, **Table** group, click **View Gridlines**.

4. Press **CTRL + P**, and note that the borders have been removed and gridlines do not display. Your finished table should look similar to this:

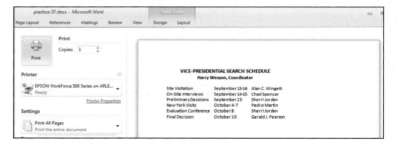

GO TO
Textbook

5. Click the **Home** tab, save changes to *practice-37*, and return to GDP.

Open Tables With Column Headings

Table—Align Bottom

Column headings describe the information contained in the column entries below them. They are centered and typed in bold using upper- and lowercase letters. Press ENTER 1 time at the desired position in a long heading to create a 2-line column heading. If a row includes both 1- and 2-line column headings, align the 1-line heading at the bottom of the cell.

To center and anchor information at the bottom of a row:

1. Select the desired row.
2. Right-click over the selected row, and click **Cell Alignment** to display a series of cell alignment buttons.

   Or: Use the cell alignment buttons found under **Table Tools**, **Layout** tab, **Alignment** group.

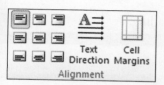

Alignment group
(**Align Top Left** button active)

3. Point to **Align Bottom Center**; if you used a right-click, note the **Live Preview**; then click **Align Bottom Center** to center the information in all selected cells, and anchor it at the bottom of the cell; then bold the selected row.

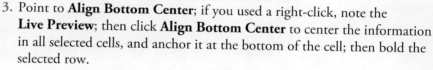

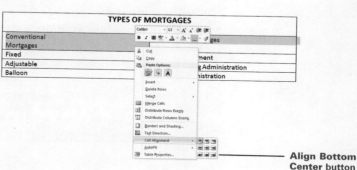

Align Bottom
Center button

PRACTICE

1. Select Row 1 and merge the cells.
2. Click in Row 1, and type the title TYPES OF MORTGAGES centered using a 14-pt. bold font.
3. Press ENTER 1 time to insert 1 blank line below the title.
4. In Cell A2, delete the space between Conventional and Mortgages; then press ENTER 1 time to create a 2-line column heading.
5. Select Row 2; align cells at the bottom, center; bold the row.
6. Right-click over the table, and click **AutoFit**, **AutoFit to Contents**. Your table should look like this:

TYPES OF MORTGAGES	
Conventional Mortgages	**Alternative Mortgages**
Fixed	Graduated payment
Adjustable	Federal Housing Administration
Balloon	Veterans Administration

Note: Keep this document open and continue reading.

Table—Center Horizontally

When you insert a table, the table extends from margin to margin and is left-aligned. If you adjust column widths, the table width shrinks and the table appears at the left margin. Horizontally center the table so it will appear centered between the document margins like this:

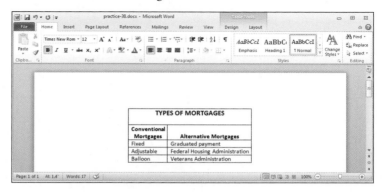

To change the horizontal alignment of a table:

1. Click inside the table.
2. Under **Table Tools**, **Layout** tab, **Table** group, click **Properties**.

   Or: Right-click the table and click **Table Properties**.

3. Click **Center** (or the desired alignment option); click **OK**.

Click **Center** to center a table horizontally.

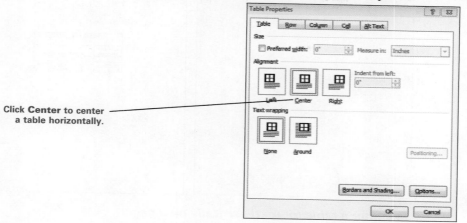

Or:

1. Select the table by clicking the **Table Move Handle** just above the top corner of Cell A1or use the **Layout** tab, **Table** group, **Select (Select Table)** button, and click **Select Table**.
2. From the **Home** tab, **Paragraph** group, click the **Center** button.

PRACTICE (continued)

1. Select the table and center it horizontally.
2. Compare it to the illustration in this section: Table—Center Horizontally.

Note: Keep this document open and continue reading.

Table—Center Page

Use the **Page Setup** command to center a table or text vertically between the top and bottom margins on a page.

Before vertical centering, the table is anchored at the top of the page.

After vertical centering, the table is centered on the page between the top and bottom margins.

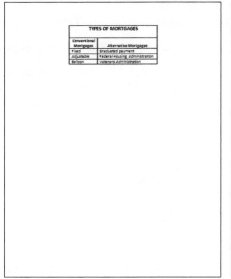
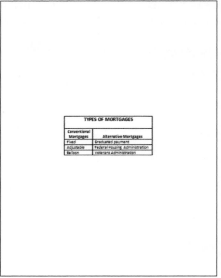

To center a table (or text) vertically on a page:

1. Position the insertion point anywhere on the page you want centered.
2. From the **Page Layout** tab, **Page Setup** group, click the **Dialog Box Launcher** to display the **Page Setup** dialog box.

   Or: Click the **View Ruler** button to display the ruler. Then double-click on any shaded part of the ruler (to the right or left of the white part of the ruler) to display the **Page Setup** dialog box.

Double-click on any shaded part of the ruler to display the Page Setup dialog box.

Click the View Ruler button to display or hide the Ruler.

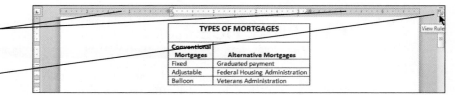

3. From the **Page Setup** dialog box, click the **Layout** tab.
4. Click the **Vertical alignment** list arrow; click **Center**, **OK**.

PRACTICE (continued)

1. Center the table vertically on the page.
2. Press **CTRL + P** to view the centered table.
3. Select the table, and remove all borders to create an open table.
4. Click the **Home** tab, save changes to *practice-38*, and return to GDP.

GO TO Textbook

Ruled Tables With Number Columns

Table—Align Text Right

To improve the readability and appearance of a table, change the alignment of column entries (the information in the cells under the column heading). Left-align text column entries. Right-align number column entries that could be used in mathematical calculations, such as dollar amounts or percentages. Phone numbers, account numbers, and so forth are aligned at the left as text column entries rather than number column entries.

To left- or right-align selected text in column entries:

1. Right-click over the selected text, and click **Cell Alignment** to display a series of cell alignment buttons.
2. Click **Align Bottom Left** to align text column entries at the bottom left of the cell, or click **Align Bottom Right** to align number column entries at the bottom right of the cell.

Or: Click the desired cell alignment button found under **Table Tools**, **Layout** tab, in the **Alignment** group.

Or: From the **Home** tab, **Paragraph** group, click the **Align Text Left** or **Align Text Right** button.

Or: On the keyboard, use one of the keyboard shortcuts CTRL + L or CTRL + R.

PRACTICE

1. Select Row 1, and merge the cells.
2. Click in Row 1, and type the title PRICE COMPARISONS centered using a 14-pt. bold font, and press ENTER 1 time.
3. Change to a 12-pt. font, type the subtitle New Cars in bold, and press ENTER 1 time to insert a blank line below the subtitle.
4. In Cell A2, delete the space between Vehicle and Category, and press ENTER 1 time to create a 2-line column heading.
5. Select Row 2; align cells at the bottom, center; and bold the row.

PRACTICE (continued)

6. Select the column entries under the column headings for Columns B, C, and D; and right-align these number entries.
7. Right-click over the table, and click **AutoFit**, **AutoFit to Contents**. Your table should look like this:

PRICE COMPARISONS New Cars			
Vehicle Category	AutoMart	SmartBuy	Dealer
Sedan	$20,861	$21,216	$23,743
SUV	28,700	29,562	32,270
Truck	18,600	20,247	21,983

Note: Keep this document open and continue reading.

Table—Borders, Ruled

REFER TO
Reference Manual

R-13C: Ruled Table

REFER TO
Word Manual

L 28: View Gridlines

Ruled tables are formatted with a border on the top and bottom of Row 2 and the bottom of the last row only. To create a ruled table, remove borders from the entire table, and then reapply them to Row 2 and the bottom of the last row. When borders are removed, use View Gridlines to see the individual table cell gridlines to guide you as you enter text.

Advanced borders and shading features are covered in these lessons:

- Lesson 51: Apply a bottom border to the first row of a resume.
- Lesson 86: Apply a border to the bottom of a header.
- Lesson 111: Apply advanced customized borders and shading.

To remove and apply borders in a ruled table:

1. Remove all borders from the table, and activate **View Gridlines** if necessary. (*Hint:* Select the table; from the **Home** tab, **Paragraph** group, click the list arrow next to the **Borders** button, and click **No Border**; click the list arrow next to the **Borders** button, and click **View Gridlines**.)
2. Select Row 2; from the **Home** tab, **Paragraph** group, click the list arrow next to the **Borders** button; then click the **Top Border** button to apply a border to the top of Row 2.
3. With Row 2 still selected, from the **Home** tab, **Paragraph** group, click the list arrow next to the **Borders** button; then click the **Bottom Border** button to apply a border to the bottom of Row 2.
4. Select the bottom row of the table.
5. From the **Home** tab, **Paragraph** group, click the **Bottom Border** button to apply a border to the bottom of the last row.

Because a bottom border was just applied, the Bottom Border is the active button—there is no need to click the list arrow to find it.

1. Remove all borders from the table, and activate **View Gridlines**.
2. Select Row 2, and apply a top and bottom border.
3. Select the last row and apply a bottom border.
4. Center the table horizontally. (*Hint:* Select the table with the **Table Move Handle**; and from the **Home** tab, **Paragraph** group, click the **Center** button.)
5. Center the table vertically. (*Hint:* From the **Page Layout** tab, **Page Setup** group, click the **Dialog Box Launcher**. From the **Layout** tab, under **Page**, click **Vertical alignment**, **Center**, **OK**.)
6. Press **CTRL + P** to view your table—it should look similar to this.

PRICE COMPARISONS
New Cars

Vehicle Category	AutoMart	SmartBuy	Dealer
Sedan	$20,861	$21,218	$23,743
SUV	28,700	29,562	32,270
Truck	18,600	20,247	21,983

GO TO
Textbook

7. Click the **Home** tab, save changes to *practice-39*, and return to GDP.

Letters With Indented Displays and Copy Notations and E-Mail With Copies

Indentation

To set off a direct quotation that has 4 lines or more of text or to emphasize a paragraph, format such text as an indented display. An indented display is indented 0.5 inch from both the left and right margins (double indent).

To format a paragraph as an indented display:

1. Insert 1 blank line above the paragraph to be displayed.
2. Type the displayed paragraph, insert 1 blank line after it, and type the paragraph immediately following it.
3. Select only the lines to be included in the displayed paragraph.
4. With the text still selected, from the **Home** tab, **Paragraph** group, click the **Dialog Box Launcher**.
5. From the **Paragraph** dialog box, click the **Indents and Spacing** tab.
6. Under **Indentation**, click the up arrow next to the **Left** and **Right** boxes to increase the paragraph indentation to 0.5 inch on both sides; click **OK**.

Set Left and Right indent boxes to 0.5".

Note the effects of the settings in the Preview box.

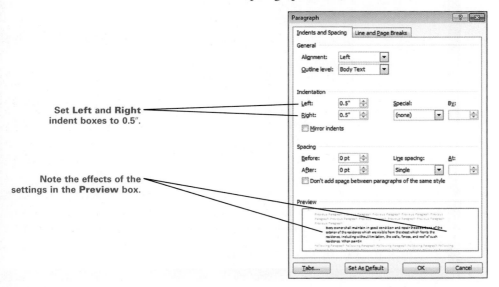

INCREASE AND DECREASE INDENT

You can increase the left indent of a paragraph to set off text, such as in a resume where you might describe your education and experience in paragraph style. You could follow steps 3 to 5 in the previous section; and in step 6, adjust the Left box setting only. However, it is faster to use the Increase Indent button.

To increase the left indent for a paragraph:

Increase Indent button

1. Click inside the desired paragraph, or click where the indented paragraph will begin.
2. From the **Home** tab, **Paragraph** group, click the **Increase Indent** button. Each click increases the indent by 0.5 inch, and subsequent lines will wrap around and conform to the adjusted left margin; or press CTRL + M.

Decrease Indent button

3. Click the **Decrease Indent** button to decrease the indent as needed, or press CTRL + SHIFT + M.

PRACTICE

REFER TO
Reference Manual
R-3A: Business Letter in Block Style (Indented display)

1. Select the second paragraph ("Every owner shall . . .").
2. Format the selected paragraph as an indented display with a 0.5-inch double indent.
3. Save and close the file.

Note: Keep Word open and continue reading.

E-Mail—Copies

REFER TO
Word Manual
L. 25: E-Mail a Document

Use the copy feature in your e-mail software to send a copy of an e-mail message to one or more recipients. The steps to send a copy will vary depending upon your e-mail program. In general, just fill in the desired e-mail address in the Copy box; separate multiple addresses with a semicolon or a comma.

Some e-mail programs hide the Copy box, and you must take some steps to display it initially. The name of the Copy box is usually abbreviated as "Cc" (carbon copy). Refer to your e-mail software's Help feature for steps to send a copy of an e-mail message.

To send a copy of an e-mail message from Word:

1. With your instructor's permission, follow the steps in Lesson 25, page 38, to send an open Word document as the actual e-mail message.
2. Click inside the **Cc** box, and type in the e-mail address of the desired recipient(s), or click the **Cc** button and select the desired name from the **Contacts** list.

Do not send an e-mail message without consulting your instructor!

1. Press **CTRL + N** to create a new blank document.
2. Type this e-mail message:

```
Hi, Mr. Morway:

Please contact Paul Fox, Association General
Manager, at 661-555-1212. I'm copying your wife so
she has this information as well.

Susan

Susan Booth
E-mail: sbooth@hoa.net
Phone: 323-555-9432
```

3. Fill in any desired address(es) in the **To** and **Cc** boxes and type Contact Information in the **Subject** box. Your document should look similar to this:

Copy box

Cc button

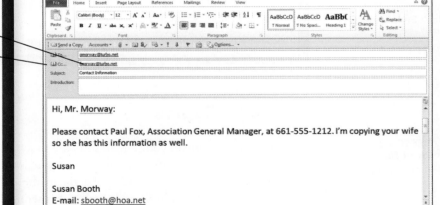

4. Save this file as *practice-44B*, send the e-mail if desired, and return to GDP.

GO TO
Textbook

Letters in Modified-Block Style

Tab Set—Ruler Tabs

Word sets automatic default tab stops every 0.5 inch starting at the left margin. When you press TAB to indent text, the insertion point moves in 0.5-inch increments to these default tab settings. When you manually set a custom tab, Word clears (deletes) all the default 0.5-inch tab stops and their corresponding tick marks to the left of the custom tab; therefore, when you press TAB, you will move directly to the new tab stop.

A custom tab is in effect from the point it was set in the document and for any text typed thereafter. If a document has already been typed, select the desired text or select the entire document (CTRL + A), and then set tabs.

Use the horizontal ruler to quickly set, move, or delete left, center, right, and decimal tabs. Other tabs must be set using menus as explained in Lesson 50. Each type of custom tab is displayed on the ruler with a different symbol. Display the ruler to see exactly where tabs have been set.

To display the ruler:

1. Click the **View Ruler** button at the top of the vertical scroll area.

   ❓ The **View Ruler** button is a toggle button. Click it once to display the ruler and again to hide it.

2. Note the tick marks that appear on the horizontal ruler every 0.5 inch.

Tick marks for 0.5-inch default tab stops

Four different kinds of tab settings are illustrated here. Below each tab marker, note the alignment of the corresponding text that was typed using each tab setting.

Click the **View Ruler** toggle button to display or hide the ruler.

Tab Selector button

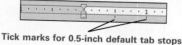

Left tab marker	Center tab marker	Decimal tab marker	Right tab marker
Digital Electronics	DEC	.76	Up 3/8
Dr. Pepper	DrPepp	1.275	Up 3/4
Consolidated Industries	CIN	12	Unchanged
Dow Chemical	DowCH	2.4	Down 3/8
Left-aligned	Centered	Decimal-aligned	Right-aligned

To set a custom tab using the ruler:

Left Tab button

Center Tab button

Right Tab button

Decimal Tab button

1. Display the ruler.
2. Position the insertion point on the line where you want the new tab to start (or select the paragraphs where you want to change the tabs).
3. Click the **Tab Selector** button on the ruler until the desired tab button is displayed.
4. On the ruler, click where you want the new tab to appear.

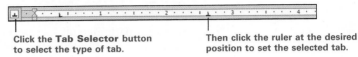

Click the **Tab Selector** button to select the type of tab.

Then click the ruler at the desired position to set the selected tab.

To clear or move a tab:

1. Position the insertion point on the desired line.

   For existing text, select the desired text and change the tabs. If you want to change the tabs throughout the document, press **CTRL + A** to select the entire document.

2. To clear (delete) a tab, drag the tab marker off the ruler. Or to move a tab setting, drag the tab marker left or right.

REFER TO Reference Manual

R-3D: Personal-Business Letter in Modified-Block Style

To set a tab to position the date, complimentary closing, and writer's identification in a modified-block style letter:

1. Set a left tab at 3.25 inches on the ruler.

   If the letter has already been typed, select all lines in the letter (**CTRL + A**) before setting the left tab.

2. Click in front of the date in the letter, and press **TAB** 1 time to begin the date at the 3.25-inch tab.
3. Click in front of the complimentary closing and writer's identification lines, and press **TAB** 1 time to begin these lines at the 3.25-inch tab.

PRACTICE

1. Select all lines of the letter, and set a left tab at 3.25 inches on the ruler.
2. Click in front of the date, and press **TAB** 1 time to begin this line at 3.25 inches; repeat this for the complimentary closing and writer's identification.
3. Turn on **Show/Hide ¶** to view formatting marks. The black arrows pointing to the right represent a tab character where you have pressed **TAB**. Your screen should look similar to the illustration that follows:

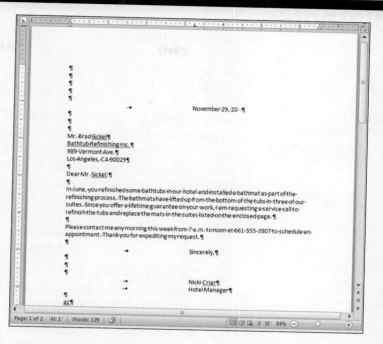

4. Move the insertion point to the end of the letter. (*Hint:* Press **CTRL + END.**)
5. Insert a manual page break. (*Hint:* Press **CTRL + ENTER.**)
6. Clear the left tab from the second page.
7. Use the ruler to set a left tab at 1.5 inches and a right tab at 4.5 inches.
8. Type the following lines—remember to press **TAB** 1 time before each building name and 1 time before each suite name.

```
Building A Grand Suite
Building B Presidential Suite
Building C Del Mar Suite
```

When you're finished with the second page, your screen should look similar to this:

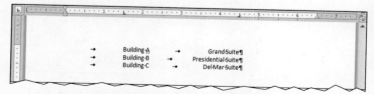

GO TO
Textbook

9. Save changes to *practice-45*, and return to GDP.

Left-Bound Business Reports With Indented Displays and Footnotes

Margins

**REFER TO
Reference Manual**
R-9A: Left-Bound Business
Report

Margins represent the distance (blank space) between the edge of the paper and the typed text on all sides of a document. Word uses 1-inch default margins all around. If you change margins, the new settings affect the entire document, not just the current page. You will need to change the left margin for a left-bound report, which uses a wider 1.5-inch left margin.

To change the left margin:

1. From the **Page Layout** tab, **Page Setup** group, click **Margins**, **Custom Margins**, to display the **Page Setup** dialog box.

   Or: Click the **View Ruler** button to display the ruler; then double-click on any part of the shaded ruler (to the right or left of the white part of the ruler) to display the **Page Setup** dialog box.

2. From the **Margins** tab, click in the **Left** box, and type 1.5 or click the arrows to increase or decrease margins as desired; click **OK**.

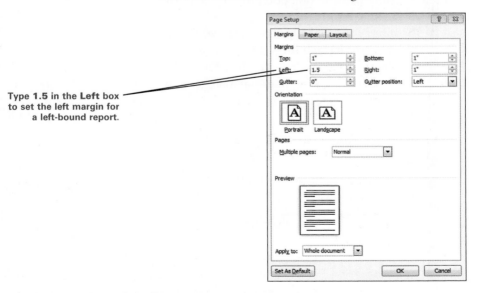

Type **1.5** in the **Left** box to set the left margin for a left-bound report.

In a multipage left-bound report, do not press TAB to position a page number using the preset tabs inside the header. Preset tabs do not adjust automatically to accommodate margin changes. Instead, click the desired page numbering from the gallery of designs.

PRACTICE

1. Display the ruler.
2. Note the line endings in each line before margins are changed.
3. Note the shaded part of the ruler indicates 1-inch left and right margins.

Before margins are changed, the shaded portion of the ruler displays 1-inch side margins.

and those workers who initially resisted the technology declare it is easy to learn and has enabled them to compete with any business that has previously published such documents as reports, newsletters, and company brochures." The cost of laying out a page has now been cut considerably with this technology. It is no wonder, then, that companies worldwide are overly enthusiastic about hiring trained personnel with these skills.

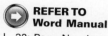

REFER TO
Word Manual

L. 32: Page Number

4. Insert a right-aligned page number set to start at "2." (*Hint:* From the **Insert** tab, **Header & Footer** group, click **Page Number**, **Top of Page**, **Plain Number 3**; from the **Design** tab, **Header & Footer** group, click **Page Number**, **Format Page Numbers**, **Start at**; type 2 in the **Start at** box; click **OK**.)
5. Close the header, and change the left margin to 1.5 inch.
6. Note that the ruler now indicates a 1.5-inch left margin.
7. Note the line endings in each line after margins are changed.
8. Note that the page number is correctly aligned at the right margin.

After the left margin is changed, the ruler displays a 1.5-inch left margin.

The page number remains aligned at the right margin.

2

and those workers who initially resisted the technology declare it is easy to learn and has enabled them to compete with any business that has previously published such documents as reports, newsletters, and company brochures." The cost of laying out a page has now been cut considerably with this technology. It is no wonder, then, that companies worldwide are overly enthusiastic about hiring trained personnel with these skills.

9. Save changes to *practice-46*.

Note: Keep this document open and continue reading.

Footnotes

When you insert a footnote, Word automatically numbers, positions, and formats the footnote for you. Do not type the footnote superscript number either in the document or in the footnote itself. The number will appear in both places automatically when you insert a footnote.

To insert a footnote:

1. Click directly after the character where you want the sequential superscript footnote number to appear. Do not insert a space between the last character in the text and the footnote number.

Position the insertion point exactly where the footnote superscript number should appear.

> technology declare it is easy t
> iness that has previously publis
> npany brochures." The cost of

2. From the **References** tab, in the **Footnotes** group, click **Insert Footnote**. A footnote superscript number appears automatically in the text just before the insertion point.

   Or: On the keyboard, press **CTRL + ALT + F**.

   Or: From the **References** tab, **Footnotes** group, click the **Dialog Box Launcher**. From the **Footnotes and Endnotes** dialog box, click **Insert**.

Footnote superscript numbers appear automatically in the text at the insertion point.

> technology declare it is easy to
> iness that has previously publish
> npany brochures."[1] The cost of

3. Note that the insertion point moves automatically to the bottom of the page, and a divider line and sequential footnote number appear.
4. Type the footnote entry at the bottom of the page where the insertion point appears—do not add or remove any spaces after the superscript.
5. When you finish typing the footnote, do not press **ENTER**. Click back inside the main text and continue typing.
6. Repeat these steps for additional footnotes. Word will automatically adjust footnote numbers when entries are added or deleted.

Note: The font size for the footnote entry is smaller than the text size in the body. Remember to italicize titles of major works, such as titles of books and magazines.

Word formats footnotes in a smaller font size than normal text and inserts 1 space after the superscript number.

> [1] Louise Plachta and Leonard E. Flannery, *Desktop Publishing Today*, 2d ed., Computer Publications, Inc., Los Angeles, 2009, pp. 558–559.
> [2] Terry Denton, "Newspaper Cuts Costs, Increases Quality," *The Monthly Press*, October 2009, p. 160.

To edit a footnote:

1. Click inside the footnote entry.
2. Make any desired changes; then click outside the footnote.

To delete a footnote:

1. Select the footnote number in the document (not in the footnote entry at the bottom of the page).
2. Press **DELETE**.
3. Note that all footnotes are renumbered to reflect the deletion.

1. Click immediately after the ending quotation mark in the first sentence, and insert the footnote shown below—do not type the footnote superscript number as it will appear automatically:

   Louise Plachta and Leonard E. Flannery, *Desktop Publishing Today*, 2d ed., Computer Publications, Inc., Los Angeles, 2009, pp. 568–569.

2. Click immediately after the period in the second sentence in the body of the document, and insert this footnote:

   Terry Denton, "Newspaper Cuts Costs, Increases Quality," *The Monthly Press*, October 2009, p. 160.

3. Edit Footnote 1 by changing the page references to pp. 558–559.
4. Delete Footnote 1, and note that Footnote 2 is renumbered.
5. Undo this action to restore Footnote 1.
6. Press **CTRL + P** to view your document; it should look similar to this:

Note the wider 1.5-inch left margin.

Note that the footnote references are positioned at the bottom of a page regardless of how much text is on the page.

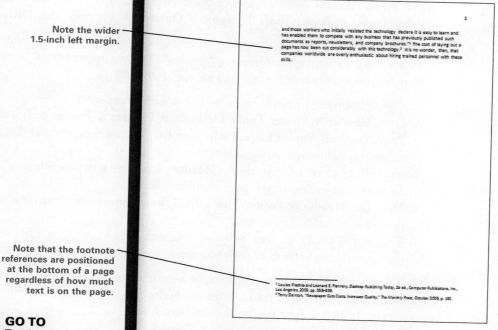

GO TO Textbook

7. Click the **Home** tab, save changes to *practice-46*, and return to GDP.

Reports in APA Style

Headers

REFER TO
Word Manual
L. 32: Page Number

REFER TO
Reference Manual
R-10A: Report in APA Style

A header is any information (such as a report title, name, page number, and/or divider line) that appears at the top of every page in a document above the body. You can suppress a header on the first page so that the header information appears only on the second and subsequent pages.

An APA-style report includes a header that begins on the first page and includes a shortened title and an automatic page number set to begin with "3" as the page number. An MLA-style report includes a header that begins on the first page and includes the author's last name and an automatic page number field that begins with "1" as the page number.

If the **Page Number** feature is not behaving as expected in any of the steps that follow, do this: right-click over the header area, and click **Edit Header**; from **Header & Footer Tools**, **Design** tab, **Options** group, verify that **Different first page** is unchecked.

To insert a right-aligned header for an APA-style report that includes text followed by an automatic page number field:

1. Right-click over the header area, and click **Edit Header**.
2. From **Header & Footer Tools**, **Design** tab, **Header & Footer** group, click **Page Number**, **Top of Page**, **Plain Number 3**, from the gallery of designs to insert a right-aligned page number.
3. Note that you are now inside the **Header** section with the document dimmed and the automatic page number inserted.
4. Note that **Header & Footer Tools**, **Design** tab appears on demand whenever you are inside a header.
5. Type any desired text, such as a shortened title, and insert a space between the text and the automatic page number.

To insert a header for an MLA-style report with right-aligned text followed by an automatic page number: Follow steps 1 through 5 in the previous steps. In step 5, type the author's last name.

To start page numbering with a different number:

1. Right-click over the header area, and click **Edit Header**.
2. From the **Header & Footer Tools**, **Design** tab, **Header & Footer** group, click **Page Number**, **Format Page Numbers**, to display the **Page Number Format** dialog box.

3. From the **Page Number Format** dialog box, under **Page numbering**, click **Start at**; type 3 in the **Start at** box; click **OK**.

To close a header and return to the document body:

1. Double-click anywhere outside the **First Page Header** area inside the document area, or from **Header & Footer Tools**, **Design** tab, **Close** group, click the **Close Header and Footer** button.
2. Note that the header is now dimmed, the document is active, and the **Header & Footer Tools**, **Design** tab disappears.

To edit a header: Double-click anywhere over the header area, or right-click over the header area and click **Edit Header**. (The document should now be dimmed and the header should be active.)

To suppress a header only on the first page of a multipage document (subsequent pages will still include a header):

1. From the **Page Layout** tab, **Page Setup** group, click the **Dialog Box Launcher**; then click the **Layout** tab.
2. Under **Headers and footers**, check **Different first page**; click **OK**.
3. Scroll down to the second page to view the header; or press CTRL + ENTER to force a page break to view the header on the second page, and then undo the manual page break.

To remove a header: From the **Insert** tab, **Header & Footer** group, click **Header**, **Remove Header**. Repeat this on the second page if you have suppressed the header on the first page.

To italicize the header or make any font changes: Click inside the header; press CTRL + A to select all text; then make any desired font changes.

To add a bottom border to a header: Click inside the header; from the **Home** tab, **Paragraph** group, click the list arrow on the **Borders** button, and click the **Bottom Border** button.

 PRACTICE

1. Type the title Toll Free Telephone Service at the top of the first page.
2. Press ENTER 1 time, type Michael Dear as the byline, and press ENTER again; center the title and byline.
3. Click at the end of the period in the first sentence, press ENTER twice, and delete the extra space at the start of the new paragraph.
4. Press TAB to indent the new paragraph, click the up arrow to move up one line, and type the main heading Analysis of Costs and Benefits; center the heading.

PRACTICE (continued)

5. Click at the end of the period in the sentence ending in "800-number calls"; then press **ENTER**.
6. Type `SmartToll Benefits` as a subheading at the left margin in italic.
7. Click at the end of the next paragraph, press **ENTER**, and type `SmartToll Fees` as a subheading at the left margin in italic.
8. Click anywhere inside the first page, and insert a right-aligned header with a page number that starts at 3.
9. Type `Telephone Service`; space once.
10. Double-click outside the header in the document body.
11. Press **CTRL + P** to view your document:

Page number on the first page is set to "3."

Centered main heading

Italicized side heading

Telephone Service 3

Toll-Free Telephone Service

Michael Dear

In order to determine the feasibility of providing a toll-free telephone service to United Manufacturing domestic spare-parts customers, the management team evaluated the costs and benefits.

Analysis of Costs and Benefits

Incoming telephone call time usage was recorded the week of November 12-17, 409 domestic customers were surveyed in October/November, and a telephone interview was conducted with a phone company toll-free representative in October. The criteria used were the costs and benefits of a toll-free service, the value customers place on a toll-free service, and how to communicate a toll-free service.

United Manufacturing currently uses Digital Connect as their long-distance telephone carrier. The required toll-free telephone service and cost analysis are based on information from, and a telephone interview with Digital Connect.

According to Art Neumann, a Digital Connect Long-Distance Network Sales Specialist, the service recommended for United Manufacturing is SmartToll. SmartToll is an inward toll-free service that utilizes the existing telephone lines to receive the 800-number calls.

SmartToll Benefits

The advantage of this service is all of the existing lines currently used to place and receive calls are available to receive the incoming 800-number calls. Because the SmartToll service distributes the incoming calls among the available lines, there is a reduction in the chance a caller will receive a busy signal. Several customers indicated in the comment section

Telephone Service 4

of the questionnaire that if United Manufacturing were to offer an 800 number, they should include sufficient service to handle the expected volume of incoming calls.

SmartToll Fees

At no additional charge, SmartToll service allows the customer to redirect a call destination over the Internet. The customer is provided with an individual Web interface. This allows the customer the flexibility to take toll-free calls on any office, home or cell phone. The customer can control where the toll-free number rings with just a click. No additional phone lines are needed. Flat rate pricing in state or out-of-state is available.

GO TO Textbook

12. Click the **Home** tab, save changes to *practice-47*, and return to GDP.

Report Citations

Indentation—Hanging

REFER TO
Reference Manual

R-9B: Bibliography

R-10B: References in APA Style

R-10D: Works Cited in MLA Style

REFER TO
Word Manual

L. 45: Tab Set—Ruler Tabs

A paragraph formatted with a hanging indent displays the first line at the left margin, and indents carryover lines 0.5 inch. The list of sources in bibliographies, reference lists, and works-cited pages are all formatted with hanging indents.

To display the ruler to verify that a hanging indent has been correctly set:

1. Click the **View Ruler** button (at the top of the vertical scroll area) to display the ruler.
2. Note that the hanging indent marker on the ruler moves 0.5 inch to the right when you format a paragraph with a hanging indent.

To format a hanging indent:

1. Position the insertion point where you want to begin indenting (or select the text you want indented).
2. From the **Home** tab, **Paragraph** group, click the **Dialog Box Launcher**.
3. From the **Paragraph** dialog box, click the **Indents and Spacing** tab.
4. In the **Special** box, click the down arrow and click **Hanging**; click **OK**.

Or: On the keyboard, press **CTRL + T**.

Under Special, click **Hanging**.

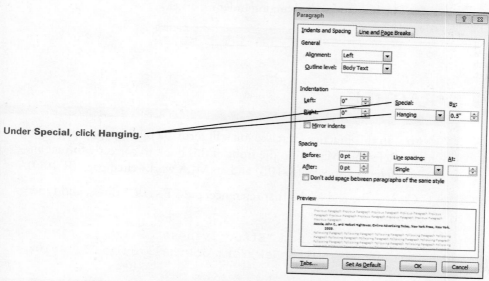

5. Begin typing the first reference. Note that the first line begins at the left margin, and when you reach the end of a line, text wraps automatically to the next line and starts at the indention point.

6. Press **ENTER** once or twice as appropriate, and type the next reference.

 If you have already typed the document and want to apply a hanging indent, select the desired text first and then apply a hanging indent.

To end a hanging indent:

1. When you finish typing the hanging-indented text, press **ENTER**.
2. From the **Home** tab, **Paragraph** group, click the **Dialog Box Launcher**.
3. From the **Paragraph** dialog box, click the **Indents and Spacing** tab.
4. In the **Special** box, click the down arrow and click **(none)**; click **OK**.

Hanging indent marker

Hanging indent applied

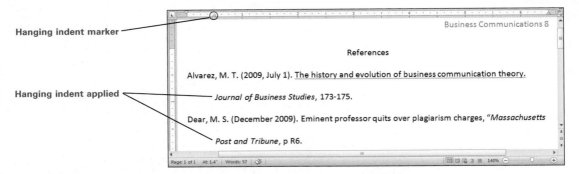

Or: On the keyboard, press **CTRL + SHIFT + T** to return the insertion point to the left margin for all lines.

To manually adjust the width of a hanging indent, drag the hanging indent marker on the ruler to the desired position—the box under it also moves. (Do *not* drag the box under the hanging indent marker.)

Drag only the hanging indent marker (bottom triangle) to adjust the width of a hanging indent.

PRACTICE

Note: In this practice exercise, you will format a bibliography page. Refer to the Reference Manual in the front of this book to correctly format an APA reference list page (R-10B) and an MLA works-cited page (R-10D).

1. Click at the end of the first reference, press **ENTER** 2 times, and type this entry.

   Choi, Byong Sang, "Effectiveness of Interactive Online Ads," *The New York Journal*, July 20, 2010, p. R6.

PRACTICE (continued)

2. Select the first two entries, and format them with a hanging indent. Your document should look similar to this:

BIBLIOGRAPHY

Acosta, John C., and Herbert Hightower, *Online Advertising Today,* New York Press, New York, 2009.

Choi, Byong Sang, "Effectiveness of Interactive Online Ads," *The New York Journal,* July 20, 2010, p. R6.

3. Save changes to *practice-49*.

Note: Keep this document open and continue reading.

AutoCorrect—Hyperlink

When you type an e-mail or Internet address and then press the SPACE BAR or press ENTER, that address is automatically converted to a hyperlink. When you type an Internet address that is surrounded by angle brackets (such as in the bibliography or footnotes for a report or in an APA reference list page) and type a punctuation mark and press the SPACE BAR or ENTER, that address is automatically converted to a hyperlink, and the angle brackets are deleted and must be manually replaced. If hyperlinks are not behaving as expected, see Appendix A: GDP—Word Settings, AutoFormat As You Type Options, to verify your Word settings.

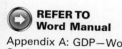

REFER TO
Word Manual

Appendix A: GDP—Word Settings, AutoFormat As You Type Options

To avoid creating an undesirable automatic hyperlink, do not insert a space or comma at the end of a Web address. However, when a space or comma must follow an electronic reference, use one of these steps to remove the hyperlink and replace any missing angle brackets:

To remove an automatic hyperlink immediately after it appears: If the **AutoCorrect Options** lightning bolt button appears, click the list arrow, and click **Undo Hyperlink**. You could also press **BACKSPACE** or click **Undo** or press **CTRL + Z**. If any angle brackets were removed, they should be automatically replaced.

AutoCorrect Options button

To remove a hyperlink later: Right-click the hyperlink; click **Remove Hyperlink**. If angle brackets need to be replaced, retype the angle brackets after removing the hyperlink.

To remove a trailing space, but still retain the hyperlink: Press the left directional arrow on the keyboard 1 time; then press **DELETE**.

PRACTICE (continued)

1. Click at the end of the last reference, and press **ENTER** 2 times.
2. Type this entry with a hanging indent; note than when you type the Internet address that is surrounded by angle brackets and type the comma, the brackets are removed and the Internet address is automatically converted to a hyperlink:

```
"Online Advertising Trends," CyberAds,
    May 11, 2010, <http://www.cyberads.com/trends>,
    accessed on June 7, 2010.
```

Your entry should look similar to this:

> "Online Advertising Trends," *CyberAds,* May 11, 2010, http://www.cyberads.com/trends,
> accessed on June 7, 2010.

3. Because this automatic hyperlink results in incorrect format, you must reverse it. Right-click over the Internet address, and click **Remove Hyperlink**.
4. Type the angle brackets at the beginning and end of the Internet address. The revised entry should look like this:

> "Online Advertising Trends," *CyberAds,* May 11, 2010, <http://www.cyberads.com/trends>,
> accessed on June 7, 2010.

5. Click at the end of the last entry, and press **ENTER** 2 times.
6. Type this entry with a hanging indent; however, immediately after you type the comma that converts the Internet address to a hyperlink and removes the angle brackets, press **CTRL + Z** or click **Undo** to reverse the undesirable results. The angle brackets should be replaced automatically. Finish typing the remainder of the entry.

```
"Web Hosting," WebHosting, June 12, 2010,
    <http://www.webhosting.com/ads.html>, accessed
    on June 15, 2010.
```

7. Verify that all lines include a hanging indent, and both Web page reference citations include the angle brackets and have not been converted to hyperlinks. Your document should look similar to the following illustration:

PRACTICE (continued)

BIBLIOGRAPHY

Acosta, John C., and Herbert Hightower, *Online Advertising Today,* New York Press, New York, 2009.

Choi, Byong Sang, "Effectiveness of Interactive Online Ads," *The New York Journal,* July 20, 2010, p. R6.

"Online Advertising Trends," *CyberAds,* May 11, 2010, <http://www.cyberads.com/trends>, accessed on June 7, 2010.

"Web Hosting," *WebHosting,* June 12, 2010, <http://www.webhosting.com/ads.html>, accessed on June 15, 2010.

GO TO
Textbook

8. Save changes to *practice-49*, and return to GDP.

Preliminary Report Pages

Tab Set—Dot Leaders

**REFER TO
Word Manual**

L. 45: Tab Set—Ruler Tabs

Before beginning this lesson, review the basics of setting tabs and using the ruler to set tabs in Lesson 45. In this lesson, you will use the menu to set custom tabs. However, you should still display the ruler, which provides a visual cue that tabs have been set correctly. To display the ruler, click the **View Ruler** button (at the top of the vertical scroll area).

**REFER TO
Reference Manual**

R-7D: Table of Contents

To format a table of contents: Set two custom tabs: a 0.5-inch left tab to position the report subheadings and a 6.5-inch right dot-leader tab to insert dot leaders automatically and to position the corresponding page number at the right margin as shown in the illustration. Menus must be used to set a dot-leader tab. Once tabs are set, you are ready to type the table of contents.

0.5-inch left tab

6.5-inch right dot-leader tab

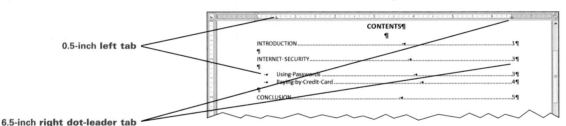

To set custom tabs for a table of contents using the menu:

1. Position the insertion point on the line where you want the new tab to start (or select the desired text where you need the tab settings).
2. From the **Home** or **Page Layout** tab, **Paragraph** group, click the **Dialog Box Launcher**.
3. From the **Paragraph** dialog box, click the **Indents and Spacing** tab, and click the **Tabs** button. The **Tabs** dialog box appears.

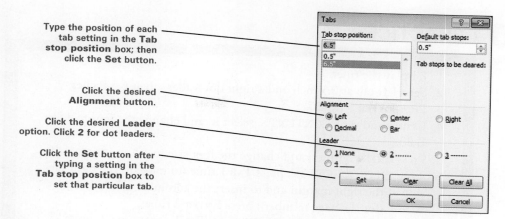

Type the position of each tab setting in the **Tab stop position** box; then click the **Set** button.

Click the desired **Alignment** button.

Click the desired **Leader** option. Click **2** for dot leaders.

Click the **Set** button after typing a setting in the **Tab stop position** box to set that particular tab.

4. Set a tab to position the subheadings:
   a. In the **Tab stop position** box, type the desired tab position. (Type 0.5 to position any subheadings.)
   b. In the **Alignment** section, click the desired alignment. (Click **Left** to position any subheadings.)
5. Set a tab to position the page numbers:
   a. In the **Tab stop position** box, type the desired tab position. (Type 6.5 to position the page number at the right margin.)
   b. In the **Alignment** section, click the desired alignment. (Click **Right** to position the page number.)
   c. In the **Leader** section, click **2** to include dot leaders.
6. Click **Set** and **OK**.

To type a main heading with dot leaders and a page number:

1. Type the main heading; then press **TAB**.
2. Note that dot leaders (consecutive periods) fill the gap to lead the reader's eye across the page to the right margin where the page number will be typed.
3. Type the page number.

To type a subheading with dot leaders and a page number:

1. Press **TAB** to indent the line 0.5 inch; then type the subheading.
2. Press **TAB** again to insert the dot leaders automatically and move to the right margin.
3. Type the page number.

PRACTICE

1. Display the ruler.
2. Set a left tab at 0.5 inch and a right dot-leader tab at 6.5 inches.
3. Press **ENTER** 5 times.
4. Center and type CONTENTS, select it, and change the font to 14 pt. Bold.
5. Press **ENTER** 2 times, and change the font size to 12 pt. if necessary.
6. Type INTRODUCTION; press **TAB** 1 time (to move to the right tab stop at the right margin and to insert the automatic dot leaders); type 1 (for the page number); press **ENTER** 2 times.
7. Type INTERNET SECURITY; press **TAB** 1 time; type 3; press **ENTER** 2 times.
8. Press **TAB** 1 time (to indent the line by 0.5 inch); type Using Passwords; press **TAB** 1 time; type 3; press **ENTER** 1 time.
9. Press **TAB** 1 time; type Paying by Credit Card; press **TAB** 1 time; type 4; press **ENTER** 2 times.
10. Type CONCLUSION; press **TAB** 1 time; type 5.

Your document should look similar to this:

CONTENTS

INTRODUCTION .... → tab 6.5″ 1

INTERNET SECURITY 3

→ tab 0.5″ Using Passwords 3
Paying by Credit Card 4

CONCLUSION 5

11. Save changes to *practice-50*, and return to GDP.

Resumes

Font

"Font" refers to the general shape of a character. A serif font has short lines extending from the edges of letters. A sans serif font does not have these lines. Word's default font is Calibri, a sans serif font. Avoid using too many different fonts in the same document. In a traditional resume, use Cambria in Row 1.

Serif Fonts	Sans Serif Fonts
Cambria	Calibri
Times New Roman	Arial

To change fonts:

1. Position the insertion point where you want to begin using the new font (or select the text you want to change).
2. From the **Home** tab, **Font** group, click the down arrow to the right of the **Font** box.
3. Click the desired font—scroll down the list if necessary.

As you change fonts, the most recent choice is added to the top of the font drop-down list under **Recently Used Fonts**.

Font box ——————

Recently Used Fonts
list with the most recently
used fonts listed first.

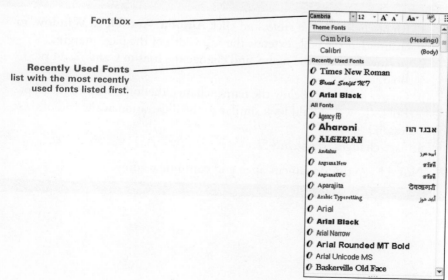

Or: From the **Home** tab, **Font** group, click the **Dialog Box Launcher** or press **CTRL + D**, and make the desired choices in the **Font** dialog box.

Use the **Font** dialog box to change any of the features you see.

To change the font or font style, size, and effect:

1. From the **Font** dialog box, **Font** tab, under **Font**, click the desired font.
2. Under **Font style**, **Size**, and **Effects**, click the desired choices; click **OK**.

If the font inside a table defaults to 11 pt. rather than 12 pt., see Appendix A, GDP—Word Settings, Default Font Size—Table, for help.

 PRACTICE

REFER TO
Reference Manual
R-12A: Resume

1. Right-click over the table, and click **AutoFit**, **AutoFit to Window**, to ensure that the table extends the full width of the page margins.
2. In Row 1, center the name, and change the font to Cambria 14 pt. Bold.
3. Center both lines below the name; change the font to Cambria 12 pt. Bold. (Row 1 should look similar to the illustration at the end of this lesson.)
4. Save changes to *practice-51*.

Note: Keep this document open and continue reading.

Table—Change Column Width

In Lesson 36, you learned to change table column width using AutoFit to Contents. However, you can also change the column width using the mouse. Whenever you adjust column widths, begin by clicking the View Ruler button to display the ruler.

To change column widths by double-clicking the right border:

Resize pointer

1. Point to the right border of the table column until the mouse changes to a resize pointer.
2. Double-click the right border of the desired column to adjust the width to the widest cell entry.

    When you double-click the right border of the last column, the width of that column will adjust to extend that column to the right margin, such as for the right border of the last column in a resume.

To change column widths by dragging on the right border:

1. Display the ruler, and point to the right border of the table column until the mouse changes to a resize pointer.
2. Click and hold the mouse button; note the dotted vertical line that appears along the full length of the border extending up to the ruler.
3. Drag the column border until the dotted vertical line points to the desired position on the ruler above.

   As long as the cell is not selected, dragging the right border adjusts the entire column width, not just the cell width. Hold down **ALT** as you drag to see the exact ruler measurements.

PRACTICE (continued)

**REFER TO
Word Manual**
L. 37: Table—Borders

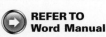

1. Press **CTRL + HOME**, and press **ENTER** 5 times.
2. Remove all table borders. (*Hint:* Select the table; from **Table Tools**, **Design** tab, **Table Styles** group, click the list arrow next to the **Borders** button, and click **No Border**.)
3. If necessary, display table gridlines. (*Hint:* From **Table Tools**, **Layout** tab, **Table** group, click **View Gridlines**.)
4. Select Row 1, and apply a bottom border to Row 1. (*Hint:* From **Table Tools**, **Design** tab, **Table Styles** group, click the list arrow next to the **Borders** button; then click **Bottom Border**.)
5. Bold all the headings in Column A.
6. In the "EXPERIENCE" section in Column B, italicize the job titles and business names.

**REFER TO
Word Manual**

L. 44: Indentation, Increase
and Decrease Indent

PRACTICE (continued)

7. Increase the indent for the job description paragraphs by 0.5 inch.

8. Double-click the right border of Column A to fit the widest entry.

9. Double-click the right border of Column B to expand it so it extends to 6.5 inches on the ruler (the right margin of the document).

    If you are unsuccessful using the mouse to adjust column widths, undo your actions; right-click over the table; and click **AutoFit**, **AutoFit to Contents**.

10. Press **CTRL + P** to view your document. Your document should look similar to this.

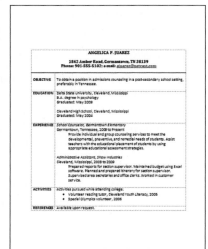

Print Layout

Print view

11. Click the **Home** tab, save changes to *practice-51*, and return to GDP.

**GO TO
Textbook**

Special Correspondence Features

Sort

You can sort text alphabetically, numerically, or by date in ascending order (for example, A to Z or zero to nine) or descending order (Z to A). Information in tables may be sorted; however, steps vary from these.

To perform a sort:

Sort button

1. Select only the paragraphs to be sorted.
2. From the **Home** tab, in the **Paragraph** group, click the **Sort** button.
3. In the **Sort by** box, click **Paragraphs**; in the **Type** box, click **Text**; then click **Ascending**.

To sort the bulleted list in the practice exercise alphabetically from A to Z, use these settings.

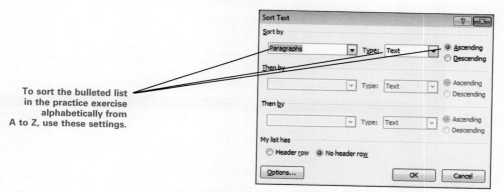

4. Click **OK**. The list is sorted alphabetically from A to Z.

To undo a sort: Click **Undo**, or press **CTRL + Z** immediately after sorting.

PRACTICE

1. Select the text to be sorted, and note the unsorted list order:

> As you know, your health care plan will be changing effective April 1. In order to help you plan for any anticipated future expenses, you should go to your *Summary Plan Description* booklet and research the following topics:
>
> - Dental plan program
> - Pharmacy co-pay structure
> - Member-managed care
> - Deductibles
> - Office visits
>
> Please contact us if you have any questions at 800-555-1212.

2. Sort the list, and note the sorted list order (alphabetical from A to Z):

> As you know, your health care plan will be changing effective April 1. In order to help you plan for any anticipated future expenses, you should go to your *Summary Plan Description* booklet and research the following topics:
>
> - Deductibles
> - Dental plan program
> - Member-managed care
> - Office visits
> - Pharmacy co-pay structure
>
> Please contact us if you have any questions at 800-555-1212.

GO TO
Textbook

3. Save changes to *practice-67*, and return to GDP.

More Special Correspondence Features

Table—Shading

To give your table a more finished look and increase readability, add shading to desired rows, columns, or cells. Shading is a design element—don't overuse it. Shading choices should be purposeful and attractive.

To add shading:

1. Select the desired cells, rows, or columns.
2. From the **Home** tab, in the **Paragraph** group, click the list arrow to the right of the **Borders** button; click **Borders and Shading**.

   Or: Right-click the selected cells, and click **Borders and Shading**.

   Or: Click inside the table; from the **Table Tools**, **Design** tab, **Table Styles** group, click the **Shading** button; then click the desired shading.
3. From the **Borders and Shading** dialog box, click the **Shading** tab.

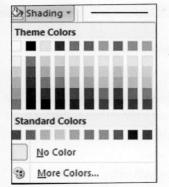

Table Styles Shading button

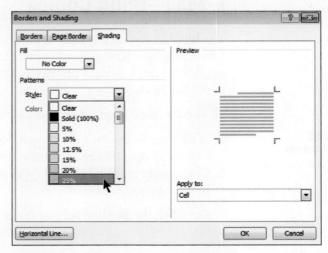

4. Select the desired shading option by clicking the down arrow in the **Style** box; then click **OK**.
   - **Clear** (the default setting) provides no shading.
   - **Solid (100%)** provides solid black shading with white text.
   - **10%**, **20%**, or **25%** shading provides gradient gray shading with black text.

PRACTICE

1. If necessary, activate **View Gridlines**. (*Hint:* From the **Home** tab, **Paragraph** group, click the list arrow next to the **Borders** button. From the drop-down menu, click **View Gridlines**.)
2. Click after the last word in the first paragraph, and press ENTER 1 time to insert 1 blank line before the table.
3. Click before the first word in the second paragraph, and press ENTER 1 time to insert 1 blank line after the table.
4. Select Row 1.
5. Right-click the selected row, and click **Borders and Shading**.
6. From the **Borders and Shading** dialog box, click the **Shading** tab, and apply a **Solid (100%)** shading style to Row 1.
7. Select Row 2, and apply a **25%** shading.
8. Apply an outside border to the entire table. Your table should now look similar to the illustration at the end of this lesson.

Note: Keep this document open and continue reading.

E-Mail—Blind Copies

The Blind Copy box is usually abbreviated as Bcc (blind carbon copy), and some e-mail programs hide it. Refer to your e-mail software's Help feature for steps to use this feature. Standard practice is to simply fill in the desired e-mail address in the Bcc box.

To send a blind copy of an e-mail message from Word:

REFER TO
Word Manual
L. 25: E-Mail a Document

1. With your instructor's permission, follow the steps in Lesson 25, page 38, to send an open Word document as the actual e-mail message.
2. Click inside the **Bcc** box, and type in the e-mail address of the desired blind-copy recipient.

   Or: Click the **Bcc** button, and select the desired name from the **Contacts** list.

PRACTICE (continued)

Do not send an e-mail message without consulting your instructor!

1. Follow the steps in Lesson 25, page 38, to send an open Word document as the actual e-mail message.

PRACTICE (continued)

2. Fill in any desired address in the **To** and **Bcc** boxes; then type `American Landscape Price List` in the **Subject** box.

Note: If you use Outlook, your message would look similar to this:

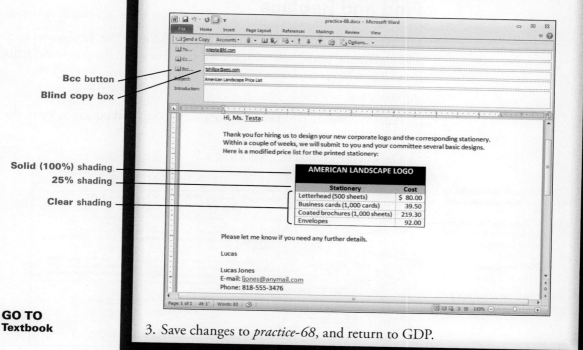

Bcc button

Blind copy box

Solid (100%) shading

25% shading

Clear shading

GO TO
Textbook

3. Save changes to *practice-68*, and return to GDP.

Multipage Memos With Tables

Find and Replace

Use Find to search for text, numbers, and so forth. Use Replace to both find and replace the found text with revised text. For example, you could replace all occurrences of "James" with "Jim" in one step.

To find text:

1. From the **Home** tab, **Editing** group, click the **Find** button to open the **Navigation** pane.

   Or: On the keyboard, press **CTRL + F.**

Click the **Find** button to open the **Navigation** pane.

Type the characters you want to find in the **Search Document** box.

Click the **Close** button to end your search.

Click the **Find Options** list arrow to explore **Options** and **Advanced Find.**

Browse through the summary of search results.

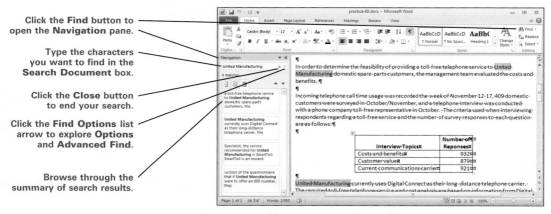

2. In the **Search Document** box of the **Navigation** pane, type the characters you want to find.
3. Note that as you type, Word matches characters and highlights matches in the document; scroll down the document to view all matches, and note the summary of all search results in the **Navigation** pane.

   💡 You can edit the text in the document without closing the **Navigation** pane, but the highlighting will disappear. To highlight text again, click inside the **Search Document** box, and press **ENTER.**

   💡 If you get unexpected search results, click the **Find Options** list arrow to the right of the **Search Document** box; click **Options**, and verify the accuracy of the selected **Find Options.**

4. Click the **Close** button to the right of the **Search Document** box to end your search; to close the **Navigation** pane, click the **Close** button on the **Navigation** bar.

To find and replace text:

1. From the **Home** tab, **Editing** group, click **Replace** to open the **Find and Replace** dialog box.

   Or: On the keyboard, press **CTRL + H**.

Type the text you want to find in the **Find what** box and the replacement text in the **Replace with** text box.

Click **Format** or **Special** to find and/or replace characters, such as a tab character or a font change.

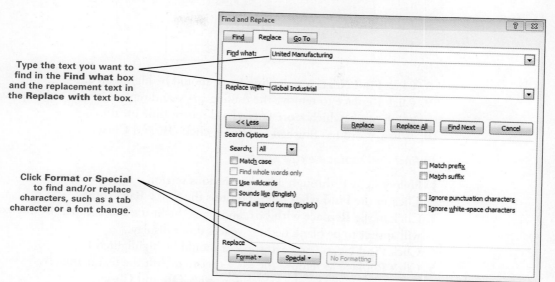

💡 Click **More** to expand the dialog box and display other options. Click **Less** to collapse the box.

2. Type the text you want to replace in the **Find what** text box.
3. Press **TAB**, and type the replacement text in the **Replace with** text box.
4. Click **Find Next**.

   💡 If Word highlights the desired text in the document, click **Replace** to replace the text; to leave the text unchanged, click **Find Next**.

   💡 To automatically change all occurrences of the text in the document without stopping to verify each change, click **Replace All**.

5. When Word finishes, click **OK** and **Close** or **Cancel**.

Use Find and Replace to find and replace incorrect spaces that might be missed when you proofread, such as an extra space between words or sentences or an extra trailing space following any punctuation in the last line of a paragraph.

To find and replace trailing spaces:

1. On the keyboard, press **CTRL + H**.
2. From the **Find** tab, click the **More** button to expand the menu.
3. Click in the **Find what** box, and if necessary, select and delete any characters in the box.
4. Under **Find** at the bottom of the dialog box, click **Special**; and click **White Space** from the list of choices.
5. Click **Special**, and click **Paragraph Mark** from the list of choices.

6. From the **Replace** tab, click in the **Replace with** box.
7. Under **Replace** at the bottom of the display, click **Special**; click **Paragraph Mark**. The boxes should look like this:

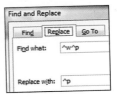

8. Click **Find Next**. Any trailing space should be highlighted.
9. Click **Replace** to remove the trailing space and replace it with only a paragraph mark, which represents a hard return (line break).
10. When Word has finished searching, click **OK** and **Close**.

To find and replace extra spaces:

1. Follow steps 1 through 3 in the previous section.
2. Click in the **Find what** box, and press the **SPACE BAR** 2 times.
3. Click in the **Replace with** box, and press the **SPACE BAR** 1 time. (Both boxes will appear to be blank because spaces don't display.)
4. Click **Find Next**. (Any extra spaces should be highlighted.)
5. Click **Replace** to remove the extra spaces, or edit the text manually.
6. When Word has finished searching, click **OK** and **Close**.

 PRACTICE

1. Use **Replace** to find all occurrences of "United Manufacturing" and replace it with "Global Industrial." (You should have 4 occurrences.)
2. Press **CTRL + HOME** to move to the top of the document.
3. Turn on **Show/Hide ¶**, and note that there is a trailing space after "President" at the end of the first line and another after the period at the end of the first paragraph.
4. Use **Replace** to find and replace both trailing spaces.
5. Press **CTRL + HOME** to move to the top of the document.
6. Note that there are 2 spaces after "Vice" in the first heading line.
7. Note the 2 spaces after the period in "October" in the second paragraph.
8. Use **Replace** to find and replace the extra spaces.
9. Click **OK** and **Close**.
10. Save changes to *practice-69*, and return to GDP.

 GO TO
Textbook

Procedures Manual

Footers

A footer is any information (such as a page number or text) that usually appears at the bottom of every page in a document below the body.

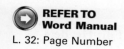

REFER TO
Word Manual
L. 32: Page Number

To insert a footer with text and a page number into every page of a document:

1. Right-click over the footer area, and click **Edit Footer**. (The document should now be dimmed and the footer should be active.)
2. Note that the **Header & Footer Tools**, **Design** tab appears on demand whenever you are inside a footer.
3. From the **Header & Footer Tools**, **Design** tab, **Header & Footer** group, click **Page Number**, **Bottom of Page**, **Plain Number 2**, from the gallery of designs to insert a centered page number.
4. Note that you are now inside the **Footer** section with the document dimmed and the automatic page number inserted.
5. Type any desired text, such as Page, and press the SPACE BAR 1 time to insert a space between the text and the automatic page number.

To start page numbering with a different number:

1. Click inside the footer.
2. From the **Header & Footer Tools**, **Design** tab, **Header & Footer** group, click **Page Number**, **Format Page Numbers** to display the **Page Number Format** dialog box.
3. From the **Page Number Format** dialog box, under **Page numbering**, click **Start at**, and type 3 in the **Start at** box; click **OK**.

To close a footer and return to the document body:

1. Double-click anywhere outside the **Footer** area, or from the **Header & Footer Tools, Design** tab, **Close** group, click **Close Header and Footer**.
2. Note that the footer is now dimmed, the document is active, and the **Header & Footer Tools**, **Design** tab has disappeared.

To edit a footer: Double-click anywhere inside the footer area. (The document should dim and the footer should be active.)

To remove a footer: From the **Insert** tab, **Header & Footer** group, click **Footer**, **Remove Footer**.

If you are having trouble removing a footer, try this: Double-click anywhere inside the footer to reopen it; press **CTRL + A**; click **DELETE**, and click outside the footer to return to the document.

To italicize the header or footer or make any font changes: Press **CTRL + A** to select all text or select the desired text; then make any desired font changes.

To add a top border to a footer: Click inside the footer; from the **Home** tab, **Paragraph** group, click the **Borders** button list arrow; click **Top Border**.

PRACTICE

REFER TO
Word Manual
L. 32: Page Number
L. 47: Headers

1. Right-click anywhere over the header area, and click **Edit Header**.
2. Click the **View Ruler** button to display the ruler; note the default header tabs—a center tab is preset at 3.25″ and a right tab is preset at 6.5″.
3. At the left margin, type this:
   `American Bistro, Employee Manual`
4. Press **TAB** 2 times to move to the right tab position; press **CTRL + I**, and type this:
   `Training Program`
5. Close the header. The header should look similar to this:

   American Bistro, Employee Manual   *Training Program*

   A high-quality dining experience doesn't happen without a careful plan. A systematic plan for
   training and then mentoring must occur. Our training program includes a structured plan for
   training for the following positions:

6. Right-click anywhere over the footer area, and click **Edit Footer**.
7. Insert a centered page number that starts at 8 for this continuation page. (*Hint:* From the **Header & Footer Tools**, **Design tab**, **Header & Footer** group, click **Page Number**, **Bottom of Page**, **Plain Number 2**; click **Page Number**, **Format Page Numbers**, **Start at**, **8**, **OK**.)
8. Type `Page` and press the **SPACE BAR** 1 time to insert a space between the text and the automatic page number.
9. Close the footer. The document footer should look similar to this:

   Closing Out. When a meal is over, the check must be presented, a method of payment must be
   determined, and a farewell statement is in order. A guest should not feel rushed when it is

   Page 8

GO TO
Textbook

10. Save changes to *practice-73*, and return to GDP.

Reports Formatted in Columns

Columns

You can prepare a document in newspaper-style columns or add columns to any part of your document. Text flows from the bottom of one column to the top of the next column.

In newspaper-style columns, text flows from the bottom of one column to the top of the next, is full-justified, and uses automatic hyphenation.

To add balanced columns to an existing document:

1. Type the document without columns.
2. With **Show/Hide ¶** on, position the insertion point where you want the columns to begin, and carefully select the text to appear in columns.
   a. Position the insertion point just before the first character in the desired text.
   b. Scroll to the end of the document, press and hold **SHIFT**, and click just *after* the last typed character in the document and just *before* the

Paragraph formatting mark. (You must exclude the Paragraph formatting mark to create a continuous section break and create balanced columns that are evenly divided on partial pages.)

3. From the **Page Layout** tab, in the **Page Setup** group, click **Columns**.
4. Then click **One**, **Two**, **Three**, and so forth, for the desired number of columns. Or click **More Columns** for more detailed choices.

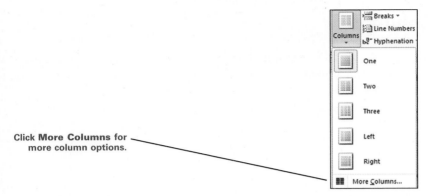

Click **More Columns** for more column options.

5. Note that a *Section Break (Continuous)* formatting code will appear at the end of the column, and the columns will be automatically balanced.

To fix any large gaps in between the words in the last line of the last paragraph in a document that uses balanced columns and justified alignment: Press **ENTER** directly after the last typed character in the line.

As you're typing, when you reach the bottom of one column, the insertion point automatically moves to the top of the next column. Sometimes, you may want to force a column to break at a certain point. Or you may want to have the text distributed equally among the columns to balance the text across the page.

To insert a column break:

1. Position the insertion point where you want to start the new column.
2. Press **CTRL + SHIFT + ENTER**.

To balance the columns:

1. Position the insertion point at the end of the text you want to balance.
2. From the **Page Layout** tab, in the **Page Setup** group, click the **Breaks** button. A list of **Page Breaks** and **Section Breaks** appears.

Breaks (Insert Page and Section Breaks) button

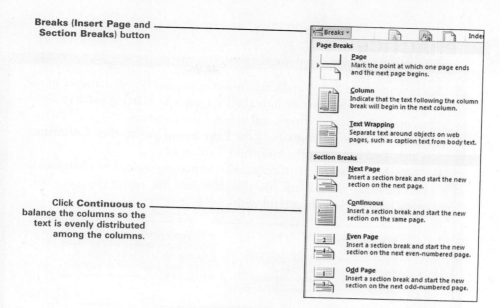

Click Continuous to balance the columns so the text is evenly distributed among the columns.

3. Click **Continuous** to divide text evenly among all the columns.

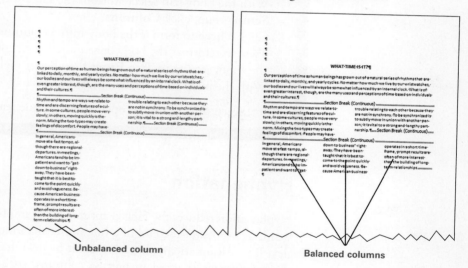

Unbalanced column   Balanced columns

PRACTICE

1. Turn **Show/Hide ¶** on; then position the insertion point just before "Time," the first word in the first paragraph.
2. Drag the scroll box down until you can see the end of the document.

PRACTICE (continued)

3. Press and hold **SHIFT**, and click just *after* the last typed character in the document—you must exclude the Paragraph formatting mark to create a continuous section break and balance the columns.
4. From the **Page Layout** tab, in the **Page Setup** group, click **Columns**.
5. Click **Two** to format the body into 2 columns.
6. Note the *Section Break (Continuous)* formatting code. The continuous section break should look like this. If it does not, repeat the preceding steps being especially careful with step 3.

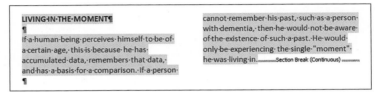

7. With the body still selected, from the **Page Layout** tab, in the **Page Setup** group, click **Columns**.
8. Click **Three** to format the body into 3 columns; then click **Columns**, **Two**, to reformat the body once more into 2 columns. (*Hint:* Change the zoom setting to **Two Pages** for a better look.)
9. With the body still selected, save changes to *practice-74*.

Note: Keep this document open and continue reading.

Hyphenation

Hyphenation reduces the ragged appearance of unjustified text because it divides words as needed at the end of a line rather than moving the entire word to the next line. Automatic hyphenation is off by default. Reserve automatic hyphenation for text formatted in narrow columns, such as a magazine article with justified text or a newsletter formatted in columns. The hyphens Word inserts in words are called "soft hyphens" because they appear and disappear as text is typed and deleted.

To hyphenate words automatically:

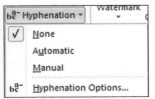

Hyphenation button

1. From the **Page Layout** tab, in the **Page Setup** group, click the **Hyphenation** button, **Hyphenation Options**.
2. In the **Hyphenation** dialog box, check **Automatically hyphenate document** if it is not already checked.

3. If desired, in the **Limit consecutive hyphens to:** box, click the up arrow until **2** is displayed; click **OK**.

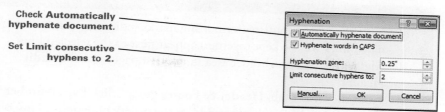

Check **Automatically hyphenate document.**

Set **Limit consecutive hyphens** to **2**.

To eliminate a widow (a one-liner at the bottom of a column), choose whichever method produces the better result:

REFER TO
Word Manual
L. 32: Widow/Orphan
Control

1. Select the lines to be kept together—for example, select the heading, the blank line below it, and the first line of the following paragraph.
2. From the **Home** tab, **Paragraph** group, click the **Paragraph Dialog Box Launcher**.
3. From the **Paragraph** window, click the **Line and Page Breaks** tab.
4. Check **Keep with next**, **OK**.

Or: Press **ENTER** above the heading to force it to the next column.

PRACTICE (continued)

1. With the body still selected, from the **Page Layout** tab, in the **Page Setup** group, click the **Hyphenation** button, **Hyphenation Options**.
2. From the **Hyphenation** dialog box, check **Automatically hyphenate document**.
3. In the **Limit consecutive hyphens to:** box, click the up arrow until **2** is displayed; click **OK**.
4. Note that line endings have changed, and note the one-line heading at the bottom of page 1.
5. With the body still selected, from the **Home** tab, **Paragraph** group, click the **Justify** button or click **CTRL + J** to justify the lines so that the line endings at the right margin are even.
6. Select the heading "LIVING IN THE MOMENT" at the bottom of page 1, the blank line that follows it, and the first line of the paragraph at the top of the next page.
7. From the **Home** tab, **Paragraph** group, click the **Paragraph Dialog Box Launcher**.
8. From the **Paragraph** window, **Line and Page Breaks** tab, check **Keep with next**; click **OK**. (Do not check **Keep lines together**, or you will get unexpected results.)

REFER TO
Word Manual
L. 31: Alignment

PRACTICE (continued)

REFER TO
Word Manual

L. 32: Page Number
L. 47: Headers

9. Note that square bullets (formatting marks indicating that the designated lines will be kept together) appear next to the selected lines.

10. Right-click over the header area in the first page, and click **Edit Header**.

11. From the **Insert** tab, **Header & Footer** group, click **Page Number**, **Top of Page**, **Plain Number 3** from the gallery of designs to insert a right-aligned page number.

12. Type Jones and press the **SPACE BAR** 1 time. "Jones" should now appear before the page number.

13. From the **Header & Footer Tools**, **Design** tab, **Options** group, check **Different First Page** to suppress the header on the first page.

14. Double-click over the body to close the header; note that the header appears only on the second page.

15. Scroll to the end of the document; note the large gaps that appear between the words in the last line of the last paragraph.

16. Click just *after* the last typed character (a period), and press **ENTER** to eliminate the gaps. Your document should look similar to this:

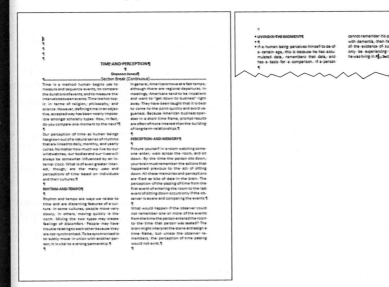

17. Turn off **Show/Hide ¶**.

18. Save changes to *practice-74*, and return to GDP.

GO TO
Textbook

Tables With Source Notes or Footnotes

Table—Text Direction

The default orientation for text in a table is horizontal. Sometimes, however, you may have a table that includes cells with long column headings that look more balanced if a vertical orientation is used.

To change the text direction or orientation of text in a table:

Text Direction button

Text Direction button
(vertical from bottom to top)

Resize pointer

1. Click the cell or select the row that contains the text to be changed.
2. From the **Table Tools, Layout** tab, **Alignment** group, click the **Text Direction** button repeatedly until you see the desired text direction. Note that the **Text Direction** button changes to give you a preview of the alignment.
3. Click the **Align Bottom Center** button.
4. Point to the bottom border of the row containing the vertical text until you see the table resize pointer.
5. Drag down using the table resize pointer until the vertical text appears in one continuous line without wrapping.

PRACTICE

1. Select Row 1.
2. From the **Table Tools, Layout** tab, **Alignment** group, click the **Text Direction** button repeatedly until you see the desired text direction set to vertical from bottom to top. (*Hint:* The button should match the one shown in the next illustration.)
3. From the **Table Tools, Layout** tab, **Alignment** group, click the **Align Bottom Center** button. Your table should appear similar to this:

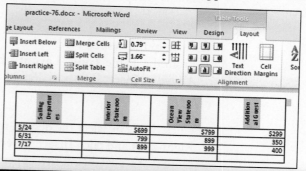

PRACTICE (continued)

4. Drag on the bottom border of Row 1 until the column headings appear in one continuous line (without wrapping text) and without leaving too much blank space above the longest item. (*Hint:* Drag the **Zoom slider** to zoom in.)

5. Click inside the table and apply the **AutoFit to Contents** feature. Your table should appear similar to this:

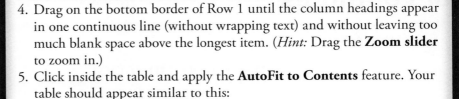

6. Center the table horizontally. (*Hint:* From the **Layout** tab, **Table** group, click **Properties**; from the **Table** tab, click **Center**, **OK**.)
7. Center the table vertically on the page.
8. Save changes to *practice-76*.

Note: Keep this document open and continue reading.

REFER TO Word Manual

L. 36: Table—AutoFit to Contents

REFER TO Word Manual

L. 38: Table—Center Horizontally; Table—Center Page

Table—Insert, Delete, and Move Rows or Columns

Table rows and columns can be inserted, deleted, or moved in a variety of ways. The on-demand Table Tools Layout tab includes buttons in the Rows & Columns group to help you.

To insert a row:

1. Click in the desired row.
2. From the **Table Tools**, **Layout** tab, **Rows & Columns** group, click **Insert Above** or **Insert Below** as desired.

Or:

1. Click inside or select the desired row.
2. Right-click and click **Insert**, **Insert Rows Above** or **Insert Rows Below**. Note that a new, blank row appears above or below the selected row.

Or: Click just to the right of the cell in the desired row, press **ENTER**, and a new row will be inserted just below that row.

To insert a new row at the end of the table, click inside the last table cell, and press **TAB**.

To insert a column:

1. Click in the desired column.
2. From the **Table Tools**, **Layout** tab, **Rows & Columns** group, click **Insert Left** or **Insert Right** as desired.

Or:

1. Select the desired column.

Point to the top border of the column you want to select and click to select the column.

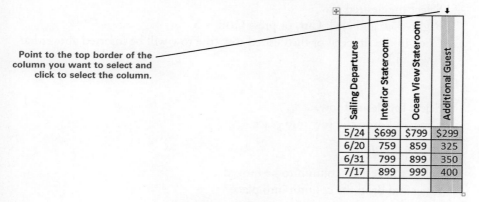

2. With the column still selected, right-click; then click **Insert**, **Insert Columns to the Left** (or the desired choice).

If any table rows were merged and a new, undesired column appears, select the row, and merge cells again for that row to remove the undesired new column. Merge cells last when creating a table to avoid unexpected results.

To delete a row or column:

1. Select the desired row or column.
2. Right-click, and click **Delete Rows** or **Delete Columns**, or press Cᴛʀʟ + **X**.

💡 If you press Dᴇʟᴇᴛᴇ, you will delete only the contents of the row or column—the blank row or column will remain.

To move a row:

1. Click in the desired row to be moved.
2. Press Aʟᴛ + Sʜɪꜰᴛ + ↑ (the directional up arrow) or Aʟᴛ + Sʜɪꜰᴛ + ↓ (the directional down arrow) as needed.

Or:

1. Select the desired row.
2. Right-click and click **Cut**, or press Cᴛʀʟ + **X**.
3. Click in the first cell of the desired row (the row will be inserted above that row), and paste.

Or:

1. Select the desired row.
2. Drag and drop the row into place.

To move a column:

1. Select the desired column to be moved.
2. Drag and drop the column into place.

Or:

1. Select the desired column to be moved.
2. Right-click and click **Delete Columns**, or press Cᴛʀʟ + **X**.
3. Click in the top cell of the desired column (the column will be inserted to the left of that column), right-click, and click **Paste Column** or press Cᴛʀʟ + **V**.

   ❓ To move a column to the right of the last column in the table, click just to the outside of the top cell of the desired column before pasting.

PRACTICE (continued)

1. Insert a new row above Row 3.
2. Type the following information in the cells of the new row:
   6/29 759 859 325
3. Insert a new column to the left of Column D.
4. Delete Row 4 with the sailing departure date of 6/31.

PRACTICE (continued)

5. Type the following information in the cells of the new column: (*Hint:* Type the dollar sign and then insert 3 spaces for "$899" to allow 2 spaces for each digit and 1 space for each comma. This action causes the dollar sign to align with the longest amount of "1,099" in the column.)

```
Junior Suite
$899
959
1,099
```

6. If necessary, align "Junior Suite" in Row 1 at the bottom center.
7. Move Row 3 down 1 row. (*Hint:* Click inside Row 3 and press **ALT + SHIFT + ↓**.)
8. Change the date from 6/29 to 8/29. The table should look like this:

Sailing Departures	Interior Stateroom	Ocean View Stateroom	Junior Suite	Additional Guest
5/24	$699	$799	$ 899	$299
7/17	899	999	1,099	400
8/29	759	859	959	325

9. Delete the blank row at the end of the table, and cut Column A.
10. Click just to the outside of the top cell of the last column. Your insertion point should be positioned like this:

Interior Stateroom	Ocean View Stateroom	Junior Suite	Additional Guest
$699	$799	$ 899	$299
899	999	1,099	400
759	859	959	325

Click just to the right of the top cell of the last column to paste a column as the last column in a table.

11. Paste the cut column. It should appear as the last table column.
12. Cut the newly pasted column and move it so it is the first column in the table. (*Hint:* After cutting the newly pasted column, click in Cell A1, the top cell of the desired column, and press **CTRL + V**.)

13. Insert a new row at the end of the table. (*Hint:* Click inside the last cell and press **TAB**; or click outside the last table cell and press **ENTER**.)
14. Merge the cells in the new row; if necessary, change to left alignment; and type this:
    `Note: Prices may change.`
15. Your table should look similar to this:

Sailing Departures	Interior Stateroom	Ocean View Stateroom	Junior Suite	Additional Guest
5/24	$699	$799	$ 899	$299
7/17	899	999	1,099	400
8/29	759	859	959	325
Note: Prices may change.				

GO TO
Textbook

16. Save changes to *practice-76*, and return to GDP.

Tables in Landscape Orientation

Page Orientation

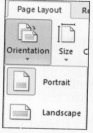

Use Word's Landscape feature to change the default page orientation for 8.5- by 11-inch paper from vertical to horizontal. Use the Portrait feature to change the page orientation from horizontal to vertical.

To change the page orientation:

On the **Page Layout** tab, in the **Page Setup** group, click the **Orientation** button, and click either **Portrait** or **Landscape**.

Or: Press **CTRL + P**; under **Settings**, next to **Portrait Orientation**, click the list arrow, **Landscape Orientation**.

Orientation button

PRACTICE

1. Change the page orientation to **Landscape**.
2. Press **CTRL + P**. Your document should look similar to this:

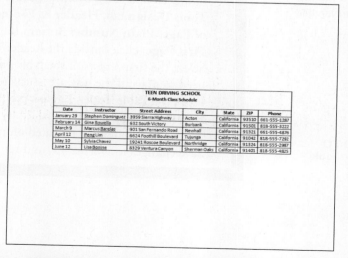

3. Click the **Home** tab, save changes to *practice-78*, and return to GDP.

GO TO
Textbook

Table—Repeating Table Heading Rows

To repeat a table heading on subsequent pages:

1. Select the rows of text (including the first row) that you want to use as a table heading.

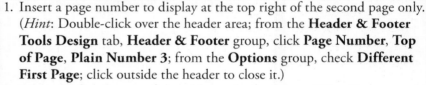

MANUSCRIPT PROCESSING McGraw-Hill Higher Education				
	Rejected		Accepted	
Short Title	Editorial	Reviewer	Editorial	Reviewer

2. From the **Table Tools**, **Layout** tab, **Data** group, click **Repeat Header Rows**. The headings are now repeated on each page.

PRACTICE

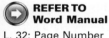

REFER TO Word Manual

L. 32: Page Number

1. Insert a page number to display at the top right of the second page only. (*Hint*: Double-click over the header area; from the **Header & Footer Tools Design** tab, **Header & Footer** group, click **Page Number**, **Top of Page**, **Plain Number 3**; from the **Options** group, check **Different First Page**; click outside the header to close it.)
2. Select the first 3 rows of the table on the first page. (*Hint*: You may need to drag all the way across the rows to select all cells.)
3. From the **Table Tools**, **Layout** tab, **Data** group, click **Repeat Header Rows**.
4. The headings are now repeated on page 2.
5. Save changes to *practice-79*, and return to GDP.

GO TO Textbook

Tables With Predesigned Formats

Table—Styles

The Table Styles feature is used to format a table with predesigned headings, borders, shading, and so forth. You can preview a wide variety of styles and choose the one that enhances the design and readability of the table's content.

In general, begin with a table with plain text (no bolding) in Row 1 and no active hyperlinks in e-mail addresses or Web addresses—the hyperlink style often clashes with the table styles and decreases readability. Then apply a table style, and customize any table formatting as desired. For example, you might wish to center the table horizontally and change cell alignment, font size, and bolding.

Use Table Style Options to format different parts of the table in unique ways to distinguish them and improve readability. For example, to distinguish a table title in Row 1, under **Table Style Options**, check **Header Row**. To distinguish text in Column A, check **First Column**. To distinguish a bottom row that includes a total line, check **Total Row**.

To format a table automatically:

1. Scroll and increase your **Zoom** level so that your table is larger and positioned at the bottom of the window so the **Live Preview** is easier to see.
2. Click anywhere in the table.
3. From the **Table Tools**, **Design** tab, **Table Styles** group, click the **More** list arrow button to the right of the **Table Styles** group to expand the gallery.
4. Point to each style, and pause to read the **ScreenTip** identifying the style name.
5. Look at the **Live Preview** of the table as you point to the desired style and as you check and uncheck **Header Row**, **Total Row**, **Banded Rows**, **First Column**, **Last Column**, and **Banded Columns** in **Table Style Options**. Note also that the design gallery changes dramatically depending upon which options are checked in the **Style Options** group.

REFER TO
Word Manual
L. 49: AutoCorrect—Hyperlink
L. 38: Table—Align Bottom
Table—Center Horizontally
Table—Center Page
L. 39: Table—Align Text Right

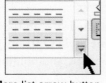

More list arrow button

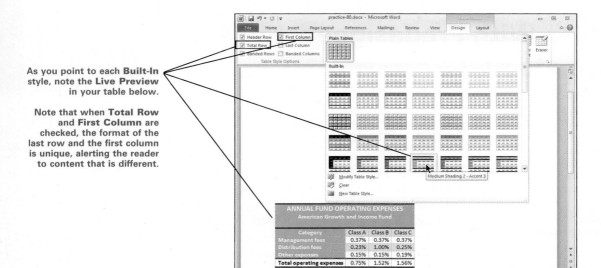

As you point to each **Built-In** style, note the **Live Preview** in your table below.

Note that when **Total Row** and **First Column** are checked, the format of the last row and the first column is unique, alerting the reader to content that is different.

6. Under **Table Tools**, **Design** tab, in the **Table Style Options** group, point to each button and read the descriptive **ScreenTip**.

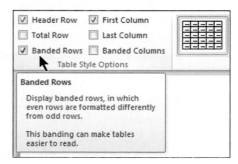

7. When you have settled on a style choice, click the desired style in the **Table Styles** group and the desired checkboxes in the **Table Style Options** group.
8. Center the table horizontally; adjust any fonts (color, size, and bolding), spacing, and alignment as desired.

To clear a table style:

1. Click anywhere inside the table.
2. From the **Table Tools**, **Design** tab, **Table Styles** group, click the **More** list arrow.
3. Click **Clear** at the bottom of the style list.

PRACTICE

1. Click anywhere in the table.
2. From the **Table Tools**, **Design** tab, **Table Styles** group, click the **More** list arrow.
3. Point to the **Medium Shading 2–Accent 3** style, and apply it to this table. (*Hint*: This style is located in the fifth row in the center.)
4. Under **Table Tools**, **Design** tab, **Table Style Options** group, point to each button and read the descriptive **ScreenTip**.
5. In the **Table Style Options** group, check and uncheck **Header Row, Total Row**, **Banded Rows**, and **First Column**; note the effect in the **Live Preview**.
6. From the **Design** tab, **Table Style Options** group, check these choices only: **Header Row** to apply a unique style to Row 1, **Total Row** to apply a unique style to the last row, and **Banded Rows** and **First Column** to apply a unique style to the rows and first column.
7. Center the table horizontally, and bold all entries in Rows 1 and 2 as necessary.
8. Verify that numerical column entries are right-aligned; adjust any settings as needed. Your table should appear similar to this:

ANNUAL FUND OPERATING EXPENSES American Growth and Income Fund			
Category	Class A	Class B	Class C
Management fees	0.37%	0.37%	0.37%
Distribution fees	0.23%	1.00%	0.25%
Other expenses	0.15%	0.15%	0.19%
Total operating expenses	0.75%	1.52%	1.56%

GO TO Textbook

9. Save changes to *practice-80*, and return to GDP.

International Formatting—Canada

Paper Size

The default paper size is the standard 8.5 by 11 inches. You can, however, change the paper size if your printer has the capability of handling different-sized paper.

To change the paper size:

1. From the **Page Layout** tab, in the **Page Setup** group, click the **Size** button.

A4 metric size paper has been selected. A4 size is only slightly narrower and slightly longer than **Letter** size; so look at the ruler carefully to note the changes after selecting this paper size.

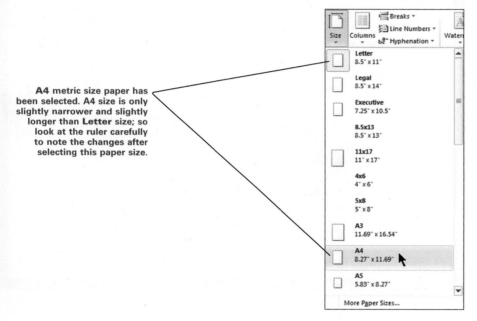

2. From the expanded list, click the desired paper size.
3. To display more sizes, click **More Paper Sizes** at the bottom of the pane.

PRACTICE

1. Display the ruler, and note the right margin is positioned at 6.5 inches.
2. Note the line ending of the first line in the first paragraph.
3. Change the paper size to **A4**.
4. Note the right margin is now positioned at 6.25 inches and the line ending of the first line has changed.
5. Save changes to *practice-81*, and return to GDP.

GO TO
Textbook

International Formatting—Mexico

Symbol—Insert

Many foreign languages use diacritical marks or a combination of characters to indicate phonetic sounds. The **Symbol** dialog box contains many of the characters needed to type words with special accents.

To insert a symbol:

1. Click where you want to insert a symbol, or select an existing letter.
2. From the **Insert** tab, **Symbols** group, click the **Symbol** button, **More Symbols**.

Once you have selected the desired **Subset**, use the down and up arrows on the keyboard—not the scroll box—to navigate through the list.

An international character can also be inserted by using a shortcut key. Microsoft Word Help provides a list of symbols and shortcut keys, or check the Internet, or see a brief list in this lesson.

The **Recently used symbols** list changes dynamically.

3. In the **Font** box, click **(normal text)**. (*Hint*: Look at the first choice directly under the **Font** box.)
4. In the **Subset** box, click **Latin-1 Supplement** to move to a character code subset for the desired symbol.
5. Click the down arrow under the scroll bar (*not* the scroll box) repeatedly until you see the desired symbol.
6. Click a symbol to see a highlighted view.
7. Click **Insert** to insert the symbol, and click **Close**.

   After you click **Insert**, the inserted symbol is automatically added to the **Recently used symbols** area under the **Symbols** button for easy insertion next time.

8. Check the capitalization of the symbol. It may be necessary to change from uppercase to lowercase.

To insert a symbol using the keyboard and the numeric keypad (not the numbers on the top row of the keyboard) with Num Lock active:

Symbol	Name	Example	Shortcut
á	a acute	Yucatán	ALT + 160
é	e acute	Querétaro	ALT + 130
í	i acute	García	ALT + 161
ñ	n tilde	Señor	ALT + 164
ó	o acute	Torreón	ALT + 162
ú	u acute	Cancún	ALT + 163
ü	u umlaut	Nürnberg	ALT + 129

PRACTICE

1. Note that your practice file opens as shown without any special symbols in Column C:

Symbol	Name	Example	Shortcut
á	a acute	Yucatan	ALT + 160
é	e acute	Queretaro	ALT + 130
í	i acute	Garcia	ALT + 161
ñ	n tilde	Senor	ALT + 164
ó	o acute	Torreon	ALT + 162
ú	u acute	Cancun	ALT + 163
ü	u umlaut	Nurnberg	ALT + 129

2. Insert symbols as shown using either the **Insert**, **Symbol** feature or the keyboard shortcuts; then delete the extra letter.

Symbol	Name	Example	Shortcut
á	a acute	Yucatán	ALT + 160
é	e acute	Querétaro	ALT + 130
í	i acute	García	ALT + 161
ñ	n tilde	Señor	ALT + 164
ó	o acute	Torreón	ALT + 162
ú	u acute	Cancún	ALT + 163
ü	u umlaut	Nürnberg	ALT + 129

GO TO
Textbook

3. Save changes to *practice-82*, and return to GDP.

Formal Report Project—A

Styles

REFER TO
Word Manual
Appendix A: GDP—Word Settings, Style Set—Word 2003
Appendix A: Style Set—Word 2010, Style Gallery—Word 2010

A default Style Set is a group of embedded styles that automatically control "normal" formatting for fonts, indents, line spacing, and so forth. When you open a Word document through GDP, the default Style Set in effect is "Word 2003." The base font is Calibri 12, the line spacing is single, and the spacing after paragraphs is 0 pt.

On the Home tab, in the Styles Group, a Style gallery is displayed on the ribbon with choices like Normal and Heading 1. Normal is highlighted in a new document because it is the default style in use. All the styles in the Style gallery change when a different default Style Set is selected. The order of styles changes based upon styles recently used.

When you modify an individual style, any text that uses that style in the current document will automatically update the text to reflect any change. Applying a style is a powerful, efficient editing tool because its use results in global changes throughout a document.

The **Normal** style is the default style in the **Styles** group. The order of the style buttons changes dynamically.

Click the **More** arrow to the right of the **Styles** group to display the **Style** gallery.

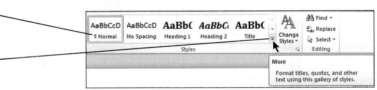

To apply an individual style:

1. Position the insertion point in the paragraph where you want the style formatting to be applied, or select the desired text.
2. From the **Home** tab, **Styles** group, click the **Styles Dialog Box Launcher**.
3. From the bottom of the **Styles** pane, click **Options**.
4. From the **Style Pane Options** window, in the **Select styles to show** box, click the list arrow, **All Styles**, **OK**.
5. Click the desired style from the **Styles** pane; then click the **Close** button on the **Styles** pane.

Or:

1. From the **Home** tab, in the **Styles** group, click the desired style; click the **More** button to see additional styles in the **Quick Styles** gallery.
2. Point to each style to see a **Live Preview** in the selected text or the entire paragraph; then click the desired style.

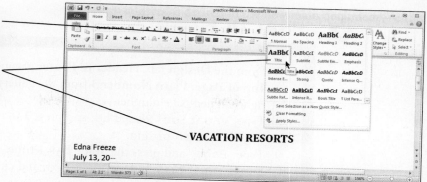

The Style gallery is dynamic and changes depending upon the default **Style Set** in use and styles recently used.

Point to the desired style in the **Quick Styles** gallery, and note the **Live Preview** in your document.

VACATION RESORTS

 After you apply a style and press **ENTER**, the next line should revert to the **Normal** style.

To remove a style:

1. Select the desired text.
2. From the **Home** tab, **Styles** group, click the **Styles Diagonal Box Launcher**.
3. From the **Styles** box, click **Normal** from the style list; then close the **Styles** box.

PRACTICE

1. Apply the **Title** style to the report title.
2. Apply the **Subtitle** style to the report subtitle and date, and bold them. (*Hint*: Click **More** to see additional styles.)
3. Apply the **Heading 2** style to the three side headings.

Note: Next, you will insert a header that looks like this:

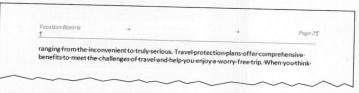

4. As a precaution before beginning, from the **Design** tab, **Options** group, verify that **Different first page** is unchecked.
5. Insert a header that is suppressed on the first page and displays on subsequent pages.
6. Right-click over the header area, and click **Edit Header**.

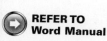

REFER TO Word Manual

L. 47: Headers
L. 32: Page Number

Lesson 86 • Formal Report Project—A   141

PRACTICE (continued)

7. From the **Design** tab, **Header & Footer** group, click **Page Number**, **Top of Page**, **Plain Number 3** from the gallery of designs to insert a right-aligned page number.
8. Type `Vacation Resorts`, and press **TAB** twice to reposition the words at the left margin.
9. Type `Page` and press the **SPACE BAR** 1 time.
10. Press **CTRL + A** to select all header text, and change font to **Cambria 10 pt. Italic**.
11. Press the right arrow on the keyboard to deselect the text and to move to the line below the header.

REFER TO Word Manual
L. 37: Table—Borders

12. To add a bottom border, from the **Home** tab, **Paragraph** group, click the list arrow on the **Borders** button, and click the **Bottom Border** button.
13. From the **Design** tab, **Options** group, click **Different First Page**.

> The **First Page Header** section should now be blank. If the page number is still in the **First Page Header**, select the page number and cut it with **CTRL + X**.

14. Scroll down to the second page to see the header, which should now contain text, a page number, and a bottom border.
15. Double-click over the document area to close the header. Your report should appear similar to this:

GO TO Textbook

16. Save changes to *practice-86*, and return to GDP.

Clip Art—Insert

One of the easiest ways to make a document interesting is to add an image, such as clip art or a photograph. Images like this (also referred to as "objects") can be sized easily and positioned within a document. A wide selection of clip art and photographs is readily available in Word. You may use other images as long as they are compatible with Word.

Clip Art pane

To add clip art or a photograph to a document:

1. Click in the document where you want to insert an image.
2. From the **Insert** tab, **Illustrations** group, click the **Clip Art** button.
3. Note that a **Clip Art** task pane opens to the right of the Word window.

   ❓ If you are online and a prompt appears asking if you want to include thousands of additional clip art images and photos from Microsoft Office Online, click **Yes**.

4. In the **Clip Art** task pane, in the **Search for** box, type a keyword or phrase describing the type of image you want.
5. If desired, specify the type of media file in the **Results should be** text box; click **Go**.
6. Scroll down to view the displayed image.
7. Click over the picture you want to insert automatically.
8. Note that the inserted picture is selected (sizing handles appear on the corners of the picture).
9. Note that the **Picture Tools Format** tab appears on demand while the clip art or picture is selected.

To find more clip art if you have an Internet connection:

1. Click the **Find More at Office.com** link at the bottom of the **Clip Art** task pane.
2. Follow the steps there to search for additional clip art.

TEXT WRAPPING

Text will wrap around inserted clip art in different ways depending upon the Text Wrapping choice in use:

- **In Line with Text**. When you first insert an image, text wrapping is set by default to In Line with Text. Text moves around the picture as if the inserted picture were another very large character in a line of text.
- **Square**. Text wraps in a square shape around all sides of the image.
- **Tight**. Text wraps around the actual shape of the image filling in any white space around the picture shape.
- **Through**. Text wraps around the actual shape of the image filling in any white space around the picture shape. This wrap is similar to but even closer than the Tight option.
- **Top and Bottom**. Text is placed above and below the image, but never beside the image.
- **Behind Text**. The image appears behind the text without rearranging the text.
- **In Front of Text**. The image appears on top of the text without rearranging the text.

To set text wrapping and visually position a picture:

1. Double-click the picture to select it and to activate the on-demand **Picture Tools** tab and **Format** tab.
2. From the **Picture Tools**, **Format** tab, **Arrange** group, click **Wrap Text**.

   Or: Right-click the picture, and click **Wrap Text**.

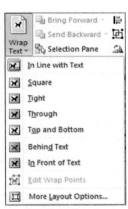

Wrap Text button

3. Click the desired text wrapping.
4. Position the mouse pointer over the selected graphic until a 4-headed move pointer displays.
5. Drag the image into position.

To position a picture precisely, relative to the document margins:

1. Double-click the image to select it and to activate the on-demand **Picture Tools** tab and **Format** tab.
2. From the **Format** tab, **Arrange** group, click the **Align** button.
3. Verify that **Align to Margin** is checked.

   ⊘ If the alignment choices are dimmed, set text wrapping to something other than **In Line with Text**, and try setting alignment again.

4. Click the desired horizontal alignment—**Align Left**, **Align Center**, or **Align Right**; or click the desired vertical alignment—**Align Top**, **Align Middle**, or **Align Bottom**.

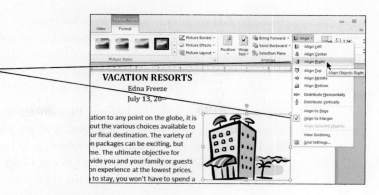

To align this clip art precisely at the right margin of the document, verify that **Align to Margin** is checked; then click **Align Right**.

To rotate and size an image visually:

1. Click the image to select it.
2. Position the mouse pointer over the green rotate dot until the pointer changes to a rounded rotate arrow; drag in a circle as desired.
3. Position the mouse pointer over any corner sizing handle until the pointer changes to a double-sided arrow; drag as desired.

   💡 Drag on a corner sizing handle, not a handle in the middle, when you visually size an image to prevent distortion of the image. Try dragging on a middle sizing handle; note the distortion to the picture.

4. Note that as you drag, a **Live Preview** shadow appears.
5. Release the mouse button when the desired size is reached.

A selected picture has top, middle, and bottom sizing handles and a green rotate dot above the center of the picture.

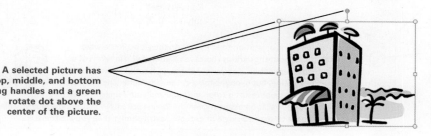

Drag the green rotate dot to rotate the image.

Drag one of the top or bottom sizing handles to adjust the height.

Drag one of the middle sizing handles to adjust the width.

Drag one of the corner sizing handles to adjust the width and height and to maintain the original proportions!

To size an image using exact measurements:

1. Double-click the image.
2. From the **Format** tab, **Size** group, type the desired size in either the **Height** or **Width** box to resize the image in proportion to the measurement entered in either the **Height** or **Width** box.

To change the overall visual style for a selected image:

Experiment freely with all the buttons and tools in these groups from the **Format** tab—**Adjust**, **Picture Styles**, **Arrange**, and **Size**. The **Live Preview** feature is very helpful as you experiment with these tools:

- In the **Picture Styles** group, point to a **Picture Effects** button for some dramatic results.

- In the **Adjust** group, use the **Recolor** button to change image colors.
- In the **Arrange** group, use the **Rotate** button to turn your image. You also can rotate by dragging the green rotate dot at the top of an image.
- In the **Size** group, use the crop tool to "cut" part of your image in the same way you would use scissors to cut a real picture.

Experiment freely with the **Format Picture** dialog box choices. Right-click the selected image, click **Format Picture**, and try **Fill**, **Line Color**, **Line Style**, **Shadow**, **Reflection**, **Glow and Soft Edges**, **3-D Format**, **3-D Rotation**, **Picture Corrections**, **Picture Color**, **Artistic Effects**, **Crop**, **Text Box**, and **Alt Text**; click any available, active **Reset** button in the right pane to undo any changes.

OBJECT ANCHOR

Object anchor

When an object such as clip art is inserted, Word anchors that object to the paragraph in which the insertion point was positioned when the object was inserted. When Show/Hide ¶ is active and an object is selected, an "object anchor" displays in the margin next to the paragraph. The object must have text wrapping set to something other than **In Line with Text** for the anchor to appear.

The object anchor appears in the margin next to the paragraph to which the object is anchored.

The object anchor can be dragged and dropped to any paragraph mark on the page. The clip art will not move when the anchor is repositioned.

If lines are added above the paragraph with the anchored object, both the paragraph and its anchored object move down the page. If you delete text and an image is unexpectedly deleted, undo the deletion, drag the object anchor, and drop it on a paragraph that is not likely to be deleted.

Object anchor with move handle

Object anchor with mouse pointer

To anchor an object, such as a text box or picture, to a particular line:

1. Display formatting marks by turning on **Show/Hide ¶**.
2. Double-click the image (or click the edge of the text box) to select it.
3. Note the object anchor in the selection bar area.
4. Point slightly to the top right side of the object anchor until you see the 4-sided move handle.

5. Drag and drop the anchor next to the desired paragraph.
6. Note that the object anchor symbol is attached to the mouse pointer as you drag the anchor into position.

PRACTICE

1. Click in front of the first word in the first paragraph.
2. Insert clip art related to resorts.
3. Change the wrap style to **Square**.
4. Set the image width to exactly 1 inch.
5. Drag the image to the middle of the first paragraph.
6. Observe changes as you change the wrap style to **In Line with Text**, then **Tight**, then **Behind Text**, then **In Front of Text**, undoing each choice as you go; change the wrap style back to **Square**.
7. Turn on **Show/Hide ¶**, and drag the image to the right to position it visually at the right margin of the first paragraph—the image should *not* extend into the right margin or above the line of type.
8. Position the selected picture exactly at the right margin. (*Hint*: From the **Format** tab, **Arrange** group, click the **Align** button; verify that **Align to Margin** is checked; click **Align Right**.)
9. If necessary, drag and drop the object anchor in the margin next to the first paragraph. The picture position and anchor position should look similar to the previous illustration.
10. Save changes to *practice-88*, and return to GDP.

GO TO
Textbook

File—Insert

To insert the contents of a Word document into the current active document:

1. Position the insertion point where the inserted contents should appear.
2. From the **Insert** tab, in the **Text** group, click the arrow next to the **Object** button; then click **Text from File**.

Click the arrow *next to* the **Object** button and *not* the **Object** button itself to display the object menu.

3. Note that the **Insert File** dialog box opens.

   Your dialog box will differ depending on your computer, your Windows version, and your Windows settings. File extensions may or may not appear. See your Windows documentation for help with displaying file extensions and browsing to files.

4. Browse to the desired location and file.
5. Double-click the desired file name to insert the file contents.

   If the desired file does not display, you likely have a file filter in effect. Consult your Windows documentation for steps to display All Files (*.*) when you are browsing.

 PRACTICE

1. Press **CTRL + END,** and press **ENTER** 2 times.
2. Insert the file named *practice-89-insert.* The last two paragraphs of your document should look similar to this:

PRACTICE (continued)

> **TRAVEL PROTECTION PLANS**
>
> You might also want to consider purchasing some sort of travel protection plan. Anyone who has traveled for any length of time knows that travel plans can be interrupted by unexpected events ranging from the inconvenient to truly serious. Travel Insurance Associates offers a variety of insurance packages with comprehensive benefits to meet the challenges of travel and help you enjoy a worry-free trip. When you think about the cost, stop also to think about how you would feel if you lost all nonrefundable fees, airfares, and so forth. The cost begins to look more and more reasonable. Visit their Web site at www.tia.com for full details.
>
> Comprehensive travel protection plans are designed for the travelers who are looking for things like trip cancellation and interruption benefits and other coverage benefits such as medical expenses, baggage and personal belongings recovery, baggage delay, travel delay, and emergency evacuation.

Note: Keep this document open and continue reading.

Bookmarks and Hyperlinks

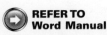

REFER TO Word Manual

L. 49: AutoCorrect— Hyperlink

If hyperlinks are not behaving as expected, see Appendix A, GDP—Word Settings, AutoFormat As You Type Options, to verify your Word settings.

A hyperlink is a linked object (usually text or a picture) you click on to jump from one place to another. When you type an e-mail or Internet address and press the SPACE BAR, that address is automatically converted to a hyperlink. Hyperlinked text is underlined, and the mouse pointer displays as a hand icon when you point to it. A manual hyperlink can be created to move quickly from the hyperlink to a bookmarked location within a document. First, the electronic bookmark, which is the destination of the hyperlink, must be created.

To create a bookmark:

1. Click at the desired position in the text—this location will become the destination of the hyperlink.
2. From the **Insert** tab, **Links** group, click **Bookmark**.
3. From the **Bookmark** dialog box, click in the **Bookmark name** box; type a descriptive, short bookmark name without spaces or hyphens; click **Add**.

Click in the **Bookmark name** box, and type the desired name without spaces or hyphens. The bookmark will be inserted where the cursor is positioned in the text.

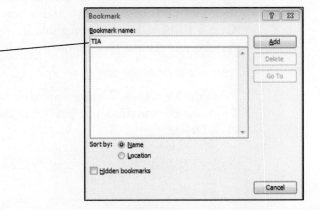

⊘ If you type a space or hyphen in a bookmark name, the Add button will dim, making it unavailable. Remove the space, and insert an underscore between words as a substitute for a space, or use different capitalization to distinguish words.

💡 To move to a bookmark without using a hyperlink, press **CTRL + G**; under **Go to what**, click **Bookmark**; under **Enter bookmark name**, select the desired bookmark, and click **Go To**.

To create a text hyperlink to an existing bookmark:

1. Select the text for the hyperlink.
2. From the **Insert** tab, **Links** group, click **Hyperlink**.
3. From the **Insert Hyperlink** dialog box, under **Link to**, click **Place in This Document**.
4. In the **Select a place in this document**, under **Bookmarks**, click the desired bookmark name; click **OK**.

Select the text to be hyperlinked, click Hyperlink, click Place in This Document, and click the desired bookmark.

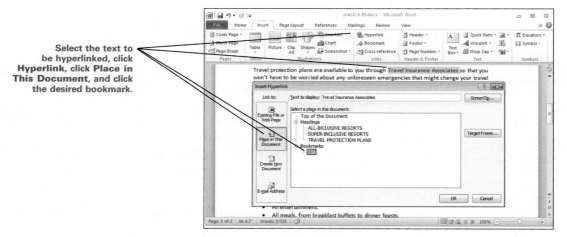

5. Note that the selected text is converted to a hyperlink.
6. Click the hyperlink to move to the bookmark.

⊘ If the hyperlinked text does not automatically convert to a hyperlink or if you click the hyperlink and a **ScreenTip** displays telling you to use **CTRL + Click** to follow a hyperlink, see Appendix A, GDP—Word Settings, AutoFormat As You Type Options, to adjust your settings.

To remove a bookmark:

1. From the **Insert** tab, **Links** group, click **Bookmark**.
2. From the **Bookmark** dialog box, select the desired bookmark name, and click **Delete**.

To remove a hyperlink:

1. Use the directional arrow on the keyboard to position the insertion point inside the hyperlinked text.
2. From the **Insert** tab, **Links** group, click **Hyperlink**.
3. From the **Insert Hyperlink** dialog box, click **Remove link**.

PRACTICE (continued)

1. Move to page 2, and click just before "Travel Insurance Associates" in the first paragraph under the side heading "TRAVEL PROTECTION PLANS."
2. Create a bookmark named "TIA" without spaces.
3. Move to page 1, and select "Travel Insurance Associates" in the first sentence of the second paragraph.
4. Create a hyperlink to the "TIA" bookmark.
5. Click the Travel Insurance Associates hyperlink to test it. The insertion point should move automatically to page 2 just before the "T" in "Travel Insurance Associates."
6. Save changes to *practice-89*, and return to GDP.

GO TO
Textbook

Cover Page—Insert

You could manually create a cover page for a formal report, but Word includes a Cover Page feature that you can use to create a preformatted, professionally designed cover page. This feature can retrieve some content from Microsoft; so the gallery list may vary.

To insert a cover page:

1. Open a blank Word document.
2. From the **Insert** tab, **Pages** group, click the **Cover Page** button.
3. From the gallery of cover pages, click the desired choice.

Depending upon your choice, a cover page will appear with fields to enter information, such as the company name, document title and subtitle, author name, year, and company address. You can click inside these fields and type the desired information or select the field and delete it.

PRACTICE

1. From the **Insert** tab, **Pages** group, click the **Cover Page** button.
2. Scroll down the gallery list, and click **Exposure** (or another suitable choice if **Exposure** is unavailable) to insert that cover page.
3. Save this document as *practice-90*.
4. Click in the **Type the document title** field, and type Tuscany Travel Guide.
5. Double-click in the **Author** box to the right to select any text that might already be entered, and with the text still selected, type Edna Freeze.
6. Click in the list arrow next to the **Year** box, and select the desired date. The current year should appear.
7. Click in the **Abstract** box, and type this:

   Picture yourself strolling through fields of sunflowers in the valleys of Tuscany, enjoying fine Italian cuisine, and dancing the night away. Italian Vacation Resorts can make that dream come true. Read on for a full description of our dream vacation packages.

8. Click in the **Type the company name** box, and type this:
Italian Vacation Resorts
9. Click in the **Type the company address** box, and type this:
italianvacationresorts.com
10. Click in the **Type the phone number** box, and type this:
800-555-3497
11. Click in the **Type the fax number** box; press **CTRL + X** to cut it.
12. Press **CTRL + END** to move to the end of the cover page, and press **BACKSPACE** twice to remove the blank page. Your cover page should look similar to this:

13. Save changes to *practice-90*, and return to GDP.

Medical Office Documents—B

Table—Tab

REFER TO
Word Manual
L. 45: Tab Set—Ruler Tabs
L. 50: Tab Set—Dot
Leaders

When you press TAB inside a table, the insertion point moves to the next cell and automatically selects any text in that cell for possible editing.

To indent text inside a table with the TAB key: Press **CTRL + TAB** to move in 0.5-inch increments to the default tab settings, or set custom tabs to indent text or to align text in a different way within the same cell. For example, if a row includes text aligned at both the left and right cell borders, set a right tab at the right cell border; type the left-aligned text; then press **CTRL + TAB** to move to the right tab; then type the right-aligned text.

To set custom tabs inside a table: When you set tabs, type all table contents first, use AutoFit to adjust the column widths to the contents, and then work with the tab settings to indent any text inside the table.

PRACTICE

Note: Begin by using default tab settings to indent text:

1. Click the **View Ruler** button (at the top of the vertical scroll area) to display the ruler, and turn on **Show/Hide ¶**.
2. In the last line of Row 1, click after the last digit in the telephone number; then press **CTRL + TAB** once.
3. In Row 2, click after the colon in each line, and press **CTRL + TAB** once.
4. In Column A, replace the "--" with the current year (in black).
5. In the last row, click after "Total Due," and press **CTRL + TAB** once.
6. Right-click anywhere in the table, click **AutoFit**, **AutoFit to Contents**.
7. Note the effects of the default tab settings on text alignment:
   - Row 1 has an acceptable amount of white space between the telephone and e-mail information.
   - In Row 2, a left tab should be set at approximately 1.5 inches to align the information after the colons.
   - In the last row, a right tab should be set at the right margin to adjust the spacing after "Total Due."

Note: Next, set custom tabs to align text attractively:

1. Verify that the **Left Tab** marker to the left of the ruler is displayed. If it is not, click the **Tab Selection** button until it displays.

2. Scroll up so that Row 2 is positioned just under the ruler, zoom in so you can see Row 2 clearly, and select the 3 typed lines in Row 2.

   ⓦ Do not select the row itself, or you will not be able to set tabs using the ruler.

3. On the white part of the ruler, hold the mouse over the 1.5-inch position.

4. Click, hold, and drag the **Left Tab** marker into position; use the dotted lines that shoot down over the table to guide you into the desired position to align the text after the colon following the longest heading. Your screen should look similar to this.

Slide the **Left Tab** marker into position until this guideline is positioned approximately 1 space after the colon following "ZIP."

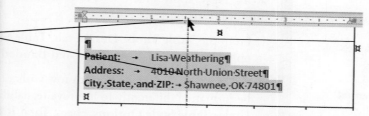

5. Release the mouse to set the custom left tab. Row 2 and the tab settings should look similar to those in the next step.

6. If the custom left tab is set incorrectly, with the lines still selected, point *carefully* to the **Left Tab** marker until the "**Left Tab**" **ScreenTip** appears; then drag the marker. (Waiting for the ScreenTip assures you that you are not going to set a new tab accidentally.)

Point to the **Left Tab** marker; wait for the ScreenTip; then slide the **Left Tab** marker into position.

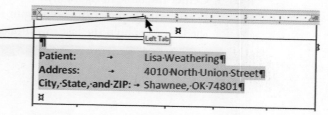

7. Click in the last row, and click the **Tab Selection** button until the **Right Tab** marker appears.

PRACTICE (continued)

8. On the white part of the ruler, point to the 3.5-inch position; click, hold, and drag the **Right Tab** marker into position until it stops at the right table border. The right tab setting should look similar to this just before you release it:

9. Note that after you release the right tab setting, the last row should be right-aligned and look similar to this.

Note: Next, apply a table style to format the table attractively and improve readability:

1. From the **Table Tools**, **Design** tab, **Table Style Options** group, check only **Header Row**, **Total Row**, and **Banded Columns**.

   If a table includes a bottom row with a total line, that row should be formatted differently to improve readability and comprehension. Under **Table Style Options**, check **Total Row** to format the last row in a unique way.

REFER TO
Word Manual
L. 80: Table—Styles

2. From the **Table Tools**, **Design** tab, **Table Styles** group, click the **More** list arrow; and apply the **Colorful List–Accent 1** style (or any desired style) to this table. (*Hint*: **Colorful List–Accent 1** is positioned in the second to the last row in the **Style** gallery, Column B.)
3. Center the table horizontally.
4. If necessary, remove any bolding in Row 1 from all typed lines except the first two; bold the last row if necessary.

5. Adjust any other fonts (color, size, and bolding), spacing, and align-ment as desired. Your table should appear similar to this:

Note the **Table Style Options** that were used to design this table.

Note the **Colorful List–Accent 1** style appears in the **Table Styles** box after it has been applied.

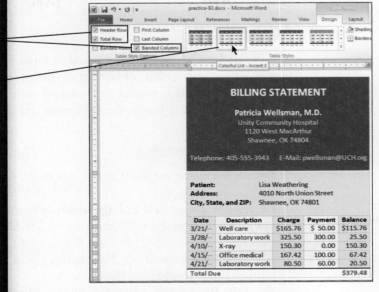

6. Save changes to *practice-92*, and return to GDP.

Line Numbering

Use Word's Line Numbering command to number lines in legal documents for ease of reference in a court of law. Line numbers can be positioned, formatted, and turned on or off as needed and restarted within a document. Word can add line numbers to every line in the document and also restart line numbering on each page.

To begin line numbering:

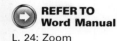

REFER TO
Word Manual

L. 24: Zoom

1. Position the insertion point at the start of the page where you want line numbering to begin.
2. Change the **Zoom** level to **Page width** so that you will be able to see the line numbering in the space between the left edge of the page and the left margin.
3. From the **Page Layout** tab, **Page Setup** group, click the **Line Numbers** button, **Line Numbering Options**.
4. From the **Page Setup** dialog box, click the **Layout** tab.
5. From the bottom of the **Layout** tab, click the **Line Numbers** button to display the **Line Numbers** dialog box.
6. Check **Add line numbering**, and click **OK** twice.

Check **Add line numbering**.

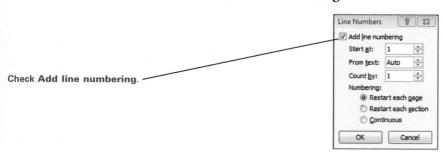

PRACTICE

1. Change the zoom level to **Page width**.
2. Add line numbering. Your document should look similar to this:

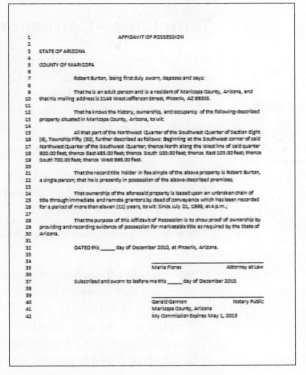

GO TO
Textbook

3. Save changes to *practice-98*, and return to GDP.

Using Correspondence Templates

Templates—Correspondence

When you create a new document, Word automatically uses its default template, also known as the "normal" template. Default margins, tabs, line spacing, and other settings are defined by the settings embedded in this template. You can also create a document by opening one of Word's predefined correspondence templates that includes formatted content, such as a memo or letter template.

 **REFER TO**
Word Manual

L. 102: Templates—Report

To download and use a memo template outside of GDP:

1. Go online; then from the **File** tab, click **New**.
2. In the center pane under **Office.com Templates**, click **Memos** to open a list of available memo templates.

   💡 In the center pane under **Office.com Templates**, click **More Templates** for additional choices.

   ❗ The list of available templates is Web-based content retrieved from Microsoft that may vary or become unavailable. Therefore, at the start of any template job, GDP will automatically open a preselected memo or report template with an assigned name ready for input. In GDP, follow steps 6–10 in this section to use a memo template. In the workplace, follow the steps 1–5 in this section to download a memo template and steps 6–10 to use it.

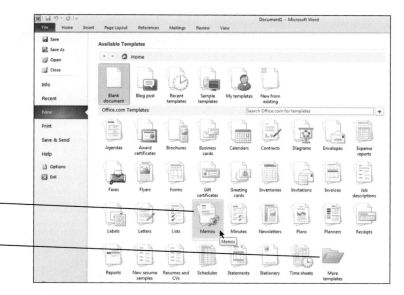

Double-click the desired category to open a list of templates for that category.

Click **More templates** for additional choices.

3. In the **Available Templates** pane, click the desired memo template.
4. Note the preview in the far right pane.

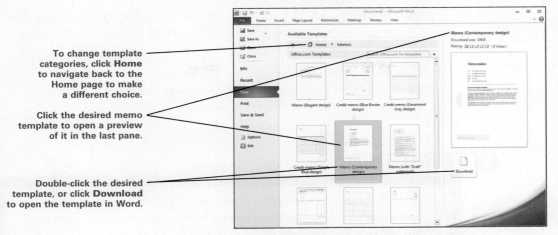

To change template categories, click **Home** to navigate back to the Home page to make a different choice.

Click the desired memo template to open a preview of it in the last pane.

Double-click the desired template, or click **Download** to open the template in Word.

5. Double-click the desired template, or click **Download** to download and open a copy of the template in Word with a generic file name.

Follow any prompts that might appear at any point to validate the status of your software. To change template categories, under **Available Templates** in the center pane, click **Home** to navigate back to the **Home** page. If you wish to reformat the template using a different style set, you would change style sets at this point.

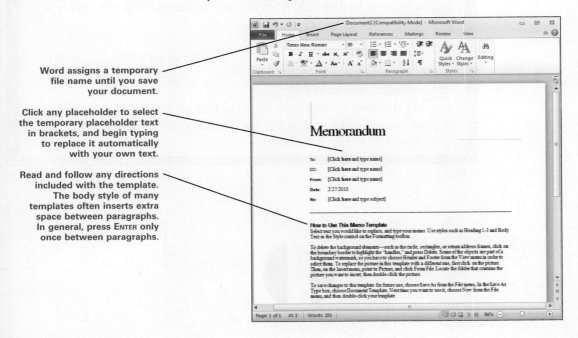

Word assigns a temporary file name until you save your document.

Click any placeholder to select the temporary placeholder text in brackets, and begin typing to replace it automatically with your own text.

Read and follow any directions included with the template. The body style of many templates often inserts extra space between paragraphs. In general, press ENTER only once between paragraphs.

6. Read the instructions on the template, and follow any that apply.
7. Click any desired placeholder text in brackets to select it.

    The date placeholder changes dynamically to display the current date. Therefore, the dates in the template illustrations will vary from those you will see when the template opens.

8. With the text still selected, type any desired replacement text.
9. Select and delete any parts of the template text you don't want to use.
10. Save the document as you normally would.

PRACTICE

1. Note that the memo template shown in the previous illustration opens automatically with an assigned name ready for input. Turn on **Show/Hide ¶** to see formatting marks.
2. Click the placeholder text after "To" to select it; with the placeholder text still selected, type Helen Lalin as the recipient's name.
3. Click the placeholder text after "CC" to select it; with the placeholder text still selected, type Jose Limon as the copy recipient's name.
4. Click the placeholder text after "From" to select it; with the placeholder text still selected, type Shannon Newsome as the sender's name.
5. Click the placeholder text after "Date" to select it.
6. Drag across the date field from the start to the end, delete it, and type this:
   February 14, 20--
7. Click the placeholder text after "Re" to select it; with the placeholder text still selected, type this:
   Luncheon Invitation
8. Select the body of the memo from the first bold line of the memo template instructions to the end of the last paragraph of instructions. Your selected text should look like this:

Re: → Luncheon·Invitation¶

How·to·Use·This·Memo·Template¶

Select·text·you·would·like·to·replace,·and·type·your·memo.·Use·styles·such·as· Heading·1-3·and·Body·Text·in·the·Style·control·on·the·Formatting·toolbar.¶

To·delete·the·background·elements—such·as·the·circle,·rectangles,·or·return· address·frames,·click·on·the·boundary·border·to·highlight·the·"handles,"·and·press· Delete.·To·replace·the·picture·in·this·template·with·a·different·one,·first·click·on·the· picture.·Then,·on·the·Insert·menu,·point·to·Picture,·and·click·From·File.·Locate·the· folder·that·contains·the·picture·you·want·to·insert,·then·double·click·the·picture.¶

To·save·changes·to·this·template·for·future·use,·on·the·File·menu,·click·**Save·As**.·In· the·**Save·As·Type**·box,·choose·**Document·Template**·(the·filename·extensions·should· change·from·*.doc*·to·*.dot*)·and·save·the·template.·Next·time·you·want·to·use·the· updated·template,·on·the·**File**·menu,·click·**New**.·In·the·**New·Document**·task·pane,· under·**Templates**,·click·**On·my·computer**.·In·the·**Templates**·dialog,·your·updated· template·will·appear·on·the·General·tab.¶

¶

9. With the instructions still selected, type this paragraph:

> I will be happy to attend the luncheon meeting of the Purchasing Managers' Association with you next Tuesday at the Friar's Club. Since I'll be at a workshop until 11:15 that morning, I'll meet you in their lobby at 12:15 p.m.

💡 If you delete the selected instructions instead of typing in the replacement text while the instructions are still selected, you will likely delete the embedded paragraph styles. If you make this mistake, click **Undo** to reverse your actions and try again.

10. Press **ENTER** 1 time; note that an extra blank line is inserted automatically.

❓ If a blank line is not inserted, press **ENTER** as needed to insert 1 blank line between paragraphs.

11. Type this as the final paragraph:
Thanks for thinking of me.

12. Press **ENTER** 1 time, and type your reference initials. Turn off **Show/Hide ¶**. Your document should look similar to this:

Memorandum

To:	Helen Lalin
CC:	Jose Limon
From:	Shannon Newsome
Date:	February 14, 20--
Re:	Luncheon Invitation

I will be happy to attend the luncheon meeting of the Purchasing Managers' Association with you next Tuesday at the Friar's Club. Since I'll be at a workshop until 11:15 that morning, I'll meet you in their lobby at 12:15 p.m.

Thanks for thinking of me.

urse

1

GO TO
Textbook

13. Save changes to *practice-101*, and return to GDP.

Using Report Templates

Templates—Report

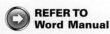
REFER TO Word Manual

L. 101: Templates— Correspondence

To download and use a report template outside of GDP:

GDP will automatically open a preselected memo or report template with an assigned name ready for input at the start of any template job. In GDP, follow steps 6–10 in this section to use a report template. In the workplace, follow the steps 1–5 in this section to download a report template and steps 6–10 to use it.

1. From the **File** tab, click **New**.
2. In the center pane under **Office.com Templates**, click **Reports** to open a list of available report templates. (You can also click **More Templates** for additional choices.)

    Follow any prompts that might appear at any point in to validate the status of your software.

3. In the **Available Templates** pane, click the desired report template.
4. Note the preview in the far right pane.

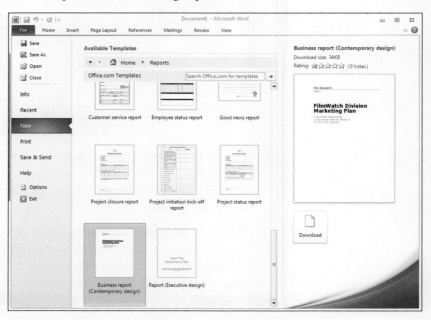

5. Double-click the desired template, or click **Download** to download and open a copy of the template in Word with a generic file name.

 If you wish to reformat the report template using a different style set, you would change any desired style set at this point.

6. Read the instructions on the template and follow any that apply.
7. Click any desired placeholder text in brackets to select it.
8. With the text still selected, type any desired replacement text.
9. Select and delete any parts of the template text you don't want to use.
10. Save the document as you normally would.

PRACTICE

1. Note that the report template shown next opens automatically with an assigned name ready for input. Turn on **Show/Hide ¶** to see formatting marks.

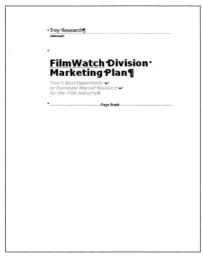

2. On the first line of the first page, select the company name "Trey Research."
3. With the name still selected, type this new company name:
   `Digital Media Associates`

   In this step or those that follow, if you delete the selected text rather than typing in the replacement text while the original text is still selected, the embedded paragraph styles will also be deleted. If you make this mistake, click **Undo** to reverse your actions, and try again.

4. On the second line of the first page, click over the "Address" place-holder to select it—the selected placeholder should look like this:

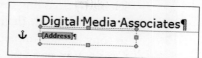

5. With the placeholder text still selected, type these lines; then click outside of the text box when you are finished.

```
4066 Main Avenue
Orlando, Florida 32806
```

6. On the first page, select both lines of the title "FilmWatch Division Marketing Plan."

💡 Although the Address placeholder also appears highlighted, it will not be deleted when you type the new title.

7. With both lines of the title still selected, type this new title:
```
Business Solutions
```

8. Select all lines of the subtitle "Trey's Best Opportunity to Dominate Market Research for the Film Industry."

9. With the subtitle lines still selected, type this new subtitle:
```
Digital Media Products
```
The first page of your unfinished report should look similar to this:

10. Move to the top of the second page of the template, select both lines of the title "FilmWatch Division Marketing Plan," and type this new title:
```
Business Solutions
```

11. Select the subtitle "Trey's Best Opportunity to Dominate Market Research for the Film Industry," and type this new subtitle:
```
Digital Media Products
```

12. Click in front of the second paragraph under the first heading that begins with "This report . . ."; hold down **CTRL + SHIFT + END** to select all remaining text in the template; press **DELETE**.

13. Triple click inside the remaining paragraph to select it; press **CTRL + C** to copy it; click immediately in front of the side heading, and press **CTRL + V** to paste the paragraph.

14. Select the first paragraph; with the paragraph still selected, type this:

    ```
    Digital Media Associates specializes in e-commerce
    and e-learning solutions. We are committed to
    designing, developing, and marketing the world's
    best digital media products.
    ```

15. Select the side heading "How to Use This Report Template"; with the heading still selected, type E-Commerce Solutions as the new side heading.

16. Select the first paragraph below the new side heading; with the paragraph still selected, type this:

    ```
    Our e-commerce solutions make buying and selling
    of goods and services on the Internet simple
    and cost effective. We deliver integrated,
    customizable online shopping cart solutions for
    companies of all sizes.
    ```

17. The last page of your finished report should look similar to this:

> ## Business·Solutions¶
> *Digital·Media·Products¶*
>
> Digital· Media· Associates· specializes· in· e-commerce· and· e-learning· solutions.· We· are· committed· to· designing,· developing,· and· marketing· the· world's· best· digital· media· products.¶
>
> • **E-Commerce· Solutions¶**
> Our· e-commerce· solutions· make· buying· and· selling· of· goods· and· services· on· the· Internet· simple· and· cost· effective.· We· deliver· integrated,· customizable· online· shopping· cart· solutions· for· companies· of· all· sizes.¶

The remaining paragraphs and headings in the report template would be completed in a similar manner—select existing side headings and paragraphs; then copy, paste, and edit them as needed. If a **Paste Options** box appears, click **Keep Text Only** or **Match Destination Formatting** so that pasted text will take on the template's styles.

18. Save changes to *practice-102*, and return to GDP.

GO TO
Textbook

Designing Letterheads

Text Boxes

Text inside a text box can be formatted, the borders and fill can be changed, and the box can be positioned and sized freely.

 The shape styles that are available for text box fills in Word 2010 vary slightly from the text box styles available in Word 2007. Because the textbook illustrations depict Word 2007 documents, the appearance of any text box fills and borders will differ slightly. This difference is not cause for concern. Use a comparable style when making a selection for a shape style in the Word 2010 document processing jobs.

To insert a text box:

1. Change the zoom to **Page Width**.
2. From the **Insert** tab, **Text** group, click the **Text Box** button; then click the **Draw Text Box** button at the bottom of the list.

Text Box button ————

Draw Text Box button ————

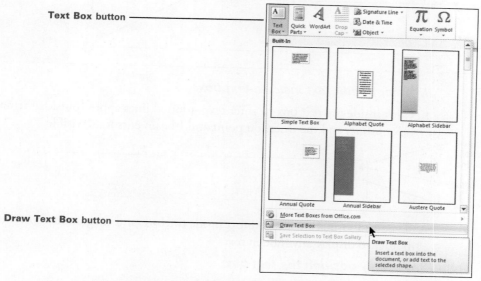

Cross hair pointer

3. Position the cross hair pointer where you want the text box to appear; then drag to insert the text box.
4. Note that an on-demand **Drawing Tools** tab with a **Format** tab below it appears when you insert or select a text box.

On-demand **Drawing Tools, Format** tab

To size a text box:

1. Display the ruler, and click on the outside border of the text box to select it—the text box outline should appear solid.
2. Position the mouse pointer on a sizing handle until the pointer changes to a 2-headed resize pointer; then drag to size the box using the rulers to help you visually size the text box.
3. Repeat this step for all sides of the box.

Resize pointer (text box)

Or: With the text box still selected, from the **Drawing Tools**, **Format** tab, **Size** group, enter exact measurements in the **Height** and **Width** boxes.

A selected text box displays a solid outline with blue sizing handles.

Use the white section of the displayed rulers to draw a text box to an approximate size, and use the **Height** and **Width** size boxes to set exact measurements. This text box is 1 inch high and 7.8 inches wide.

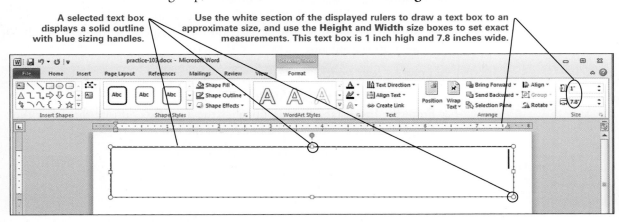

To enter or edit text inside a text box:

1. Click inside the text box to enter text—dotted lines appear outside the text box outline, and the insertion point and I-beam cursor are visible.

Dotted lines appear outside the solid text box outline.

Insertion point

I-beam cursor

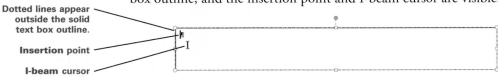

2. Type and format the desired text inside the box, and drag on the bottom border to display any hidden text.

To visually position the text box:

1. Change the **Zoom** level to **Page width**.
2. Click on the outside border of the text box to select it—the text box outline should appear solid.
3. Position the mouse pointer on any edge of the text box until the pointer changes to a 4-headed move pointer; then drag the text box to position it. Note that an outline of the box appears as you drag the text box.

Move pointer

? If you lose sight of the desired text box, change the **Zoom** level to **Page width** or click the **Zoom Out** or **Zoom In** button or drag the **Zoom** slider.

Or: Select the text box, and use the directional arrows to position the box.

REFER TO Word Manual

L. 88: Clip Art—Insert, Text Wrapping

To precisely position a text box relative to the document margins:

1. Double-click the border of the text box to select it and to activate the on-demand **Drawing Tools** tab and **Format** tab.
2. From the **Format** tab, **Arrange** group, click the **Align** button.
3. Verify that **Align to Margin** is checked.
4. Click the desired horizontal alignment—**Align Left**, **Align Center**, or **Align Right**; or click the desired vertical alignment—**Align Top**, **Align Middle**, or **Align Bottom**.

If you are using clip art, insert it before you change the text box outline, shape, line style, and fill. In this way, you can coordinate text box settings described next with the clip art to create a unified, attractive design.

To change the text box shape in a selected text box:

1. Under the **Drawing Tools** tab, click the **Format** tab.
2. Under the **Insert Shapes** group, click the **Edit Shape** button and click the desired shape.

? To remove the border, under **Drawing Tools**, **Format** tab, **Shape Styles** group, click **Shape Outline**, **No Outline**.

This text box **Shape Outline** is set to **Rounded Rectangle**.

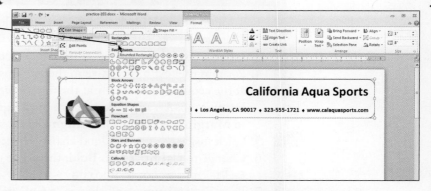

California Aqua Sports

♦ Los Angeles, CA 90017 ♦ 323-555-1721 ♦ www.calaquasports.com

To change the text box fill and shape outline in a selected text box:

1. Under the **Drawing Tools** tab, click the **Format** tab.
2. Under the **Shape Styles** group, click the **Shape Fill** button and click the desired fill color, picture, gradient, texture, and pattern—experiment freely with all choices.
3. Under the **Shape Styles** group, click the **Shape Outline** button and click the desired color, weight, pattern, and so forth—experiment freely with all choices.
4. Under the **Shape Styles** group, click the **Shape Effects** button—experiment freely with all choices.

To make the text box fill transparent, from the **Shape Styles** group, **Shape Fill**, click **No Fill**.

To change the overall visual text box style in a selected text box: Under **Drawing Tools**, **Format** tab, **Shape Styles** group, click the **More** list arrow at the right of the gallery of styles; point to one of the predefined styles, note the **Live Preview**, and click the desired style.

To change the overall design of the entire document including any text boxes within it: From the **Page Layout** tab, in the **Themes** group, point to the **Colors**, **Fonts**, or **Effects** button as desired and watch the **Live Preview**. Click the desired choice(s).

This **Text Box Style** is set to **Subtle Effect— Orange, Accent 6.**

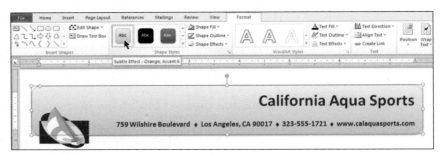

 PRACTICE

1. Turn on **Show/Hide ¶**, and display the ruler.
2. Change the top, left, and right margins to 0.3 inch.
3. Insert a text box at the top of the page 1 inch high and 7.8 inches wide.
4. Position the text box relative to the margins by aligning it horizontally at the center and vertically at the top. (*Hint*: From the **Drawing Tools**, **Format** tab, **Arrange** group, click the **Align** button; verify that **Align to Margin** is checked; click **Align Center** and **Align Top**.)
5. Click inside the text box, and change the text alignment to right.
6. Change to **Calibri 24 pt. Bold**; then type this:
   California Aqua Sports
7. Press ENTER 1 time, and change to **Calibri 11 pt. Bold**.
8. Press ENTER 1 time, and type this:
   759 Wilshire Boulevard
9. Press the SPACE BAR 2 times, insert a diamond-shaped Wingding symbol, and press the SPACE BAR 2 times. (*Hint*: From the **Insert** tab, **Symbols** group, click **Symbol**, **More Symbols**; from the **Symbols** tab, **Font** box, select **Wingdings**; scroll down about 6 rows until you see the diamond-shaped symbol; click it, and click **Insert**.)

10. Type this information in one continuous line inserting the 2 spaces, the Wingdings symbol, and 2 spaces between each one:

    ```
    Los Angeles, CA 90017
    323-555-1721
    www.calaquasports.com
    ```

REFER TO Word Manual

L. 49: AutoCorrect—Hyperlink

11. If necessary, remove any active hyperlinks from the URL. (The hyperlink style often clashes with the design.)
12. Select each Wingdings symbol, change the font size to 7, and click outside the text box to close it.

REFER TO Word Manual

L. 88: Clip Art—Insert, Text Wrapping

13. Insert clip art related to sailing or water sports, and change the wrap style to **In Front of Text**.
14. Drag the clip art to the lower left side on top of the text box as shown in the preceding illustration.
15. Set the width of the clip art to approximately 1 inch.
16. Change the text box shape to **Rounded Rectangle**.
17. Change the text box style and font color to coordinate with the clip art.
18. Click anywhere inside the first line of text.
19. From the **Home** tab, **Paragraph** group, click the arrow next to the **Borders** button, and click **Borders and Shading**.
20. From the **Borders and Shading** dialog box, **Borders** tab, **Color** box, select a color that coordinates with the font and clip art.
21. Under **Preview**, click on the **Bottom Border** button (second button to the left of the diagram) to apply a bottom border to the diagram, or click on the bottom of the diagram directly to apply a bottom border; click **OK**.
22. Save changes to *practice-103*.

Note: Keep this document open and continue reading.

Font—Small Caps

You can vary the appearance of text by changing the font to small caps. Compare the normal text with text typed in small caps:

Normal	Small Caps
ALL CAPS	ALL CAPS
Initial Caps	INITIAL CAPS
Lowercase	LOWERCASE

To apply small caps:

1. Position the insertion point where you want to begin using small caps, or select the text you want to change.
2. From the **Home** tab, click the **Font Dialog Box Launcher**; from the **Font** dialog box, **Font** tab, **Effects**, check **Small caps**; click **OK**.

   Or: Press **CTRL + SHIFT + K**.

PRACTICE (continued)

1. Select the first line of text in the text box, and apply small caps. Your document should look similar to this:

CALIFORNIA AQUA SPORTS

759 Wilshire Boulevard ♦ Los Angeles, CA 90017 ♦ 323-555-1721 ♦ www.calaquasports.com

GO TO
Textbook

2. Save changes to *practice-103*, and return to GDP.

Designing Notepads

Print Options

To print: From the **File** tab, click **Print** to view the **Print** pane with print options.

Or: Press **CTRL + P** to go directly to the **Print** pane.

The Print pane allows you to set the desired number of copies, select a printer, and adjust other settings. Clicking the **File** Tab, **Print**, **Print** button, sends all pages of the document directly to the default printer. The document preview in the right pane allows you to see how your document will look when printed.

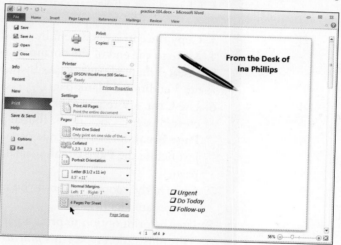

For easier access to printing options, you can add the Quick Print and Print Preview and Print buttons to the Quick Access toolbar. Click the list arrow to the right of the **Quick Access** toolbar, and click any desired choices to add that button to the **Quick Access** toolbar.

You can print specific pages, all pages, or use a specific paper size. For example, if you have created a 4-page document, such as the notepad illustrated on page 177, and you wanted all 4 pages to print on one sheet of paper, under **Settings** (the last option), select **4 Pages Per Sheet**, and click **Print**. The 4 pages will be automatically scaled down and reduced to fit on the selected paper size.

To access print options:

1. From the **File** tab, click **Print**.

   Or: Press **CTRL + P**.

2. Under **Settings** (the last option), select **4 Pages Per Sheet**, and click **Print**.

 If your pictures or text boxes won't print, you may need to adjust your print settings. Click the **File** tab, **Options**; from the **Word Options** left pane, click **Display**; under **Printing options**, check **Print drawings created in Word**; click **OK**.

PRACTICE

Note: Always check with your instructor before printing.

1. Display formatting marks by turning on **Show/Hide ¶**.
2. Change to a whole-page view, click outside any objects, and select the entire document by pressing **CTRL + A**.
3. Copy the entire document by pressing **CTRL + C**.
4. Move to the end of the document by pressing **CTRL + END**.
5. Insert 3 manual page breaks by pressing **CTRL + ENTER** 3 times to create 3 additional blank pages.
6. Use **CTRL + V** to paste the copied document into each of the 3 newly created pages: Click in the fourth page and paste; click just before the **Page Break** formatting code page on the third page, and paste; click just before the **Page Break** formatting code on the second page, and paste.
7. Change the zoom level until you can see all 4 pages, and note that all 4 pages are identical.
8. Use the print option to print 4 pages per sheet on 8.5- by 11-inch paper. This illustration represents *practice-104* after using the **Print** option, **4 Pages Per Sheet**, which causes all 4 pages to print on a single page.

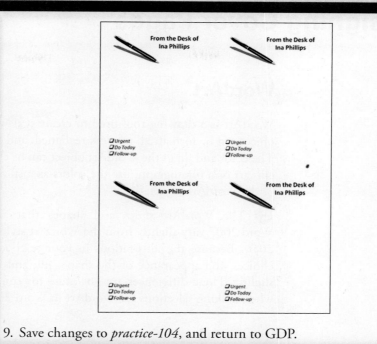

GO TO
Textbook

9. Save changes to *practice-104*, and return to GDP.

Designing Cover Pages

WordArt

WordArt is a drawing tool used to create text with special effects. A WordArt object can be formatted, rotated, realigned, and stretched to predefined shapes. The color and fill of the WordArt object can be changed. If your design includes clip art or a photograph, use the colors as inspiration for the colors and design of the WordArt object.

The WordArt styles and shapes that are available for WordArt in Word 2007 vary slightly from the WordArt styles and shapes available in Word 2010. Because the illustrations in your textbook show Word 2007 WordArt choices, the appearance of the shape, fill, and outline of WordArt will differ slightly. These differences are not cause for concern. Use comparable choices when making selections for WordArt in Word 2010.

To insert and format a WordArt object:

1. From the **Insert** tab, **Text** group, click the **WordArt** button; then click the desired style from the **WordArt** gallery.

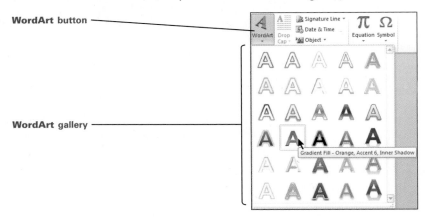

WordArt button

WordArt gallery

2. Note that a **WordArt** object appears in the document with highlighted text, and an on-demand **Drawing Tools** tab appears with a **Format** tab below it.

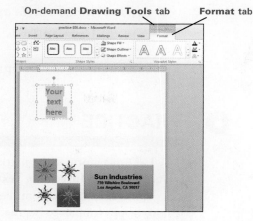

3. With the generic text still highlighted, type the desired text, and adjust the text box size to accommodate the new text as desired.
4. With the desired text selected, point to the top part of the selected text until the brightened **Mini Font** toolbar appears; then click the **Grow Font** button as desired and make any other desired font choices.

When you click inside a WordArt object to edit text, note that the appearance of the text changes. When you click outside the WordArt object, the text represents its final stylized appearance.

From the **Drawing Tools**, **Format** tab, click on the various tools, and experiment freely with these features:

1. From the **Arrange** group, click the **Wrap Text** button, and click **In Front of Text** to drag the WordArt freely.
2. In the **WordArt Styles** group, click the list arrow to view other gallery styles; point to each style, look at the **Live Preview**, then click the desired style to change it.
3. In the **WordArt Styles** group, click the **Text Fill**, **Text Outline**, and **Text Effects** buttons to change fills, outlines, and effects. Under **Text Effects**, click **Transform** to display a gallery of shapes. Point to a shape to display the shape name. Look at the **Live Preview** as you point; then click the desired choice.
4. From the **Shape Styles** group, click the **More** list arrow to display the style gallery; point to different styles and note the effect.
5. From the **Shape Styles** group, experiment with **Shape Fill**, **Shape Outline**, and **Shape Effects** buttons.

To edit text in your WordArt: Click inside the text box, and edit the text as desired.

To align the WordArt horizontally:

1. Click inside the **WordArt** text box.
2. From the **Drawing Tools**, **Format** tab, **Arrange** group, click the **Align** button; and click the desired alignment.

To see the WordArt style name:

1. From the **Drawing Tools**, **Format** tab, **WordArt Styles** group, point to a style button.
2. Pause until the **ScreenTip** displays the style name.

PRACTICE

1. Display formatting marks by turning on **Show/Hide ¶**.
2. From the **Insert** tab, **Text** group, click the **WordArt** button; then click the desired style from the **WordArt** gallery for the new WordArt object.
3. Type "Employee" as the WordArt text; repeat step 2, and position the new WordArt object below the first one; then type "Benefit Plan" in the second WordArt object.
4. Select the text inside each WordArt object, and make any desired font changes.
5. Experiment with all features from the **Drawing Tools**, **Format** tab.
6. Drag each **WordArt** object to the top of the page until each one is positioned approximately as shown in the next illustration; align each one horizontally at the center.
7. Arrange your finished document similar to the next illustration, or change the design as desired.

WordArt Styles: Gradient Fill—Orange, Accent 6, Inner Shadow; Text Effects, Transform, Chevron Up

Font, Calibri (Body) 48

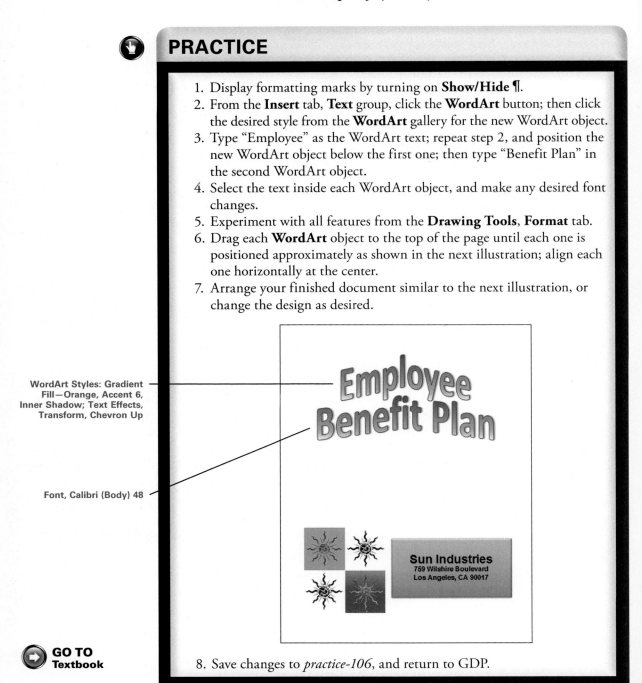

8. Save changes to *practice-106*, and return to GDP.

GO TO
Textbook

Designing Announcements and Flyers

Table—Move

Table move handle

The easiest way to move a table is to point to it until the table move handle appears just above the top left-hand corner of Cell A1. Next, point to the table move handle, and drag the table into position. To add overall style and design to your table, use the Table Tools Design tab groups.

On-demand **Table Tools** tab   **Design** tab   **Layout** tab

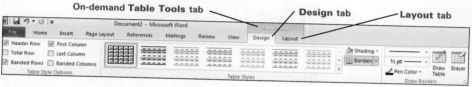

To move a table:

Mouse pointer over **table move** handle

1. Place the mouse pointer over the table until the 4-headed table move handle appears.
2. Point to the table move handle until the mouse pointer displays a 4-headed move handle over the table move handle.
3. Drag the table to the new location.

 Reduce the **Zoom** level if necessary for a better view of the table position on the page.

PRACTICE

1. Move the mouse pointer to see the **table move handle**.
2. Point to the **table move handle**, and drag the table to position it as shown in the illustration at the end of this exercise.
3. Click inside the table, and use the **Table Tools**, **Design** tab, **Table Styles**, to add overall style and design to your table; customize the text and any other design elements as desired.
4. Save changes to *practice-107*.

Note: Keep this document open and continue reading.

Page Color

To add a background page color: From the **Page Layout** tab, **Page Background** group, click the **Page Color** button; click the desired color from the color palette.

Or: Click the **Page Color** button, **More Colors** to display the **Colors** dialog box; experiment with settings in the **Standard** and **Custom** tabs.

Or: Click the **Page Color** button, **Fill Effects** to display the **Fill Effects** dialog box; experiment with settings in the **Gradient**, **Texture**, **Pattern**, and **Picture** tabs.

PRACTICE (continued)

1. Add a page background color or fill effect.
2. Click **More Colors** to display the **Colors** dialog box.
3. Experiment with settings in the **Standard** and **Custom** tabs.
4. Click **Fill Effects** to display the **Fill Effects** dialog box.
5. Experiment with settings in the **Gradient**, **Texture**, **Pattern**, and **Picture** tabs.
6. Experiment with table styles, borders, shading, fonts, and spacing.
7. Your finished document should look similar to this illustration:

WordArt Styles: Fill—Red, Accent 2, Matte Bevel; Text Effects, Glow, Glow Variations, Blue, 5 pt glow, Accent color 1; Text Effects, Transform, Deflate

Font, Arial Narrow 80

Table Styles, Table Simple 2 (with changes)

Page background, Page Color, Fill Effects, Texture tab, Water droplets

United Auto Club

SERVICE DEPARTMENT
Employees of the Month

Luis J. Bachman
Austin Engerrand
Louise Chang
Robert Romero

GO TO Textbook

8. Save changes to *practice-107*, and return to GDP.

Designing an Online Resume

Table—Borders and Shading, Custom

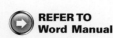

REFER TO
Word Manual

L. 89: Bookmarks and
Hyperlinks

An online resume uses advanced formatting features, such as customized borders, customized shading, and themes. If desired, you can create electronic hyperlinks to items noted in the text shown in brackets, such as [Transcript]. You will not create hyperlinks in this practice exercise. But if you wish to do so for your own purposes, review Lesson 89.

> EDUCATION
> Allied Medical College, [accredited by CAAHEP], Frankfort, Kentucky
> Associate of Science Degree
> • Graduated: June 2010
> • Major: Medical Assistant
> • GPA: 3.9 in major on 4.0 scale [Transcript] [Skills Checklist]

**Text shown in brackets
would be converted to a
hyperlink to jump to the
related item or document
in an electronic resume.**

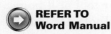

REFER TO
Word Manual

L. 37: Table—Borders
L. 68: Table—Shading

To apply the same border with customized colors and widths to a selected row, column, or cell:

1. Select the desired row, column, or cell.
2. From **Table Tools**, **Design** tab, **Draw Borders** group, click the list arrow next to the **Line Style** button.
3. Click the desired **Line Style**—the first choice is the solid line style.
4. From **Table Tools**, **Design** tab, **Draw Borders** group, click the list arrow next to the **Line Weight** button.
5. Click the desired weight from the drop-down list.
6. From **Table Tools**, **Design** tab, **Draw Borders** group, click the list arrow next to the **Pen Color** button.
7. Point to a color from the drop-down color palette, and pause until the **ScreenTip** with the color name appears.

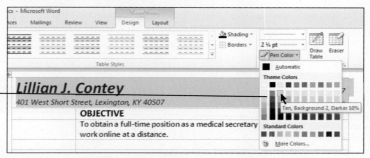

**Point to a color square
on the color palette to
see a ScreenTip display
the color name.**

8. From **Table Tools**, **Design** tab, **Table Styles** group, click the list arrow next to the **Borders** button, and click the desired border.

To apply the same border with customized colors and widths to a deselected cell immediately after following the preceding steps:

1. Click in the desired cell.
2. Click the desired **Line Style**, **Line Weight**, and **Pen Color** as explained in the previous section.
3. The mouse pointer should change to a **Pen Color** tool; when it does, point to any desired border, and click to apply the new border choices.

   (?) Experiment with selecting a group of desired cells to apply borders more efficiently for large areas.

When the mouse pointer changes to the Pen Color tool, click any desired border to apply the border choices.

4. If necessary, press **Esc** to drop the **Pen Color** tool.

   (?) If the mouse pointer does not change to a **Pen Color** tool or if border choices are not behaving as expected, do this: from **Table Tools**, **Design** tab, **Table Styles** group, click the list arrow next to the **Borders** button; then click the desired border to apply the border choices to the selection. Click and release the border button, or remove the border button and try again until the desired border appears.

5. If desired, change to a different **Line Style** and/or **Line Weight** and/or **Line Color**, and repeat the preceding steps until all desired borders have been applied.

To apply shading with a customized color:

1. Select the desired row, column, or cell.
2. From **Table Tools**, **Design** tab, **Table Styles** group, click the list arrow next to the **Shading** button.
3. Point to a color from the drop-down color palette, pause until the **ScreenTip** with the color name appears, and note the **Live Preview**.

Point to a color, pause to see the ScreenTip with the color name, and note the Live Preview.

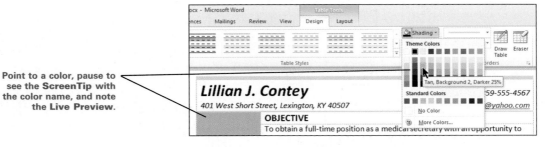

4. Click the desired color to apply the shading to the selection.

THEME

After you have applied customized borders and shading, you can apply a theme color palette to change border and shading colors and/or a theme font selection to change font styles.

To apply a theme color:

1. From the **Page Layout** tab, **Themes** group, click the list arrow next to the **Colors** button.
2. Point to any color palette under **Built-In**, and note the **Live Preview**.
3. Click the desired selection.

To apply a theme font:

1. From the **Page Layout** tab, **Themes** group, click the list arrow next to the **Fonts** button.
2. Point to any theme name noting the font changes in the **Live Preview**.
3. Click on the desired selection.

PRACTICE

REFER TO
Word Manual
L. 45: Tab Set—Ruler Tabs
L. 50: Tab Set—Dot Leaders

1. Turn on **View Gridlines**, and remove all table borders.
2. Select Row 1 and apply italic.
3. In Row 1, select "Lillian J. Contey," and change the font to Calibri 24 pt. Bold.
4. Carefully drag across to select only the text in Row 1 (do not select the entire row), and set a right tab at the right margin. (*Hint*: Display the ruler, click the **Tab Selector** button until the **Right Tab** button displays, click just before the right margin on the ruler, and drag the tab marker over to the right margin.)

   Or: From the **Home** tab, **Paragraph** group, click the **Dialog Box Launcher**; from the **Paragraph** dialog box, **Indents and Spacing** tab, click the **Tabs** button; in the **Tab stop position** box, type **6.5**; in the **Alignment** section, click **Right**; click **OK**.

5. Note that the phone number and e-mail address are now aligned at the right margin.
6. Select each heading, and change the font to Calibri 14 pt. Bold.

   Or: From the **Home** tab, **Clipboard** group, double-click the **Format Painter** tool to apply identical formatting to the remaining headings. Press **Esc** to release the tool.

PRACTICE (continued)

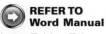

REFER TO
Word Manual

L. 92: Table—Tab

7. Select all bulleted items, and change the font to Calibri 11 pt.

8. Italicize the two job titles, "Medical Secretary" and "Volunteer," in the EXPERIENCE section and the business names that follow them.

9. Increase the indent on the line under the REFERENCES section to align with the text following the bullet in the bulleted lists. (*Hint*: Press **CTRL + TAB**; or from the **Home** tab, **Paragraph** group, click the **Increase Indent** button.)

10. Select the last line of text in the resume, center it, and change the font to Calibri 9 pt. Italic.

11. Select Row 1; select a solid **Line Style** with a **6-pt.** width and this **Pen Color: Tan, Background 2, Darker 25%**; apply these choices using the **Top Border** button or the pen.

12. Deselect Row 1, and change the **Line Weight** to **2¼-pt.**; leave all other border settings the same.

13. When the **Pen Color** tool appears, point to the bottom border of Cell B1, and click to apply the new line width; repeat this for the bottom border in Cell A1; release the **Pen Color** tool when finished.

    If the border is not applied as expected, make sure you are pointing the pen directly to the top of the gridline before clicking the pen; or try releasing the active **Border** button, and then try again until you achieve the desired results.

14. Select the last row in the table, and use the **Border** button to apply a **Bottom Border** with a **2¼-pt.** width; leave all other border settings the same.

15. Click in Cell A2, scroll down, hold down **SHIFT**, and click in the last cell of Column A to select the range of cells.

16. From **Table Tools**, **Design** tab, **Table Styles** group, click the list arrow next to the **Shading** button.

17. Point to **Tan, Background 2, Darker 25%**, from the drop-down color palette; then click that color square to apply the shading to the selection.

18. Change the font color of "Lillian J. Contey" in Row 1 and the font color of each heading to **Tan, Background 2, Darker 50%**.

19. From the **Page Layout** tab, **Themes** group, **Colors** button, point to the various choices, and observe the changes in the **Live Preview**.

20. Apply the **Colors** for the **Median** theme to warm up the brown colors.

21. Apply the **Colors** for the **Verve** theme for a gray color palette.

22. With the **Verve** color theme still applied, change the font color for the name in Row 1 and all the headings to **Pink, Accent 1, Darker 50%**.

23. Apply the **Colors** for the **Median** theme again, and notice the font color change to the name in Row 1 and to all the headings.

24. From the **Page Layout** tab, **Themes** group, click the list arrow next to the **Fonts** button and point to various custom theme fonts; note the **Live Preview** but do not apply the fonts.

25. Turn off **View Gridlines**. Your resume should look similar to this:

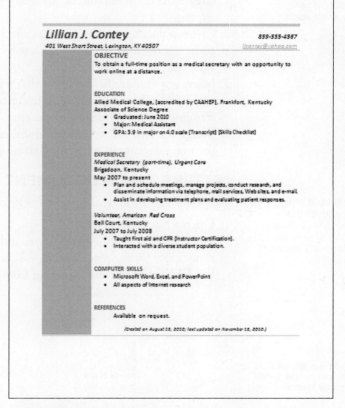

GO TO
Textbook

26. Save changes to *practice-111*, and return to GDP.

Form Letters—A

LESSON

112

Mail Merge—Letters

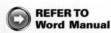

**REFER TO
Word Manual**

L. 115: Mail Merge—
Envelopes and Labels

To execute a mail merge, follow four basic steps:

1. Create the main document (such as a form letter) that includes standard content.
2. Create a data source file (such as a recipient list with the names and addresses of those receiving the letter) that contains unique information that varies in each merged document.
3. Insert placeholder fields (codes that will be replaced with actual text) in the main document that link unique content from the data source file to the standard text in the main document.
4. Merge the two files to create a number of finished documents that combine the main document with the variable text (the inside address and greeting).

LETTERS—MAIN DOCUMENT

To create the main document for a form letter:

Before creating a main
document and its data
source file, always close
any open Word files to
avoid linking data sources
to an open file!

1. Open a blank document.
2. Press **ENTER** 5 times, type the date, and press **ENTER** 8 times after the date to allow space for the placeholders, which will insert the variable information for the **Address Block** and **Greeting Line** placeholder fields later in the merge.

The **Address Block** field
placeholder for the inside
address will be inserted here.

The **Greeting Line**
field placeholder will
be inserted here.

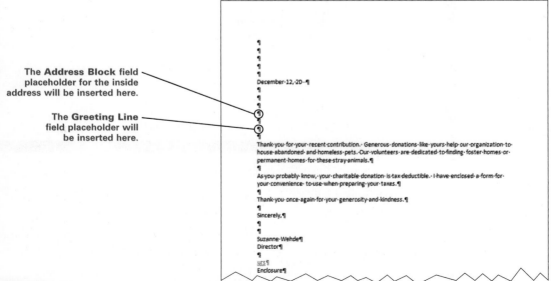

3. Type the rest of the letter (the body, closing, and so forth), save the main document, and name it descriptively (use "main" in the file name) so it will be easy to recognize later—for example, *practice-112-main-letter*.

LETTERS—DATA SOURCE FILE

To create the data source file with an address list:

1. Open the main document for the letter. Click **Yes** if you see a warning that opening the document will run an SQL command.

   This warning occurs after the main document and data source files are created and linked and is expected behavior. When a main document is created and an existing data source file is specified as described in the next section, the two files will be "linked" to each other. Thereafter, when you open the main document, a warning appears regarding an SQL command. Click **Yes** to open the main document.

   If you accidentally create a link to a normal Word file and try to open the file, you will see the message about running the SQL command. Click **Yes** to open the file and then break the link.

   To detach (unlink) a main document (or a document mistakenly linked to a data source file) from the data source: From the **Mailings** tab, **Start Mail Merge** group, click the **Start Mail Merge** button, and click **Normal Word Document**.

2. From the **Mailings** tab, **Start Mail Merge** group, click the **Select Recipients** button; then click the **Type New List** button.

3. In the **New Address List** dialog box, type the information for the first recipient in each of the desired fields, press **TAB** to move from field to field, and skip any fields that are not applicable.

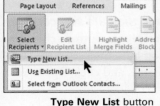

Type New List button

The insertion point is in the Title field ready for input.

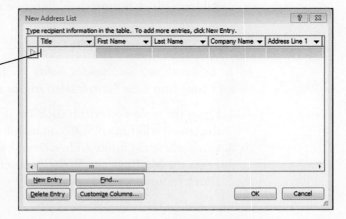

4. When you finish with one entry, click **New Entry** to begin the next address block until all entries are completed; then click **OK**.

5. Note that the **Mailings** tab, **Write & Insert Fields** group, is dimmed behind the open dialog box. This group will become active when you save the address list in the next step.

6. From the **Save Address List** dialog box, in the **File name** box, type a name that will be easy to recognize later (use "data" in the file name)—for example, *practice-112-data-letter.mdb*.

7. Click **Save** to save the file in the default **My Data Sources** folder, or browse to the desired location. See GDP Help for details on the location of the directory in which mail merge data source files are stored.

   Microsoft Office Address List files are stored as a *.mdb file (Access database file) in the **My Data Sources** folder by default. In this way, that data source can be used by all Microsoft Office applications. The "mdb" file extension will be added automatically.

8. Note that the **Write & Insert Fields** group on the **Mailings** tab is now active; therefore, you can now insert merge placeholder fields.

   If the **Address Block** button is dimmed, browse to the data source again to reestablish a link from the main document to the data source.

   To reestablish a link from the main document to the data source: From the **Start Mail Merge** group, click the **Select Recipients** button; click **Use Existing List**; from the **Select Data Source** dialog box, browse to the location of your data source *.mdb file, click the file name, and click **Open**. Your **Address Block** button should now be active.

LETTERS—PLACEHOLDERS

To add merge placeholder fields for the Address Block (inside address) and Greeting Line (salutation) in the main document:

1. Open the main document; click **Yes** if you see a warning that opening the document will run an SQL command.

2. Click where the inside address would normally be typed.

3. From the **Mailings** tab, **Write & Insert Fields** group, click the **Address Block** button.

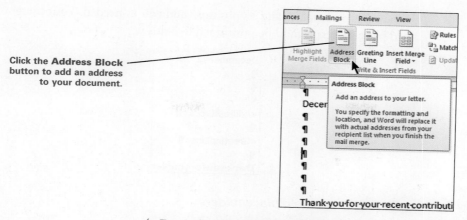

Click the **Address Block** button to add an address to your document.

4. From the **Insert Address Block** dialog box, review the choices, make any desired changes, and click **OK**.

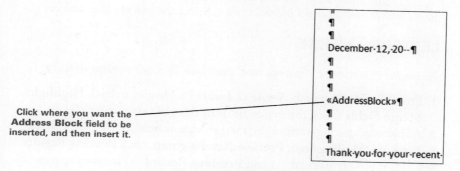

Click where you want the **Address Block** field to be inserted, and then insert it.

5. Click where the salutation would normally be typed.
6. From the **Mailings** tab, **Write & Insert Fields** group, click the **Greeting Line** button.
7. From the **Insert Greeting Line** dialog box, review the choices, make any desired changes (such as choosing a colon for the salutation), and click **OK**.

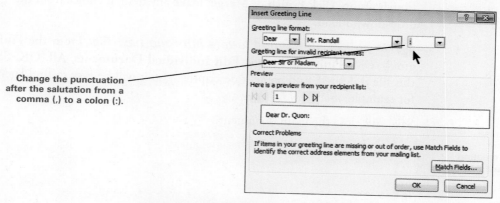

Change the punctuation after the salutation from a comma (,) to a colon (:).

8. From the **Mailings** tab, **Write & Insert Fields** group, click **Highlight Merge Fields** to view the inserted placeholder fields.

9. Review the placeholder and its position, and edit as needed. Your merge field placeholders should be positioned like this:

```
December·12,·20--¶
¶
¶
¶
«AddressBlock»¶
¶
«GreetingLine»¶
¶
Thank·you·for·your·rec
```

To edit any merge field placeholders:

1. Right-click the placeholder.
2. Click **Edit Address Block**, **Edit Greeting Line**, and so forth.

To delete a merge field placeholder: Select the placeholder and cut it.

LETTERS—MERGE

To begin the merge process and preview or save merge results:

1. From the **Mailings** tab, **Write & Insert Fields** group, click **Highlight Merge Fields** to see the merge fields in the main document clearly.
2. Adjust any spacing around the merge fields as needed.
3. From the **Mailings** tab, **Preview Results** group, click **Preview Results**.
4. Click the **Next Record** (>) and **Previous Record** (<) buttons to page through your finalized merge files.
5. From the **Mailings** tab, **Preview Results** group, click **Preview Results** to toggle it off and to view the placeholders in main document again.
6. Edit the main document or data source as needed; preview your results.
7. When you're satisfied with the merge results, from the **Mailings** group, **Finish** group, click **Finish & Merge**; make any desired choice from the drop-down menu.

    🔘 *To collect all merged letters into one new file:* From the **Finish** group, click **Finish & Merge**, **Edit Individual Documents**, **All**, **OK**. Save this file if desired, and name it descriptively so it will be easy to find later—for example, *practice-112-letter.*

8. Save and close the main document.

Always save and close your main document before opening or creating any other Word files!

To edit the data source:

1. Open the main document; click **Yes** if you see a warning that opening the document will run an SQL command.

   (?) If you move the data source file after creating a merge document, the link to it will be broken and error messages will appear when you try to open the main document.

   To reestablish a broken link from a main document to the data source: Open the main document file. Click **Yes** to the warning regarding an SQL command. Browse to the data source as described in this paragraph; or if necessary, click **OK** to the warning that the *.mdb file could not be found. Click **Cancel** to close the **Data Link Properties** dialog box. Click **OK** to the warning regarding a database engine error. Another dialog box will appear prompting you to find the data source file for a mail merge main document—click **Find Data Source**. In the **Select Data Source** dialog box, browse to the location of the *.mdb file, click the file, and click **Open**.

   (?) *To detach (unlink) a main document from the data source:* From the **Mailings** tab, **Start Mail Merge** group, click the **Start Mail Merge** button, and click **Normal Word Document**.

2. From the **Mailings** tab, **Start Mail Merge** group, click **Edit Recipient List**.
3. In the **Select Data Source** dialog box, browse to the desired data source; click **Open**. (By default, data source files are saved in the **My Data Sources**. See GDP Help for details on the location of the directory in which mail merge data source files are stored so you will browse to the correct location if necessary.)
4. In the **Mail Merge Recipients** dialog box, under **Data Source** (in the bottom half of the dialog box), click the data source file name; click **Edit**.
5. In the **Edit Data Source** dialog box, click in any desired field; edit data as needed. (You can also click **New Entry** and **Delete Entry** if needed.)
6. Click **OK** when you're finished, and answer **Yes** to the prompt to update your recipient list and save changes to the data source file; click **OK**.
7. Preview your merge results again; repeat this process as needed.

PRACTICE

Note: Close any other Word files that might be open outside of GDP before beginning! You will now create a new data source file, insert placeholder fields, and finish creating the main document.

1. Turn on **Show/Hide ¶**; then create a new data source file. (*Hint*: From the **Mailings** tab, **Start Mail Merge**, click **Select Recipients**, **Type New List**.)

Title	First Name	Last Name	Address Line 1	City	State	ZIP Code
Dr.	Michael	Quon	1501 East Capitol Avenue	Bismarck	ND	58501
Ms.	Maryanne	Coldwell	31 Anthony Avenue	Augusta	ME	04330

2. From the **Save Address List** dialog box, save the data source file as *practice-112-data-letter*. The extension "mdb" will be added to the file name automatically.
3. Click **Save** to save the file in the **My Data Sources** folder or browse to the desired location.
4. In the main document, click in the blank line where you would normally type the inside address (the fourth blank line under the date).
5. Insert an address block field placeholder. (*Hint*: From the **Mailings** tab, **Write & Insert Fields** group, click **Address Block**, edit any choices, and click **OK**.)

   ❓ If the **Address Block** button is dimmed, refer to the Letters—Data Source File section, step 8, page 190.

6. Click where you would normally type the salutation, and insert a greeting line field placeholder. (*Hint*: From the **Mailings** tab, **Write & Insert Fields** group, click the **Greeting Line** button; under **Greeting Line Format**, select the desired punctuation, and click **OK**.)

Note: Now you will begin the merge process and preview your merge results.

PRACTICE (continued)

7. Preview your results; edit the main document or data source as needed. The address block and greeting line areas of the first letter should look like this:

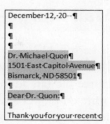

```
December·12,·20--¶
¶
¶
¶
Dr.·Michael·Quon¶
1501·East·Capitol·Avenue¶
Bismarck,·ND·58501¶
¶
Dear·Dr.·Quon:¶
¶
Thank·you·for·your·recent·c
```

8. From the **Finish** group, click **Finish & Merge**, **Edit Individual Documents**.
9. From the **Merge to New Document** dialog box, click **All**; click **OK**.
10. Note that a new document opens with a generic file name, such as *Letters1*.
11. Save the merged letters file as *practice-112-letter*.
12. Save changes to *practice-112-main-letter*, and return to GDP.

GO TO
Textbook

Form Letters With Envelopes and Labels—D

Mail Merge—Envelopes and Labels

REFER TO
Word Manual

L. 112: Mail Merge—Letters

In Lesson 112, you learned how to use mail merge to create a main document file (a form letter with inserted placeholder fields) and its corresponding data source file (an address list). That same data source file could be used again to create envelopes and labels. However, in this lesson you will continue to create new data source files and new main documents for envelopes and labels.

To execute a mail merge for envelopes and labels:

1. Create the main document file (such as an envelope or label) that includes boilerplate content that is the same in the finalized merged documents.
2. Create a data source file (such as a recipient list with the names and addresses of those receiving a mailing) that includes unique information for each merged document.
3. Insert placeholder fields (codes that will be replaced with actual text) in the main document to link unique content from the data source file to the main document.
4. Merge the two files to create finished documents (envelopes and labels with addresses) that combine the main document with the variable text, such as an inside address block.

ENVELOPES—MAIN DOCUMENT

Before creating a main document and its data source file, always close any open Word files to avoid linking a data source to an open file!

To create the main document for an envelope:

1. Open a blank document.
2. From the **Mailings** tab, **Start Mail Merge** group, click the **Envelopes** button.

REFER TO
Word Manual

L. 28: Envelopes and Labels

3. From the **Envelope Options** window, **Envelope Options** tab, make any desired changes, and click **OK** to close the dialog box

4. Edit the return address as desired in the new main document—either delete the existing one or type a new one.

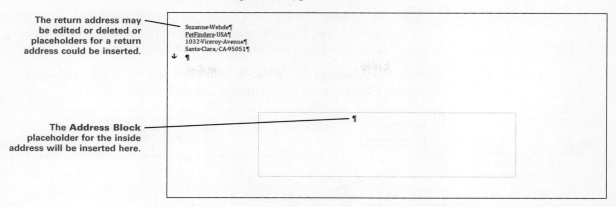

The return address may be edited or deleted or placeholders for a return address could be inserted.

Suzanne·Wehde¶
PetFinders·USA¶
1032·Viceroy·Avenue¶
Santa·Clara,·CA·95051¶
¶

The **Address Block** placeholder for the inside address will be inserted here.

¶

5. Save the main document for the envelope, and name it descriptively (use "main" in the file name) so it will be easy to recognize and reuse—for example, *practice-115-main-envelope*.

ENVELOPES—DATA SOURCE FILE AND PLACEHOLDERS

To add the Address Block merge field placeholder from a new data source file to the main document for the envelope:

1. Open the main document for the envelope.
2. If you see a warning that opening the document will run an SQL command, click **Yes**.
3. From the **Mailings** tab, **Start Mail Merge** group, click the **Select Recipients** button; then click the **Type New List** button.
4. In the **New Address List** dialog box, type the information for the first recipient in the desired fields, pressing **TAB** to move from field to field, skipping any fields that are not applicable.
5. When you finish with one entry, click **New Entry** to begin the next address block until all entries are completed; then click **OK**.
6. From the **Save Address List** dialog box, save the data source file; in the **File name** box, name the file descriptively (use "data" in the file name) so it will be easy to recognize later—for example, *practice-115-data-envelope.mdb*.
7. Click **Save** to save the file in the **My Data Sources** folder or browse to the desired location. See GDP Help for details on the location of the directory in which mail merge data source files are stored.
8. Click on the envelope data source file where the inside address would normally be typed.
9. From the **Mailings** tab, **Write & Insert Fields** group, click the **Address Block** button.

10. From the **Insert Address Block** dialog box, review the choices, make any desired changes, and click **OK**.

🛈 If the **Address Block** button is dimmed, browse to the data source again to reestablish a link from the main document to the data source. Refer to the Letters—Data Source File section, step 8, page 190.

11. From the **Mailings** tab, **Write & Insert Fields** group, click **Highlight Merge Fields** to view the inserted placeholder field.

An envelope with a return address and an **Address Block** placeholder field for variable addresses.

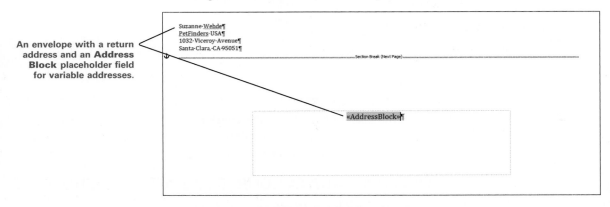

12. Edit any placeholder position as needed.

LABELS—MAIN DOCUMENT

To create the main document for labels:

1. Open a blank document.
2. From the **Mailings** tab, **Start Mail Merge** group, click the **Labels** button.

Labels button

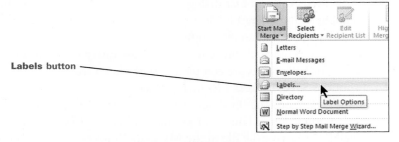

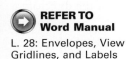
REFER TO Word Manual

L. 28: Envelopes, View Gridlines, and Labels

3. From the **Label Options** window, under **Label vendors**, click **Avery US Letter** (or the desired label vendor).
4. Under **Product number**, click **5160 Easy Peel Address Labels** (or the desired product number).

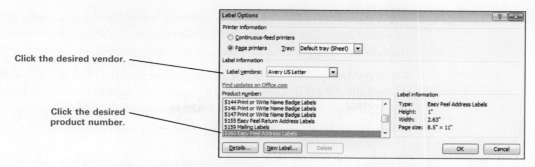

Click the desired vendor.

Click the desired product number.

5. Click **OK** to create a page of blank labels. (Turn on **View Gridlines** if necessary.)

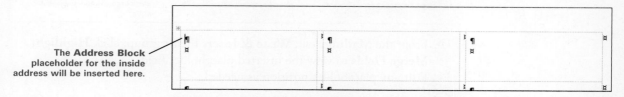

The **Address Block** placeholder for the inside address will be inserted here.

6. Save the main document for the labels, and name it descriptively (use "main" in the file name) so it will be easy to recognize and reuse—for example, *practice-115-main-label*.

LABELS—DATA SOURCE FILE AND PLACEHOLDERS

*To add the **Address Block** merge field placeholder from a new data source file to the main document for the labels:*

1. Open the main document for the labels. (If you see a warning that opening the document will run an SQL command, click **Yes**.)
2. From the **Mailings** tab, **Start Mail Merge** group, click the **Select Recipients** button; then click the **Type New List** button.
3. In the **New Address List** dialog box, type the information for the first recipient in the desired fields, press **TAB** to move from field to field, and skip any fields that are not applicable.
4. When you finish with one entry, click **New Entry** to begin the next address block until all entries are completed; then click **OK**.
5. From the **Save Address List** dialog box, save the data source file; in the **File name** box; name it descriptively (use "data" in the file name) so it will be easy to recognize later—for example, *practice-115-data-label.mdb*.
6. Click **Save** to save the file in the **My Data Sources** folder or browse to the desired location. See GDP Help for details on the location of the directory in which mail merge data source files are stored.
7. Click in the first label cell where the address block will be inserted. From the **Mailings** tab, **Write & Insert Fields** group, click **Address Block**.

? If the **Address Block** button is dimmed, browse to the data source again to reestablish a link from the main document to the data source. Refer to the Letters—Data Source File section, step 8, page 190.

8. From the **Insert Address Block** dialog box, review the choices; click **OK**.
9. To include the same **Address Block** placeholder field in each label, from the **Mailings** tab, **Write & Insert Fields** group, click **Update Labels**.

A sheet of labels with an **Address Block** placeholder for variable addresses appears in each cell after clicking **Update Labels**.

10. From the **Mailings** tab, **Write & Insert Fields** group, click **Highlight Merge Fields** to view the inserted placeholder field.
11. Edit any placeholder position as needed.

📍 *To create a full page of the same label:* From the **Mailings** tab, **Create** group, click **Labels**. From the **Envelopes and Labels** dialog box, **Labels** tab, type the address in the **Address** box. Click **New Document**.

ENVELOPES AND LABELS—MERGE

To begin the merge process and preview merge results:

1. From the **Mailings** tab, **Preview Results** group, click **Preview Results**.
2. Click **Next Record** (>) and **Previous Record** (<) to page through the finalized merge files for the envelopes; for labels, review the page of labels.
3. From the **Mailings** tab, **Preview Results** group, click **Preview Results** to toggle it off and return to the main document with the placeholders.
4. Edit the main document or data source as needed, and preview results again.
5. When you're satisfied with the merge results, from the **Mailings** group, **Finish** group, click **Finish & Merge**; make any desired choice from the drop-down menu.

📍 *To collect all merged envelopes or labels into one new file:* From the **Finish** group, click **Finish & Merge**, **Edit Individual Documents**, **All**, **OK**. Save this file if desired, and name it descriptively so it will be easy to find later.

6. Save and close the main document with the desired merge results.

PRACTICE

Note: In the first part of this exercise, you will create the data source file (*practice-115-data-envelope*) for the main document (*practice-115-main-envelope*) for envelopes.

1. Close any Word files that might be open outside of GDP before beginning.
2. Turn on **Show/Hide ¶**.
3. Create a new main document for envelopes. (*Hint:* From the **Mailings** tab, **Start Mail Merge** group, click **Envelopes**. From the **Envelope Options** window, **Envelope Options** tab, make any desired changes, and click **OK**.)
4. Edit the return address in the main document envelope to this address:

```
Suzanne Wehde
PetFinders USA
1032 Viceroy Avenue
Santa Clara, CA 95051
```

5. Save the main document as *practice-115-main-envelope*.
6. Create a new data source file with this information. (*Hint:* From the **Mailings** tab, **Start Mail Merge** group, click the **Select Recipients** button; click the **Type New List** button.)

Title	First Name	Last Name	Address Line 1	City	State	ZIP Code
Mr.	Samuel	Keller	155 North Franklin Street	Juneau	AK	99801
Mrs.	Maude	Arthur	200 Chopin Plaza	Miami	FL	33131

7. From the **Save Address List** dialog box, save the data source file as *practice-115-data-envelope* in the **My Data Sources** folder or browse to the desired location, and click **Save**. The extension "mdb" will be added to the file name automatically.
8. On the envelope data source file, click in the blank line where you would normally type the inside address.
9. From the **Mailings** tab, **Write & Insert Fields** group, click **Address block**; click **OK**.

   ❓ If the **Address Block** button is dimmed, browse to the data source again to reestablish a link from the main document to the data source. Refer to the Letters—Data Source File section, step 8, page 190.

10. Preview results; edit the main document or data source as needed.
11. From the **Finish** group, click **Finish & Merge**, **Edit Individual Documents**, **All**, **OK**.
12. Save the merged envelopes as *practice-115-envelope*. Your first finished, merged envelope should look similar to this:

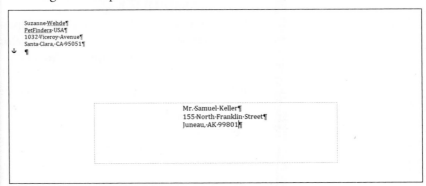

13. Save *practice-115-envelope*, and close the file.
14. Save changes to *practice-115-main-envelope*, and close the file.

Note: Next, you will create the data source file (*practice-115-data-label*) for the main document for labels (*practice-115-main-label*).

1. Open a new, blank document. (*Hint*: Press **CTRL + N**.)
2. Save the main document for the labels as *practice-115-main-label*.
3. From the **Mailings** tab, **Start Mail Merge**, click **Labels**.
4. From the **Label Options** window, **Label vendors**, click **Avery US Letter**.
5. Under **Product number**, click **5160 Easy Peel Address Labels**; click **OK** to create a page of blank labels; turn on **View Gridlines** if necessary.
6. Save the main document for the labels as *practice-115-main-label*.
7. Create a new data source file. (*Hint*: From the **Mailings** tab, **Start Mail Merge** group, click the **Select Recipients** button; click the **Type New List** button.)

Title	First Name	Last Name	Address Line 1	City	State	ZIP Code
Mr.	Ismael	Juarez	1212 Champa Street	Denver	CO	80202
Dr.	Byron	Orey	420 East Sixth Street	Topeka	KS	66607

PRACTICE (continued)

8. From the **Save Address List** dialog box, save the data source file as *practice-115-data-label* in the **My Data Sources** folder or browse to the desired location. The extension "mdb" will be added to the file name automatically.

9. Click in the first label cell where the inside address would normally be typed.

10. From the **Mailings** tab, **Write & Insert Fields** group, click the **Address Block** button.

   ❓ If the **Address Block** button is dimmed, browse to the data source again to reestablish a link from the main document to the data source. Refer to the Letters—Data Source File section, step 8, page 190.

11. From the **Insert Address Block** dialog box, review the choices, make any desired changes, and click **OK**.

12. Highlight the merge field placeholders and edit as needed.

13. To include the same **Address Block** placeholder field in each label, from the **Mailings** tab, **Write & Insert Fields** group, click **Update Labels**.

14. Preview your results, and edit the main document or data source as needed.

15. From the **Finish** group, click **Finish & Merge**, **Edit Individual Documents**, **All**, **OK**.

16. Save the merged labels as *practice-115-label*. Your finished, merged labels should look similar to this:

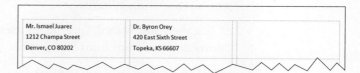

GO TO
Textbook

17. Save changes to *practice-115-main-label*, and return to GDP.

Using Microsoft Word in the Workplace

REFER TO
Word Manual
L. 21: Orientation to Word
Processing—A

When you first install and launch Word outside of GDP, some initial default (automatic) settings, such as margins, line spacing, and font choices, are in effect. However, initial defaults do not have lasting impact because most users customize Word. This appendix focuses specifically on workplace settings that might differ from those used in GDP.

Start Word From Windows

To start Word from Windows:

Microsoft Word 2010 icon

1. On the Windows **Start** menu, point to **Programs** (or **All Programs**), **Microsoft Office** to expand the menu.
2. Click the **Microsoft Word 2010** icon.

   Or: On the Windows desktop, double-click the **Word** icon.

3. Note that Word opens a blank document with a generic file name in the title bar, such as *Document1*, ready for input.

Quit Word From Windows

To quit Word from Windows:

1. Click the **Close** button (the "X" in the upper right-hand corner of the window) to close Word from Windows.

   Or: On the keyboard, press **ALT + F4**.

REFER TO
Word Manual
L. 22: File—Save

2. If you have not saved your document, Word prompts you to save it.

GDP—Word Settings

In order to create a standardized, trouble-free computing environment, GDP automatically opens Word documents with the Word 2003 Style Set already in place. (See Style Set—Word 2003 in the next section for details.) However, before you begin typing any practice exercise or document processing job, you must manually set (or verify) certain Word options. After you change these Word settings, they will hold until you reset them.

Read the following sections carefully: STATUS BAR, AUTOCORRECT OPTIONS, AUTOFORMAT AS YOU TYPE OPTIONS, and SPELLING. Then, open Word, and verify or change your settings to match the ones described in each section. If you have maintained the "out-of-the-box" Word settings, the only ones you will have to change are those shown with the 🔧 icon.

STYLE SET—WORD 2003

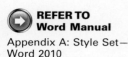
REFER TO
Word Manual
Appendix A: Style Set—
Word 2010

A default Style Set is a group of embedded styles that control "normal" formatting for fonts, indents, line spacing, and so forth. When you open a Word document via GDP, the "Word 2003" Style Set is in effect, which uses conventional document formats found in standard style manuals. The "Normal" style in the Word 2003 Style Set controls the general settings shown in the highlighted column. Compare them to the Word 2010 Style Set defaults:

	Word 2003 Style Set	Word 2010 Style Set
Font	Calibri 12	Calibri 11
Margins	1 inch	1 inch
Line spacing	Single	Multiple at 1.15
Spacing after paragraphs	0 pt.	10 pt.

🔧 You should use only the Word 2003 Style Set in GDP. If you wish to use the Word 2010 Style Set to format documents in other environments, refer to the next section, Style Set—Word 2010, for the appropriate steps.

To change the default Style Set to Word 2003, do this:

1. From the **Home** tab, in the **Styles** group, click **Change Styles**.
2. From the drop-down list, click **Style Set**; from the expanded menu, click **Word 2003**.
3. From the **Home** tab, in the **Styles** group, click **Change Styles**.
4. From the drop-down list, click **Set as Default**.

DEFAULT FONT SIZE—TABLE

The font size inside a table should default to 12 pt. If the font size inside a table is not 12 pt., see Word Help for instructions on changing the default font size; or select the desired text, and change the font size manually.

STATUS BAR

🔧 *To display the Vertical Page Position button on the status bar:*

• Point to Word's status bar and right-click.
• From the **Customize Status Bar** pane, click **Vertical Page Position**.

AUTOCORRECT OPTIONS

REFER TO
Word Manual
L. 24: Spelling and
Grammar Check,
AutoCorrect

🔧 *To disable the capitalization of the first letter of a new line:*

1. From the **File** tab, click **Options** at the bottom of the drop-down menu.

2. From the **Proofing** group, under **AutoCorrect options**, click the **AutoCorrect Options** button.
3. From the **AutoCorrect** tab, uncheck **Capitalize first letter of sentences**; click **OK** twice.

To undo the capitalization of the first letter of a new line immediately after it happens: On the keyboard, press CTRL + **Z** or click **Undo** on the **Quick Access** toolbar.

AUTOFORMAT AS YOU TYPE OPTIONS

To change any of these **AutoFormat As You Type** options in effect in GDP, open the **AutoFormat As You Type** tab as explained next; then complete the bulleted steps that correspond to each option. (If an **AutoCorrect Options** lightning bolt button appears as you type, click the button's list arrow to display **AutoFormat Options** you might wish to stop or control.)

AutoCorrect Options button

To open the AutoFormat As You Type tab:

1. From the **File** tab, click **Options**.
2. From the **Proofing** group, under **AutoCorrect options**, click the **AutoCorrect Options** button.
3. Click the **AutoFormat As You Type** tab.
4. Under **Replace as you type**, adjust the desired option; then click **OK** twice.
5. Return to the document; then delete and retype the text in question.

- Straight single or double quotes ("straight") will be converted to smart quotes ("curved") automatically:

  If you type a quotation mark or an apostrophe, curved double or single quotes should automatically appear. If they do not, under the **AutoFormat As You Type** tab, **Replace as you type**, check **"Straight quotes" with "smart quotes."**

  💡 To change a smart quote to a straight quote to type a measurement (such as 1"), press CTRL + **Z** immediately after typing the quotes.

REFER TO Word Manual
L. 49: AutoCorrect—
Hyperlink

- Internet and network paths will be converted to hyperlinks automatically:

  If you type an e-mail or Internet address and then press the SPACE BAR or ENTER, an automatic hyperlink should appear. If it does not, under the **AutoFormat As You Type** tab, **Replace as you type,** check **Internet and network paths with hyperlinks**.

  💡 To create a manual hyperlink, select the desired text, right-click, click **Hyperlink**, type the address to be hyperlinked in the address box, and click **OK**. If the shortcut menu does not display **Hyperlink**, see Lesson 89, Bookmarks and Hyperlinks, for steps to create a hyperlink using the Insert tab.

  💡 To click to follow a hyperlink, from the **File** tab, click **Options**. From the **Advanced** group, under **Editing options**, uncheck **Use CTRL + Click to follow hyperlink**; click **OK** twice.

- Ordinal numbers will be converted to superscripts:

    If you type an ordinal number such as "1st" or "2nd" and press the SPACE BAR, the ordinals should appear as "1st" and "2nd." If superscripts do not appear, under the **AutoFormat As You Type** tab, **Replace as you type**, check **Ordinals (1st) with superscript**. Or select the desired text; press CTRL + SHIFT + = or on the **Home** tab, in the **Font** group, click **Superscript**.

- Double hyphens will be converted to a solid, formatted dash:

    If you type text followed by two hyphens (--) followed by more text and then press the SPACE BAR, a solid em dash (—) should appear. If a solid dash does not appear, under the **AutoFormat As You Type** tab, **Replace as you type**, check **Hyphens (--) with dash** (—). Return to the document, and delete and retype the text in question.

    (?) If you insert two hyphens between two words you have already typed, click immediately after the second word and press the SPACE BAR 1 time to create a formatted dash.

- (!) Paragraphs will not be indented automatically:

    If you press TAB to indent the first line of the paragraph and then press ENTER and the second paragraph is indented automatically, do this: under the **AutoFormat As You Type** tab, **Automatically as you type**, uncheck **Set left- and first-indent with tabs and backspaces**.

SPELLING

To activate the spelling tool to check spelling automatically as you type:

1. From the **File** tab, click **Options**; click **Proofing**.
2. Under **When correcting spelling and grammar in Word**, click **Check spelling as you type** and **Use contextual spelling**; click **OK**.

Style Set—Word 2010

REFER TO Word Manual

Appendix A: GDP—Word Settings, Style Set—Word 2003

If you prefer to use the Word 2010 Style Set outside of GDP to type documents, simply change the default style set once, and it will be in effect from that point forward.

To change the default Style Set to Word 2010:

1. From the **Home** tab, in the **Styles** group, click **Change Styles**.
2. From the drop-down list, click **Style Set**; from the expanded menu, click **Word 2010**.
3. From the **Home** tab, in the **Styles** group, click **Change Styles**.
4. From the drop-down list, click **Set as Default**.

If you use the Word 2010 Style Set, you must make some adjustments to maintain conventional document formats. Because line spacing is multiple (1.15) rather than single and spacing after paragraphs is 10 pt. rather than 0 pt., you must make some generic adjustments.

To accommodate the extra spacing used by the Word 2010 Style Set:

1. Press **ENTER** 3 times (rather than 6) to begin a document 2 inches from the top of the page.
2. Press **SHIFT + ENTER** to single space lines.
3. Press **ENTER** 1 time (rather than 2 times) to insert a 10-pt. blank line between paragraphs and headings.
4. In a letter, press **ENTER** 2 times (rather than 4 times) after the date and complimentary close.
5. Experiment with the **No Spacing** style button from the **Home** tab, **Styles** group, to adjust the spacing.

For more help on the Word 2010 or Word 2003 Style Set, visit http://gdpkeyboarding.com/.

REFER TO Word Manual

L. 86: Styles

STYLE GALLERY—WORD 2010

A style is a set of formatting commands (fonts, line spacing, and so forth) with an assigned name such as Heading 2, Title, and Subtitle. The Style gallery choices change significantly depending upon which default Style Set is in use. Word documents opened via GDP use the Word 2003 Style Set and its corresponding Style gallery. Compare the Style gallery and Title Style used in the Word 2010 Style Set with the same styles in the Word 2003 Style Set.

Templates

See Lesson 101, Templates—Correspondence, and Lesson 102, Templates—Report, for steps to use templates in the workplace.

Using GDP Features in Document Processing

GDP features that you will use when you begin to type practice exercises and document processing jobs are introduced in this manual on a "need-to-know" basis. The order of introduction of these relevant GDP features is shown in the GDP feature index that follows.

GDP—Feature Index

GDP—Word Settings . . . . Getting Started; Appendix A
GDP—Help . . . . .Getting Started
GDP—Start Word . . . . .Lesson 21
GDP—Quit Word . . . . .Lesson 21
GDP—Scoring . . . . .Lesson 25
GDP—Proofreading Viewer . . . . .Lesson 25
GDP—Reference Manual . . . . .Lesson 25
GDP—Reference Initials. . . . . Appendix B

GDP—Reference Initials

In Lesson 26, business letters with reference initials are introduced. Because reference initials are unique for each person, GDP must compare the initials you specify as your own against the ones typed in the document for scoring purposes. The initials must match exactly to avoid a scoring error.

See GDP Help for details on entering your unique reference initials.

Saving a Word File in PDF Format

You might want to save a Word file, such as a resume or newsletter, in a fixed-layout format that is easy to share and print and hard to modify. You can now convert your files to PDF format directly from Word without installing an add in.

To save a Word file in PDF format:

1. Click the **File** tab, and click **Save As**.
2. From the **Save As** dialog box, click the list arrow next to the **Save as type** box, and click **PDF** or **PDF (*.pdf)**, depending upon your Windows settings.
3. Type the desired name in the **File name** box.
4. Check **Open file after publishing** if you wish to view the PDF file after publishing.
5. Under **Optimize for**, click either **Standard (publishing online and printing)** or **Minimum size (publishing online)** if the print quality is less important than the file size.
6. Click **Save**. (If you checked **Open file after publishing** in step 4, the file should open in a PDF reader. Close the reader when finished.)

Do not send an e-mail message without consulting your instructor!

To send a copy of a Word file in an e-mail message as an attachment in PDF format:

1. Follow the applicable steps in Lesson 25, E-Mail Messages, to send an open Word document as an e-mail attachment.
2. Click the **File** tab, and click **Save & Send** to expand the menu.
3. Under **Send Using E-mail**, click **Send as PDF**. (If you see an error message regarding MAPI compliance, open your e-mail software outside of Word and send the saved PDF file as an attachment.)